HAND ON HEART

Trevor and Nicola Hall

We dedicate this book to the wonderful people who supported us through this period. We feel particularly grateful to Dr Rob Bain for his willingness to drop everything, delve deep and diagnose. He saw what others didn't. To Dr Guy MacGowan for his faith, belief and patience in the assessment and preparation phase. To the brilliant surgeons, Mr Shah and Professor Schűle, for 'doing the plumbing.' To Dr Gareth Parry for believing that those kidneys would come back when the cry from elsewhere was a resounding, 'Abandon ye all hope!' To Dr Lucy Attenborough for her role in 'sense-making' and her tireless support in re-threading the head. To our friends and family who supported us with visits, phone calls, letters and emails, and for helping to smooth some of the rockier parts of our journey. But our most precious thanks go to a donor who made his wishes clear, and a courageous family who said 'Yes' in the midst of unimaginable pain and anguish.

All proceeds from the sale of this book will go to The Freeman Children's Heart Unit Fund (CHUF). When things looked bleak for Trevor, he often saw gravely ill children being wheeled to theatre, with desperately anxious parents clinging to the trolley and to hope. This was all the perspective he needed.

Hand on Heart Copyright © 2018 Trevor Hall and Nicola Hall. All Rights Reserved.

All rights reserved. No part of this publication may be reproduced in any form or by any electronic or mechanical means including information storage and retrieval systems, without permission in writing from the authors. The only exception is by a reviewer, who may quote short excerpts in a review.

Cover designed by Cover Designer

This book is a work of non-fiction.

The right of Trevor Hall and Nicola Hall to be identified as co-authors of this work has been asserted by them in accordance with the Copyright, Designs and Patents Act 1988.

Printed in the United Kingdom

First Printing: April 2018

ISBN-9781980905141

CONTENTS

Part I 1
CHAPTER ONE 2
CHAPTER TWO 11
CHAPTER THREE 28
CHAPTER FOUR 35
CHAPTER FIVE 61
Part II 65
CHAPTER SIX 66
CHAPTER SEVEN 85
CHAPTER EIGHT 88
CHAPTER NINE 122
CHAPTER TEN 136
CHAPTER ELEVEN 144
CHAPTER TWELVE 155
Part III 193
CHAPTER THIRTEEN 194
CHAPTER FOURTEEN 205

PROLOGUE

Newcastle Beach, New South Wales, Australia: waist deep in water, I brace myself against the incoming tide. My arms reach out to form a crucifix, head tilted upwards, basking in the warmth of the sun cradled in an endless sapphire sky. As the wave hits me, despite the grit of my determination to hold ground, I'm driven back two, maybe three metres. This force of nature laughs in the face of my futility; paradoxically, striking me brutally whilst tenderly wrapping me in its protective cloak of exquisite rawness. Struck by the immense power of the ocean – with just a flick of its wrist, it engulfs my mind, my body, my soul; swallowing me up for those few seconds of satisfaction, maybe sanctuary, before disgorging me back into this harsh physical world. Its roar deafening above this salty surge; swirling, chuckling and gurgling below. I envy the unceasing constancy and regularity of its ebb and flow; the dependable, reliable pulse coursing through the oceans of the Earth, a pulse on which all life depends.

Over many months in 2015/16, my thoughts and dreams were frequently consumed by the ocean. Memories of its beauty, its power and fury: an immense hidden world, so totally different from the one we know, and where I've had the opportunity to glimpse just a handful of its many mysteries. Even now, each time I lie on the cold hard trolley, bright lights illuminating scrupulously clean tools and surfaces, cardiologist preparing to enter my carotid artery so as to retrieve a snippet of heart, nurses chatting in the background, I head off to Fly Point. Scuba diving 'Fly' is something so familiar that I can just go there, submerge – aaah, the wait for weightlessness is over – and in my mind's eye conjure up the reeds, the rocks, the contours, the shelf over there on the left under which the pineapple fish hide. Are they here today? Direct my torch. Yes, two of them, amid a few other species, each of which prefers the darkness and safety of a ledge. I'll push on; no doubt the large, aged parrotfish will check me out any moment. I glance at my air supply: plenty left, I'm pretty shallow after all. The cardiologist manoeuvers instruments inside my body; I notice the abrasion of one tube inside another but no pain. No longer does he check my comfort level: he knows I'm away with the fishes, under the ocean, my place of refuge, where I go to escape the world.

PART I

A Failing Heart

CHAPTER ONE

Something's Gotten Hold of My Heart

Friday, 24th July 2015

Nicola and I have just finished a meeting with Dr MacGowan and his team at The Freeman Hospital, Newcastle-upon-Tyne, England. The good doctor summarised the results of three days of tests carried out to assess my suitability for transplantation. In short, it seems I need a heart transplant, but the availability of a suitable organ is by no means guaranteed. Wow. I'm not sure where that leaves us. Me.

So, after 55 years of maintaining some sort of rhythm, the life has finally been beaten out of my heart. Apparently, the only beating it's currently doing is a path to death's door, where, within the foreseeable future, it will deliver a short, firm rap to be let in. If I'm to continue being alive, I need the heart of another person transplanted into me. A thought so alien, it never really entered my conscious before I was diagnosed with heart disease. Like most people, I've given fleeting thought to those stories of transplant patients reported on the news, my main impression being huge admiration for the surgeons who've made transplantation a reality. But, even after my diagnosis - even after cardiomyopathy had been presented as a label on which to hang what is wrong with me - if I'm entirely honest, it's not something I thought would ever be an option for me. Like I said, I'm 55 years old. Surely, heart transplants are something for people in their twenties? To my astonishment, Dr MacGowan has asserted that I'm, "relatively young," and, under the circumstances, remarkably fit and this most certainly is an option for me.

The team spoke of a 'window of opportunity' - Dr MacGowan sketched it - and suggested the results of the extensive tests indicate it's just about to open for me. Apparently, this window frames the optimal time for a transplant so it's neither too early nor too late to operate. Too late has a final ring that I don't want to linger on right now. Put simply, if I deteriorate further, that window closes as I'll be too ill to operate on.

Toward the end of the meeting, I was particularly struck by the empathy of two members of the team - the cardiac nurse and the social worker. I could feel their sympathetic emotions rippling wave-like, silently across the room, communicating how sorry they felt for us. No words, just an awkward silence.

The Transplant Coordinator assigned to me for the duration of the assessment, looked a little sheepish. When she'd first set eyes on me two days earlier, she'd announced there was 'no way' I'd need a transplant, that she could tell this just from looking at me. No need to be sheepish, my appearance has fooled many-a-medical-professional. Dr MacGowan told us that I'd receive a letter in two or three weeks, asking us to return for a briefing on what 'being placed on a heart transplant list' means in practical terms. He said kindly, that we could use this time to think about whether or not we wish to proceed, that all this information is often too much for couples to digest in the moment. With an assertiveness and confidence that surprised me, I took one glance at Nicola and said to the team that there's nothing to think about. They are each professionals in their chosen field, they've assessed me, discussed my case as a team, and reached a conclusion. I said that I'm ready to commit. Now. Let's get on with it. Where do I sign? Dr MacGowan, who'd obviously seen it all before, gently acknowledged my sense of urgency, and confirmed we'd meet again in a few weeks. This would give Nicola and I time to process the information, consider our options, and make a decision. But, in all honesty, there are no other options. That has been made clear.

As the team quietly filed out of the room, we shook hands with each and thanked them for their efforts.

Alone with Nicola in that grim, windowless meeting room, I struggled to rationalise what we'd just heard. Stream of consciousness thoughts ricocheted around my head, all apparently in opposition: oscillating between absolute shock, and massive, unbridled relief. Shock because this kind of thing just doesn't happen to me - I've led a pretty healthy life; hardly a day off work in over thirty years. Shock because someone proposes to take what I imagine to be a droning circular saw and cut open my chest, right down the middle, lift out my heart, and replace it with someone else's. I couldn't speak those words. When I tried, my tongue and lips seemed to swell as though neither they nor the words were connected with my mouth.

Relief? The relief that something, I'm not sure what, is finally over. A huge burden prised from my shoulders and shared out amongst the people in that room. Relief because professional, qualified people have done some tests and have told me I'm seriously ill. I don't need to hide anything anymore: the dizziness when I stand after tying my shoelaces; the crafty pause to look in a shop window halfway up a hill because really I'm out of breath; the avoidance of needing to lift my arms above my head; and the many other tricks I've mastered.

My request for permission to go ahead with our planned tour of Italy in September had been met with unqualified refusal. I'm not sure whether it was the time we'd put into planning, or the non-refundable money we'd shelled out, but that denial of liberty really stung. However, Dr MacGowan had strongly counselled against travel and I already respected his opinion. My life will be in his hands. Let's not start off on the wrong foot.

We sat for a while in stunned silence, drinking tea, holding hands and occasionally shedding tears as we hugged. I felt distraught for Nicola. I wasn't bothered about me, I'd either come through it or I wouldn't, but exactly one month ago she'd committed to our relationship through marriage just a couple of years after losing her late-husband to an unrelentingly aggressive brain tumour. My heart problem is something we'd discussed, but neither of us had a clue how serious it was...until now. She must have been staring down an abyss: the prospect of going through all of that again. I couldn't begin to imagine how she was feeling, she hid it so well; the archetypal swan, calmness personified on the surface, but what the hell's going on underneath? I'll probably never know. Yes, we're honest with each other, but I know her well enough to be sure that she won't tell me some awful news that might have escaped me. With a background in nursing and NHS management she's able to understand medical terminology and interpret the nuances of doctors - the value of which I could never have foreseen at that moment.

I feel sadness too. An immense sadness that this illness which first struck me down in late 2010 has gradually removed most of the agreeable aspects of my life. One by one. It's denied me the ability to run; to scuba dive; to make love to Nicola how I wish; to enjoy a meal; to drink a pint of beer; to play rough and tumble with our grandchildren; to clean the car, to work in the garden ... And now, it's robbing me of my freedom to travel: one of my few remaining pleasures. Eventually, if Nicola's understanding is correct, it will incarcerate me in The Freeman.

Returning solemnly to the bed I'd been allocated for the three days, we took our possessions, checked out at the nursing station and left the hospital. Overcome by a strong desire to escape, we considered driving up to Scotland, or maybe Northumberland, finding a hotel and checking in. Remaining there until it had somehow all gone away. But, deciding that the draw of a night in our own bed was too strong, we opted to make our way to the coast and check out a couple of seaside towns – the draw of the ocean - before heading home. Sub-consciously we must have felt that taking up the mantle of holidaymakers at the coast offered some respite from the torture of sense-making. Remarkably, the coastline we happened upon is almost exactly the same as Newcastle, New South Wales, where I'd lived for almost six years, and where I'd first fallen ill. Was that irony or a very strange full circle of travel? The coal seam running through the cliffs, the swimming pool that uses sea water and tides for daily replenishment, and the rocky outcrops, all replicated and visible from my apartment balcony in Australia. We took a walk to clear our heads and get some sea air in our lungs, drank tea in a cafe and finally, the aroma from Longsands fish restaurant in Tynemouth being too tempting to resist, we decided to share a piece of haddock. I felt closer to Nic than ever before.

As the adrenalin coursing through our veins rescinded and flight became a less instinctive response, Nicola took a piece of paper from her bag and we drew up a bullet point list of what we'd learnt. A means of us beginning to gather our armory for whatever battle ensued, we also felt this would help us to be consistent when updating family and friends.

- I have a serious heart condition which is incongruous with my appearance.

- Around six months ago, a significant deterioration in my heart's performance occurred.

- More deterioration is likely, but when is not known. It is generally a case of gradual deterioration, meaning my performance drops, then recovers a bit, plateaus, then the same thing happens: three steps down, two steps up, then two steps down, one step up.

- Physically, I look in good shape because I have managed my own condition so well, which basically means I've done as doctors have instructed: taken my medication accurately and on time; shown up for appointments; and particularly I have limited my fluid intake.

- After a comprehensive series of tests, the transplant team has determined that my heart, body and mind are suitable for a heart transplant.

- Transplant is the only realistic option but there is a shortage of suitable donors. The donor needs to be at least as big as me, as well as having the same blood-type and no conflicting antibodies. In the UK, a 60kg woman has a much better chance of a donor organ being available than a 90kg man.

- I was assessed by a team of experts at The Freeman Hospital, Newcastle-upon-Tyne, one of the leading transplant centres in Europe. The team is headed by Dr Guy MacGowan, a softly spoken Irishman.

- I will be recalled to the hospital within the next three or four weeks and placed on a transplant waiting list. It's not a 'first come, first served' system; it's much more complicated than that as numerous factors are taken into consideration.

- At some stage, I'll be admitted to hospital to wait for a heart to become available and I'll be transferred to the 'urgent transplant list.' When I'll be admitted is not known but it's likely to be sooner rather than later.

- If a heart comes available, they'll transplant; the hospital stay is open-ended, but if I deteriorate significantly before a donor heart becomes available, I will be discharged.

We drove the three-hour journey home and I felt strengthened by Nicola's frequent reminders that we are in this together, all the way through. We unpacked, had an early night and for the first time in many weeks, I slept well.

The Broken Heart (John Donne – 1573-1631)

After the information shared with Trevor and me the previous day, I hadn't imagined that anything Dr MacGowan might say could alarm me. We'd spent part of the afternoon touching and feeling a cumbersome lump of metal that we both felt would be more at home in the hands of a mechanic, but, were assured by the Transplant Coordinator, Neil, was the latest innovation in heart pumps. This 'Left Ventricular Assist Device' (LVAD), it was confidently explained, would most probably need to be implanted into Trevor's heart. Now, whilst I have strong views on the need for honest and frank dialogue between clinicians and their patients, I have to say that Neil's considerable passion for the prospect of an LVAD seemed incongruent. How could anybody think the possibility of having one of these shoved into you was in any way a positive prospect? And before we'd had time to begin to digest this thought, we found ourselves sitting in front of a laptop watching a real surgeon inserting a real LVAD into a real person. As an ex-nurse, I'm not the type to shy away from watching, in the name of education, a hole being drilled into the heart of someone I don't know. These programmes can be very interesting. Enlightening. But, in the current context, even the notion that a person with an LVAD doesn't have a pulse failed to stimulate much interest. Being handed this weighty contraption, and graphically shown how it will be implanted into my husband's heart is anathema to me.

Neil's attempts to make the idea more appealing didn't really help; he showed us that attached to the heavy metal pump is a length of cable that leads from the heart, through the chest, and plugs into an external battery the size of a house brick. This can be conveniently carried, along with a spare house brick and a computer, in a handy case which, Neil helpfully reassured us, 'Can be replaced with a more fashionable man-bag, if you prefer.'

I noticed that Neil didn't elaborate on how we might become aware that it would be a good idea to switch over to the spare battery. Or, just how long it would take us to acquire a speed and fluency of changeover associated with F1 tyres. Neil's passion bubbled over as he explained that whilst originally these pumps were intended to provide support to patients awaiting an urgent heart transplant - a bridge to transplant - they're now becoming recognised as a form of treatment.

It seemed to me that Neil's job was to make sure we had an opportunity to come to terms with the prospect of a heart pump before the news of its necessity was confirmed by the Cardiologist the following day. However, whilst Dr MacGowan's ultimate recommendation rescued us from the notion that Trevor's heart journey may involve a pump that would provide a 'bridge' which might turn into a 'destination,' the bombshell he actually dropped was more disturbing.

Firstly, Dr MacGowan explained that an LVAD isn't an option since Trevor's heart failure is predominantly right-sided, whereas an LVAD is primarily used in left-sided heart failure. (The clue being in the 'L'!) I didn't fully understand the clinical detail, but it was something to do with the LVAD taking over the pumping on the left side of the heart which would force more blood through the right side thus requiring it to work harder. Since the right side of Trevor's heart is seriously damaged, this would make his condition worse, as opposed to better. Next, Dr MacGowan explained that Trevor's heart is so irreparably damaged he requires an 'urgent heart transplant.'

Other members of the team must have added their insight; I'm not sure what they said. Dr MacGowan's words - 'urgent heart transplant' - repeated on a loop inside my head. It felt as though we were in a room full of spectators, who were observing Trevor and me closely as we fought to maintain some serenity while struggling to absorb what seemed like devastating news. Absurdly, in that moment I felt very alone. Isolated. Conscious that Trevor and I had somehow been separated as we each found ourselves in entirely different situations. Trevor, as the main protagonist, confronted with his own mortality, and I apparently typecast in a painfully familiar, extreme supporting role.

In that extraordinarily *British* way, we thanked the team for their attention over the three days of Trevor's assessment. Trevor made a short speech about how impressed we had both been with their professionalism and expertise, and warmly praised their efficiency.

Once the multi-disciplinary team had left the meeting room, the only word I can think of to describe our reaction is 'numb.' Like most people, I'd never considered what I might say to somebody who's just been told they need an urgent heart transplant. Although several decades have passed since Christiaan Barnard introduced this as a treatment option, it's still very rare. Doesn't happen to anybody you know personally. And is very, very scary.

Nicola-2, who'd helped us throughout the three days, made us a cup of tea and told us to take our time. She could see how shocked we were. And it was a shock. On the first day of the assessment, the Transplant Coordinator had told us that Trevor looked too well to need a transplant and would probably be kept in the system and reviewed periodically. By the second day, the results of some investigations had been obtained and Neil, who had previously been a Transplant Coordinator but now dealt with LVADs, had indicated that Trevor would require major heart surgery to implant a complex device to keep him alive, hopefully give him a better quality of life, and possibly provide respite to allow his heart to recover.

None of this had prepared us for day three.

The tears I had been resisting came. Trevor gave in too. We hugged. We tried to be gentle with each other. We tried to find some positives. My overriding memory is a sense of deep sadness.

Escaping from the hospital became our priority - as though we could somehow leave all of this behind. And yet, neither of us was keen to go home. Maybe we needed a little time off to prepare ourselves before we processed the idea of a heart transplant. We'd been told that a follow-up appointment would be arranged in a few weeks, which would allow us time to digest the information and decide if Trevor wished to be considered for transplant. So, we collected his belongings and argued over who should carry his bags to the car. It seemed that Trevor desperately needed to hang on to his independence, almost to prove to himself that they were all wrong and he was fine. When he asked whether I minded if he drove, I told him that of course I didn't. Thoughts of Trevor's parents who, in their twilight years, died together in a car crash entered my conscious. At that precise moment, this seemed an appealing option - I wanted the pain to end before it ever began.

As we'd planned to drive up the coast after we left The Freeman, it seemed a good idea to still do this. Trevor drove us to Blyth, I think. If I'm honest, I struggle to remember where we went. We parked and had a short walk near a seafront somewhere.

By chance, we ended up in Tynemouth where we had a cup of tea in a small café. Having both agreed that we need to ensure a consistent, objective and unemotional approach to how we communicate the news to family and friends, we decided to write a list of key points. It's funny that throughout our years of friendship we've so often relied on the written word: emails, poems, postcards, lists – words seem to make 'us.' On this occasion, the only piece of paper I could find was the receipt from the Premier Inn at Holystone where we'd stayed each night of the assessment. Our important list of key points about Trevor's heart transplant was literally written on the back of a receipt.

As we left the café, Trevor noticed a fish restaurant across the road. Realising that we were both ravenous, we decided to share a piece of haddock. Coming from Grimsby, we'd both always believed the local hype that the best fish in the country, and possibly the world, is dished-up there. But, in Tynemouth that sunny late-summer afternoon, we discovered how wrong we were. The best haddock we have ever tasted is in fact in Longsands Fisheries. It's possible that the acute pain of our emotions made the pleasure of that fish so memorable, but hell we enjoyed it. I think we learnt something else too: in the bleakest of times it is possible to enjoy simple in-the-moment pleasure and submerge into a strong sense of connection and love.

Friends often say, 'You've been through such a lot, Nicola,' and maybe they have a point, I do sometimes wonder whether I'm jinxed and that anything I touch turns to stone, or salt, or the acrid whiff of a hospital ward. Trevor tells me not to think like that. He gets annoyed if I say that I fear these things happen because of something I've done. To be honest, it's difficult not to sometimes think like that when crap happens, but I'm neither religious nor believe that our futures are determined by fatalism. I'm conscious that thoughts of 'Why me?' and 'Why us?' can easily lead down that rocky road towards victim mode. Even though we're taught as children that life should be fair, in reality it isn't and the question we should ask is, 'Why not me?' Right now, I feel anxious that I won't be able to cope; although I don't have a clue what 'coping' will look like. And, as with so many situations we face in life, I really don't have any choice other than to get on with it.

CHAPTER TWO

Pouring My Heart Out

Sunday, 26th July 2015

The bullet point 'crib sheet' Nicola and I drew up was more useful than we'd anticipated. Over the weekend, we spoke either in person or on the phone to most friends and family, and I emailed the list to friends in Australia. We didn't read from it, but instead just cast our eye down the list to check we hadn't missed anything. It felt important to give exactly the same information to everyone. The biggest surprise was the energy-draining extent of the exercise. I felt bad for people because no-one knows what to say when they're given such news. There were awkward pauses, comments on the unfortunate timing, how difficult it must be, and many genuine offers of help. But there really isn't anything anybody can do at the moment. The energy drain gave us more determination to communicate to everyone over as short a period as possible, and in hindsight that was a wise move. When I received email responses, I decided not to reply. Although part of me felt bad about this, I saw that I needed to move on, and dragging out a discourse didn't serve any purpose.

Nicola said something that stayed with me - we can't change the final outcome of this, meaning transplant or death; we have no control over what, how or when it happens. But we do have control over the period between now and that event. We can either choose a path of melancholy and despair, or a path of seeking joy and happiness from the positives.

With this in mind, we bought and shucked oysters, and opened a bottle of champagne. Probably more an act of defiance than anything else, but we made a pact at that moment to seek out pleasure wherever we could. A friend once told me that champagne tastes much better when it's drunk during the normal course of life's events, and not only at points of celebration. Arguably, the current situation can't strictly be termed 'normal course of events,' but the champagne certainly hit the spot!

This Heart That Flutters near My Heart (James Joyce – 1882-1941)

Despite Trevor and me rarely being apart throughout his transplant assessment, we somehow walked out of The Freeman with entirely different recollections of what Dr MacGowan had actually told us. Trevor understands that he needs a heart transplant and will be added to a waiting list. I understand that Trevor is more unwell than he or I could ever have imagined and needs an *urgent* heart transplant; if there is any hope of achieving this, in the next few weeks he will be admitted to The Freeman Hospital in Newcastle where he will remain until a suitable donor heart becomes available.

Urgent transplant or not, we've both come away acutely aware that suitable hearts are at a premium. As Dr Bain pointed out when he told us he was referring Trevor for heart transplant assessment, "People aren't exactly queueing up to give you their heart." Dr MacGowan stressed that there are not enough hearts to go round, and they are in especially short-supply for larger framed men. Apparently, if you're a small-framed woman, you're far more likely to receive a heart. This, I understand, is partly because women are more likely to die from a brain haemorrhage than men (at the risk of sounding macabre, hearts are only generally suitable from people who are brain-dead.) Also, since the donor heart needs to be the same size or larger than that of the transplantee, there are inevitably more options for women.

We're both finding it tricky to properly address the elephant that's rampaging around the room – what happens if a heart doesn't become available? Trevor and I have boxed and weaved around this issue for the last few days. Does he spend whatever time he has left in a hospital bed and when he becomes too ill for a heart transplant, return home to die? Or does he die in a hospital bed in Newcastle? It feels like a massive gamble: Dr MacGowan made it quite clear that there is no guarantee of a suitable heart, so in effect Trevor is required to forfeit any remaining time in which he has some quality of life in the hope that a heart does become available. We're finding this difficult to talk about.

Since we arrived home, my learning on the subject of heart transplants has been less a curve and more a perpendicular line; each time I think I can see the top, I realise I'm simply clinging to a precipice and there's a steeper incline ahead. Doctors generally view non-medical people's research of online clinical information somewhat negatively, and I agree that sometimes the range and scope of information available at the touch of a few buttons can be overwhelming. But, my response to a crisis is generally to search for answers to the incessant stream of questions my mind generates. Fortunately, I have some understanding of medical terminology, and, probably more importantly, a reasonable aptitude for establishing the validity of information I find. Wrapping myself in the comfort blanket of material spewed up by my iPad also serves the purpose of making me feel as though I'm actually doing something: whenever emptiness threatens, I pluck a question and diligently research until I understand not just the answer to the initial enquiry, but also the answers to all supplementary questions that arise during the process.

Trevor has developed a tendency to look to me for explanations and reassurance. So, I consume heart transplant data; heart transplant stories; heart transplant research; heart transplant guidelines; heart transplant clinical practice recommendations; as well as organ donation data and reports; survival data; national and international statistics. There's a mass of information at my fingertips from Royal Colleges, NICE (The National Institute for Health and Care Excellence), NHS Blood and Transplant Organisation, NHS Trusts, US hospitals, Nursing Times, British Heart Foundation, and many other sites. Some of this information I share with Trevor, and other, less reassuring findings, I keep to myself.

When we left the Freeman, we were told that Trevor would be seen again in a couple of weeks which would give us time to consider whether he wanted to be placed on the Transplant Waiting List. Whilst I am very conscious that in the NHS two weeks is more likely to be a minimum of four, it seems important to do as much research as possible before this so we can participate in an informed discussion at the appointment.

During this time, our relationship seems to have begun some kind of transition from husband and wife, towards patient and carer. Trevor is gradually accepting that he's seriously ill, and coming to terms with his own mortality (while hoping - albeit anxiously - for a transplant), and I've taken on the role of ally and advocate. I need to know and understand the risks and benefits, the process for allocation of organs, the data on outcomes at different transplant units, the support he will need before and after transplant. Having said that, I'm also a newly-married wife, terrified of a future that's beginning to look a lot like Groundhog Day. Sadly, I notice that for the first time in our relationship, we seem to be on completely different pages. Different books even. Sometimes, Trevor asks a question and although I know the answer, I feel it won't be in his best interests for me to share this. That feels wrong. One of the fundamental principles of our relationship is honesty. We pride ourselves on our ability to talk about anything and everything. And yet I find myself needing to distinguish between those things I can tell Trevor and those I need to internalise and worry about secretly.

While we wait to hear from The Freeman, we've tried to get on with the priorities we agreed. It's important to us both to maintain some sense of normality. Sometimes, I find it difficult to let Trevor do things I think may harm him, but he absolutely doesn't want me to treat him as some kind of invalid. It's interesting, I've never really thought about the etymology of the word 'invalid' before - in-valid, not valid, not effective. So, are people who are invalid, ineffective? Or is just a part of them ineffective? Trevor's heart is ineffective. He isn't. I can't become his parent. Trevor is a valid adult; he has to be allowed to make his own decisions.

The Story of a Broken Heart (Johnny Cash 1961)

The story of my broken heart began when I fell ill in Australia in October 2010. For several days I experienced flu-like symptoms - lethargy, aching bones and muscles, and a preference for inactivity over activity. After the third night of feeling dreadful, I called the Occupational Health Doctor at my place of work; he instructed me to get myself into work so he could do an ECG and look at the results. To this day, I don't know how I managed to drive the fifty minute journey. He wasn't in when I arrived, so I sat at my desk. Fairly soon, I felt the need to lie on the floor and go to sleep.

When the Doctor arrived, he did the ECG, took a quick look at the results, put me in his car, and drove me somewhat hastily, to the John Hunter Hospital in Newcastle. Here, the nurses questioned me and seemed somehow annoyed, or maybe perplexed, when I explained I felt no chest pain. The only pain I could honestly report was under my sternum, but it was just a dull ache. To my intense frustration, it later transpired that despite my insistence that I had no chest pain, the triage nurse wrote 'chest pain' on my record. It seems some clinical staff have a preference for patients who fit into boxes.

An angiogram was carried out urgently, and I remember the technician commenting that my arteries were in 'pristine condition.' Those were his words. I was questioned about my lifestyle (smoking, eating, drinking, illicit drug-taking) and family history. It seemed that I was ticking all the right boxes for someone who leads a healthy lifestyle, but this was only creating more puzzlement and head-scratching. I was then placed on a ward with other men, where I was connected up to lots of wires and machines and told to stay in bed.

About 2pm (I think), the machines started buzzing, flashing and generally setting off alarms. I drifted off with a feeling of indifference, of complete abandonment of worry; vaguely aware of people shouting and running, of bodies gathering around me. I'm a bit embarrassed to write the next part as I've never done so before, and have only told one or two people. I remember hovering above the bed and below the ceiling, looking down on about six women who were working at an electric pace with no sense of panic...on me. Through my post-grad studies and my Organisation Consulting role with Hydro, I've observed teams and how they work, and supported many teams in developing their skills. Perhaps that explains why I remember being so impressed as I looked down at the seamless working of this all-female team. There was a clear leader and everyone knew their role and responsibilities. Information was being passed around the team verbally, and although hurried, it was unswervingly calm and efficient.

Meanwhile, the overpowering sense of indifference I was experiencing persisted. There were no bright white lights to move towards, only a feeling of relaxation, of release, of freedom as I looked upon the scene from above. I next remember waking up in the same bed, with the same wires, same machines, and same nursing staff just going about their normal business. Later, a Doctor came to my bed, asked how I was feeling, and told me I'd had a cardiac arrest.

I remained an in-patient in the John Hunter Hospital for about two weeks. Visitors, when they came to see me, expressed shock at my appearance and one pair of close friends later told me they'd had a discussion as to whether I was going to make it at all. But I didn't realise the seriousness of my condition, had no clue what I looked like, and thought I'd be out in a few days with some pills to take for a couple of weeks until I was fully recovered. In early November I was due to tour South America with a good friend, and was convinced I'd make that.

After ten days in 'the Hunter,' a male nurse asked me to get out of bed and walk a distance of about 10m. He disconnected me from various technological paraphernalia and I swung my legs over the side of the bed. I remember the shock at the effort of walking. It rocked my world when he coldly informed me that the old Trevor had died and I needed to get used to the new Trevor, who has serious limitations. Returning to scuba diving was, in his opinion, out of the question. I could hardly believe my ears as my mind was flung into a spinning, confused trajectory. At no stage had anyone communicated that I'd be unable to recover from this condition and return to a normal life. Surely he's wrong? Surely I should listen only to heart doctors? Or is he doing me a favour and telling me how it is because they dare not? Back in bed and reconnected, he told me I'd soon be transferred to St Vincent's Private Hospital in Sydney. I recall clinging onto this forthcoming transfer as a shred of hope: maybe a different hospital could offer a better outcome.

Later, a Cardiologist confirmed my transfer, stating that my case was a complete mystery to him and I needed to be in the care of clinicians with more experience and better technology. She asked if I'd ever seen a TV programme called 'House' starring Hugh Laurie. I hadn't so she explained the basic concept of a medical-type detective who has to solve extremely puzzling cases. Her analogy was that a cross-functional team at the John Hunter Hospital had tried to put together the pieces of my puzzle and failed - they just couldn't figure out what had gone wrong and why.

On my second day in St Vincent's, a cardiologist called Professor Peter Macdonald (pictured) visited me with his entourage in close attendance. He introduced himself and explained he headed the heart transplant team at the hospital. 'Whaaaat??!!' On examining me, he enquired after a couple of minutes if it was normal for me to perspire so much. I explained that it only happens when I'm feeling tremendously anxious, and that his introduction of the word 'transplant' had hit me like a speeding truck, head-on. He smiled, apologised and reassured me that his team also carries out other aspects of heart disease treatment. He came across as a pleasant, courteous character, and it seemed that his team thought the world of him: they hung on his every word. Professor Macdonald explained that I'd undergo a series of tests, but in the short term his greatest concern was a blood clot that was sitting at the bottom of one of the chambers of my heart. Some of the medication he'd prescribed was aimed at negating the risk of this becoming dislodged and causing a blockage.

A few days later, I had just finished eating a pasta bake for lunch when my eyesight began to go crazy. Both of my eyes had become kaleidoscopic as though looking into one of those toys we played with as children. I vomited the entire pasta bake as the room swam and moved around in sections. I managed to feel for the alarm button and nurses came running. As several nurses leaned over my bed, I could only see fragments of faces in a disjointed puzzle. The left eye and forehead of a nurse was in the top right corner, but her mouth and jaw was in the bottom left, her nose and one cheek somewhere over to the right, and so on. Again, I was conscious of a group of people working on me, calling out data and the like. No out-of-the-body experience this time, though. Twenty minutes later, I felt completely well. And hungry.

The next day Professor Macdonald visited and explained that I'd had a stroke - the blood clot had been released from my heart, arrived at my brain and broken up safely. Again, I'm not sure I understood the seriousness or implications of what had happened. You see, I never experienced any pain throughout my six-week stay in the two hospitals, and I always thought that cardiac arrests and strokes were painful.

Professor Macdonald explained that he'd like to fit a pacemaker/ defibrillator/ computer into my chest, which would be connected to my heart to monitor it. I consented. He thought it wise and I trusted him absolutely.

Within a few days, I was discharged from hospital, told to make an appointment urgently with my GP to arrange ongoing medication, and given a rehabilitation plan. Insomnia in hospital had resulted in me spending the early hours of most mornings pacing up and down the corridors of St Vincent's, which were about 100m long. I knew I was already capable of walking 2km per day as I was doing it most nights along clear, quiet, equipment-free corridors. I'd withdrawn from the tour of South America, and was distraught at the prospect of never being able to scuba dive again, especially since the cause of my illness remained a mystery. Professor Macdonald explained at my discharge that he suspected a virus had caused cardiomyopathy, a form of chronic heart disease in which the heart muscle becomes thickened and rigid and struggles to pump blood efficiently. The only way to prove a virus as the cause was to take a biopsy of my heart, but he was reluctant as the organ was too weak to undergo an operation. Noting that he knew perfectly well how to treat my condition, he explained that knowing the cause didn't add much to the equation. He arranged to see me every three months, and emphasised the importance of building up the strength and resilience of my heart through exercise which would directly improve something called my 'ejection fraction.' Ejection fraction appeared to be a big deal with the Professor and in answer to my questions he explained that simply put, it gave an indication of the pumping power of my heart. When I'd been admitted, the fraction was around 15%, and now, six weeks later, it was around 30-35%. To get my heart into the safe zone, and avoid the need to be considered for transplant, I needed to bring it up to 50%.

A healthy heart ejects at a rate of about 75%. This performance indicator would be measured through an echo test each time he saw me. Characteristically, I set about exceeding all aspects of the rehabilitation plan; I would drag that ejection fraction up through exercise if it killed me.

Over the next twelve months, I built up my strength to a remarkable extent, even participating in forty-five minute 'spin classes' at the company gym, and working out there five times each week. In contrast to my appearance, and to the perplexity of the Professor, every quarterly check-up at St Vincent's produced depressing results - my muscle tone built up, my stamina and resilience recovered to a large degree, but still the ejection fraction remained steadfastly rooted at 35%. Professor Macdonald seemed embarrassed at being unable to explain it, but did concede that I was putting plenty of blue water between me and a transplant. However, since strict adherence to a rigorous exercise programme failed to improve my ejection fraction, I decreased gym sessions to one or two per week and focused on enjoying life and friends.

Medical advice cautioned against a return to diving for two reasons; first, the risk of a bleed (one of my medications was Warfarin, the anti-clotting agent), and second, the possibility of my ICD delivering a shock whilst under water. Not to be beaten, I asked two great friends and hugely experienced divers, Dr Dave Harasti and Ian Moore, to take me to Fly Point and accompany me on a dive. They were hesitant, perhaps a bit nervous, but humoured me. The dive went like a dream, absolutely no hitches at all, and in returning to the water, I believe I increased my quality of life significantly. I was back at work, back in the water with dive friends, back in the land of the living.

4th August 2015

I've felt saddened over recent days, for a couple of reasons. I've had gout again for the first time in many months since I started to take Allopurinol on the advice of Cardiologist, Dr Bain. It's extremely painful and causes me to have difficulty in walking and generally moving about. My weight has increased - which suggests that my body is retaining fluid - by about 1.5kg. Furthermore, I feel painted into a corner in terms of my life and this affects my morale and my ability to remain positive about the outlook. My spirit declines further as we set about cancelling the different elements of our planned holiday in Italy in September. It's not just the money - we've lost about £800 - rather it's the restriction on international travel, which used to be a major source of enjoyment for both of us. We rarely bought a package holiday as we took a lot of pleasure from the planning and preparation of an overseas holiday, as well as enjoying it when it came. Now, I'm being slowly strangled as the ligature of restrictions gradually tightens. Restrictions on mobility, travel, and the extent of exercise, as well as on a wide range of food and drink.

The meeting with Dr MacGowan has introduced a question into my mind whenever I notice breathlessness. I had asked him what a further deterioration in my condition would look and feel like. To which he'd replied that the main symptoms would be an increase in breathlessness and an increased likelihood of my ICD delivering shock therapy. Now, I seem to be permanently on the alert, looking for, and perhaps expecting these inevitable changes. At the top of the stairs, am I more breathless than usual? If yes, have I started to deteriorate? Could it be the result of my increased fluid retention and gout? Is it temporary or permanent? I find it impossible to answer these questions with any degree of accuracy. I'm sure the introduction of 'inevitability' into my thoughts has raised the spectre of 'possibility.' I don't think this is anyone's fault - I always want medical professionals to be totally honest with me - it's just an observation of the psychology of this illness.

5th August 2015

I was called to Grimsby Hospital for an appointment with a Renal Consultant from Hull Royal Infirmary's Nephrology Dept. Although I had no idea why I'd been called in, I dutifully went. The doctor was pleasant enough, but he too seemed not to know why I was there. He had in front of him a file containing only two pieces of paper. He knew nothing of my heart condition, of my visit to The Freeman Hospital, of my previous and scheduled appointments with his colleague who's been overseeing my kidneys for the past year, or of what medication I took. Once again, I had to begin my story from scratch while he made notes. It was obvious that any administrative support he might reasonably expect was non-existent. Eventually, he found my recent blood test results, gathered his thoughts and went through the options open to me for the treatment of chronic kidney disease. He agreed that Dr MacGowan should indeed be allowed to take the lead with my case, and that any treatment of my kidneys will fall under The Freeman Hospital as the staff there treat me for cardiomyopathy.

Although he knew little of my background and had limited information to hand, the Consultant chose to deliver what felt like a bombshell. In his opinion, even if a donor organ is found, and even if a successful heart transplant is performed, I will still need kidney dialysis both during the operation, and subsequent to it, three times per week for the remainder of my life. My mind raced as I imagined the walls closing in even further on my quality of life. Having apparently warmed to his theme, he went on to explain that if I do not receive a new heart, it's most likely my death will be the result of chronic heart failure, chronic kidney failure, or a combination.

The Consultant then assured me that the painful gout I have been experiencing will fade over the next few days and advised me to reduce my Furosemide medication by 50% daily. Nicola explained that we'd prefer he spoke with Dr MacGowan who had stressed no medication changes should be made without his prior approval. Initially, the doctor contended that what he's suggesting is only a minor change, but he eventually figured that Nicola can be quite insistent and agreed to put his proposal in writing to the various medical professionals treating me. He recommended that I should still see his colleague for the planned appointment on 9th September. It's frustrating that so many different people in the renal department at Hull Royal Infirmary are treating me. And even more that healthcare professionals both within and between organisations seem reluctant to communicate with one another.

The flare-up of gout has now lasted five days and it's so ridiculously painful. Apparently, the theory is this: my heart fails to pump sufficient blood to my kidneys so they struggle to process uric acid. When this acid accumulates, it turns into crystals that, owing to gravity, appear most often at the feet, or sometimes other extremities. The crystals make walking painful and difficult, so this affects my mobility, my exercise tolerance, and the level of fluid in my body which, in turn, places additional stress on my heart. I can hardly leave the house as I struggle to walk. It's hard to stay positive. Thank goodness for the Ashes series being televised.

The Busy Heart (Rupert Brooke – 1887-1915)

One issue on which Trevor and I disagree - and it's a red line for me - is the advice from Dr MacGowan that our planned holiday to Italy must be cancelled. We spent a long time at the beginning of the year planning a tour of Tuscany and the Amalfi Coast. Some of the accommodation has been paid for in full and flights have been bought on a non-refundable basis. It's difficult to cancel everything: we'd both looked forward to this holiday and Trevor feels he's well enough to cope with it particularly since it's only a month since our honeymoon in New York. I think it must be very difficult for him to admit to himself how ill he is. And I know he feels responsible for it being necessary to abandon our plans. It has to be less painful for me to *do* the cancellations, so I'm just getting on with it. I've even managed to get some refunds: Ryanair are considerably more compassionate than their reputation would have you believe. Sadly, the same can't be said for EasyJet. But, on the whole, I have to say when I explain our predicament most people are sympathetic and try to help.

Telling family and friends the news about Trevor's heart has been a challenge. We agreed in the café in Tynemouth the key messages we want to convey. We've generally stuck to those. The main focus has been on the facts as we know them; we've tried to avoid emotion, and haven't attempted to respond to questions we can't answer yet. We do seem to have had to go through the details a lot of times, and we can feel pretty flaky by the end. Sometimes, we've sat and cried together. Other times, I've gone for a bath or somewhere else quiet where I can privately lick my wounds. I guess Trevor does the same. I don't think we always want to burden each other with our fears.

Today we visited my Dad to give him the news and I think we've become fairly fluent in our script. We even managed to laugh about some of the things that happened at The Freeman. It's strange that humour can be found even in the most difficult situations. That always surprises me. Whenever I hear that something tragic has happened, whether through the media or about someone I know, I have an image in my mind of people who are entirely focused on their dire situation and permanently morose. Experience has shown me that's not necessarily the case. Even in the darkest, most absurd situations, it's possible to find humour and I think this type of humour can be cathartic. Maybe it's linked to self-preservation. When my late husband was in a hospice, shortly before his brain tumour had the final word, some of the things that happened to him, and us, were indescribably awful. But even during the most difficult times, there were things to smile about. Kevin's hallucinations could be quite bizarre, but in a way funny too. After responding to his question asked in all seriousness: "How will I access my bank accounts when I'm dead?" my choices really were only to either smile or weep. Maybe people will find that shocking, but I don't think it's disrespectful. Those close friends with whom I could share humour helped to prop me up. And that seems relevant here too.

On that note, I feel very conscious that the distance between Newcastle and my family and friends at home in Lincolnshire will pose an additional challenge in whatever the future holds. My coping strategy tends to involve those long sense-making conversations women so often have. But to be fair, there's the phone and the internet. Like my daughter said recently, she's only ever a phone call away.

It's funny, but as Trevor and I said goodbye when we left my Dad this afternoon, we all realised that we'd had a genuinely pleasant interlude. Trevor and I both felt relaxed and we laughed a lot. As we left Dad said, "You've really cheered me up," but as his words hovered in the air around us, he realised how they might come across. We all laughed again. Dad added, "Not the heart transplant. Obviously, I'm worried about that. But we had such a lovely conversation, I feel much brighter. Thank you."

I know Dad's going to find it difficult with us being away in Newcastle. He's very independent and looks after himself remarkably well considering how frail he's become, but I think he's come to depend on Trevor and me a little. He feels reassured that we're nearby. I know my son and daughter will do what they can, and my brother lives close to Dad. I just wish with all my strong and healthy heart that I could be in two places at once.

16th August 2015

The fight is over, or perhaps it's only just beginning. Perhaps 'fight' is the wrong metaphor. Certainly for the past eighteen months or so, I've been denying a gradual deterioration in my condition, especially in terms of my symptoms and my physical performance levels, always hoping that a setback is temporary. When my deterioration is on a 'three steps down, two steps up' basis, it becomes much more difficult to monitor. I've always passionately believed in the power of my mind, and how staying positive and upbeat can delay or cancel-out certain aspects of deterioration. I take a holistic view which recognises which my mind and body is one, not two. If we accept that both comprise one inter-dependent entity, then we're taking a holistic view of our own health. You can't neglect one and not the other - that's simply impossible. Physical fitness and a strong, resilient attitude go hand-in-hand, as do physical illness and low spirits, sometimes even depression.

I received a copy of the letter from Dr MacGowan to Dr Bain, which summarised my visit to The Freeman Hospital and my heart transplant suitability assessment. The letter contained nothing I didn't already know, but it struck me how different it felt to hold a 'hard copy' of something that had been verbally communicated to me. My mind had two dominant thoughts: first, this transplant is truly real, and second, I can put down my sword of struggle against heart disease as someone is going to share the load now - some really nice people are going to try to help me. Relief.

A few months ago, I had an unsatisfactory conversation with my sister-in-law, who's a GP. Anne, her husband Andrew, my wife Nicola and I were relaxing and chatting and the subject of my heart condition came up. After a while, Anne commented that in her opinion part of my problem is that I don't tell the truth about my condition. This riled me as I felt it implied I'm a liar, so I felt my values were being challenged. I tried to explain that my condition is not a 'black and white' subject; there are lots of grey areas. My life has taken on a pattern of three steps down, two steps up and I keenly focus on what I can do, not what I can't. I've reflected on that conversation a lot as it's rare for me to ask - as I did then - for the discussion to end, for fear that rising emotions might cause me to say something I'd later regret. Anne chose some clumsy words, because what she was perhaps referring to was my tendency to put a brave face on, be 'upbeat' and at times disguise some of my symptoms. That much is true.

To be fair, it's difficult for me to explain, or even fully understand, the trajectory of my cardiomyopathy. I think it's easy to normalise your condition in your mind and to justify or fail to recognise gradual deterioration; especially when you're frightened of what that might mean. Maybe some people would refer to that as denial, but I think it's a less conscious process. For example, after returning to the UK, I suffered a number of cold viruses and often these culminated in chest infections. Although I recovered from the virus itself, it seems there was a subsequent drop in my fitness level from which I never recovered – the three steps forward two back and plateau I mention in the first chapter.

Curiously, my relationship with Nicola's Labrador, Charlie, sticks in my mind as one measure of my deterioration. It seemed as though his and my health decline were somehow in unison. On one occasion, I recall Charlie's doleful eyes stared up at me. The two of us stood at the foot of the stairs, simultaneously glanced up to the top, and then looked each other in the eye again. It was as if we stood at the foot of Everest, sizing up the challenge ahead and weighing up if we've got what it takes to reach the summit. With a cup of tea in each hand, I nodded a goodbye and headed up, taking a step at a time, blowing and puffing a bit by the time I hit the top. Safely delivering the teas to our bedside tables, I climbed into bed alongside Nicola for our customary morning chat. It took only a minute for my bad conscience to get the better of me; I climbed out and headed back down.

Nothing had changed in his expression. As only dogs can do, his look communicated his wishes. "I want to be with my Mum," he said.

"Ok," I replied aloud, "Let's give it a try." Free of encumbrances this time, I positioned myself behind him and with an almighty heave Charlie placed his forelegs on the second stair. I knelt behind him, put two hands on his rump and pushed. With great timing, the moment his hind legs hit the first stair, he heaved his forelegs to the third, at which moment I heaved his ass to the second. We slipped once or twice, but in the main kept the rhythm going. Halfway, and I needed a rest, puffing as if I'd just done a half-marathon. I didn't need to tell him. Somehow he knew. He waited patiently, panting himself, turning his head to see when I was ready to start again.

Off we went, same technique, same rhythm; him hopping his forelegs up with a gasp, me simultaneously pushing his hind legs up with a grunt. With a final spurt of exertion, we reached the top. He lay down on the landing panting, while I knelt on the penultimate stair – I found kneeling the best position for getting my breath back – and after a couple of minutes we were both good to go. He looked gratefully at me, I said "That's ok," and he headed off, nudged the bedroom door open and walked over to Nicola's side of the bed. By now recovered – whenever totally exhausted, I needed only minutes to go from gasping for air to being fully ok again – I walked over to him, he lifted his forelegs onto 'his' rug on the bed and I pushed up one last time. He was as happy as Larry. After being on his own all night, he was now settled in his favourite place in the whole world: Nicola's side.

Charlie was in his thirteenth year. Increasingly, his back legs were failing; he became morose and somehow uninterested in life itself. He had lived with her an awful lot longer than I, had been her constant and faithful companion while she cared for her dying husband, had listened attentively to her sense-making monologues on their long walks, and had always been there for her. Both Nicola and I knew that she was putting off the inevitable, but for now, at that moment, all three of us were warm, safe and had sufficient breath to get us through another day.

It's only events such as this which allow me to measure the level of my deterioration. And then only in hindsight. I couldn't have said in that moment, as I knelt at the top of the stairs with Charlie lying beside me, "This is a clear indication that my heart disease is worsening."

The letter from Dr MacGowan, when it sat in my hands, seemed to pull back the floodgates within me, gates that have held back the reality of how ill I've become. I can now use the word 'transplant' where previously I couldn't bring myself to do it. I had erased it from my vocabulary. When I use it now, I'm comfortable with it, mentally and verbally; whereas, previously the sound of it when spoken or thought would disturb me greatly.

On a more positive note, the gout that flared up almost three weeks ago has now almost left me. When acute pain leaves my body, it's such a feeling of relief. There were times when I couldn't walk as I had gout in both feet. Yesterday, Nicola and I walked about a mile at the seaside. It was a beautiful day and the air was fresh. We find the dynamic of our conversation changes when we walk side-by-side. We spoke of our hopefulness; our questions around being admitted to hospital; how we might deal with the waiting; the likely effect on our relationship; techniques and strategies for coping; and more.

CHAPTER THREE

Big Hearted

We've managed over the last couple of weeks to do some things that don't have the words 'heart transplant' at their root. Lunch with friends offered Trevor and me a pleasant opportunity to listen to stories about the trials and tribulations of other people's lives. It's tempting at the moment to become totally self-absorbed, but I think it's important to try to maintain some perspective: life is still going on outside of us, and other people face their own difficulties. We're not special. It's so easy to forget that and believe what's happening to us is at the centre of the universe. I remind myself that things can always be worse: Trevor might have been assessed as unsuitable for transplant and then we really would be without a paddle.

When I have that thought - the one about 'things could always be worse' - I often ponder on where the most dreadful situation lies. What is the ultimate 'worst'? And who has the undesirable accolade of having achieved it? I invariably shudder, though, when someone uses the phrase, 'Well, things can't get any worse.' My experience is that they so can! Rubbish stuff happens. And sometimes more rubbish stuff follows it. That's life. And sometimes death.

As we drove into town today, we came across an accident involving a motorcycle and a car. An ambulance was in attendance as well as the police. I looked at the scene and commented to Trevor that we really should carry donor cards to hand out when we come across an opportunity of this type. We both laughed. Inappropriate humour? Maybe.

As the days pass, I become increasingly convinced that Trevor's review at the Transplant Clinic is more likely to be in early September, than mid-August. I know from many years of infuriating delays that achieving anything in the NHS during the school summer holidays is very difficult. It makes me smile when Jeremy Hunt is quoted as promising a 7-day NHS. Maybe a more realistic starting point would be a

52-week, Monday-Friday NHS. Each school holiday is difficult because at any one time, there's always at least one crucial member of staff absent. And, despite the NHS workforce being of similar proportion to McDonalds' worldwide, it seems that nobody is ever available to provide adequate cover.

Having mulled it over for a while, I've decided we need something other than transplants to think about - the time waiting for Trevor's review will be the same whether we spend it at home worrying, or elsewhere doing something enjoyable; we may not have much longer together; we will be unable to get away once Trevor is in the system; I've actually been allocated tickets for a Radio 4 recording at Broadcasting House; and we need a break. I've suggested that I look for a really lovely hotel in central London, where Trevor and I can go for a few nights of luxury. Maybe see a show in the West End. Maybe attend the recording of Dead Ringers. Maybe just relax in the hotel. And definitely feel like we've been away. Trevor agrees, so I've done some research and found a hotel in Charing Cross; the Amba, which has an Executive Lounge, luxurious rooms, and regularly re-stocked mini-bar. Sounds perfect. We can have breakfast in the lounge and won't have to contend with too many people. The hotel is very central so we won't need to navigate the Tube or many taxis. I've booked three nights, plus First Class Rail tickets so we can use the Lounge at King's Cross, which all means little physical exertion will be necessary and we should have a relaxing break. And a bonus is that our mini-break gives us something positive to focus on. We've agreed that, in the meantime, if The Freeman contacts us and offers a date, we'll explain we're not available until after the end of August. It feels a little like we've regained some shreds of control.

Meanwhile, the concept of 'things can always be worse' seems to have come to fruition: Trevor has a flare up of gout in both ankles. It seems exceptionally cruel that on top of everything else he has to suffer such acute pain. He got some kind of medication from the GP that's supposed to relieve it, but a side-order of diarrhoea meant that he couldn't tolerate the drug, so he's battling on. Or hobbling on. I just hope that my London plan isn't a step too far.

Trevor also had an appointment with a Renal Consultant at Grimsby Hospital this week. In the days leading up to the appointment, we had a fairly heated discussion about whether he should attend. I believe The Freeman is now overseeing his care and he doesn't need any more fingers in the pie, but Trevor felt it would be disrespectful not to attend. At the appointment, the Renal Consultant was fairly direct. Well, brutally direct. In his opinion (a stock-phrase for some doctors - nobody can deny them their opinion, or criticise them if it's subsequently found to be wrong, since it's just their 'professional opinion') Trevor's kidneys are damaged beyond any hope of repair and, even if he gets a heart, Trevor will subsequently require permanent dialysis or a kidney transplant. And in the meantime, he will probably die of multiple organ failure. The Consultant was up for sending a

Community Dialysis nurse to our house to demonstrate the equipment that would be used for peritoneal dialysis. He also explained in rather more detail than either Trevor or I desired, just what peritoneal dialysis involves. Having noticed that Trevor's colour had deteriorated to a paler shade of grey, I asserted that a home visit from the nurse wouldn't be helpful at this time.

Trevor's mood was badly affected by this consultation. I feel frustrated that while we're struggling to come to terms with the prospect of a heart transplant, a Renal Consultant who doesn't have access to the complete clinical information has added to our woes. The timing is really poor. What benefit does this information have at this time? I think Trevor's care should be focused on the Transplant Service at The Freeman Hospital; they have the experience of heart transplants and can explain appropriately the implications and potential risks.

All that, and I can't even play the, "I told you so," card!!

25th August 2015

Sleep deprivation leaves me absolutely shattered and I don't feel I'm in good shape at all. My physical condition seems to be dependent on two issues; either a direct symptom of my cardiomyopathy, or a side-effect of the medication I take. At night, it's common for me to experience insomnia, violent disturbing nightmares, itching over my whole body, and restless legs. With any or all of these, or a combination, I struggle to find the rest I so badly need. My weight has increased by around 2kg and this is fluid being retained around my stomach and heart. My heart hasn't the strength to pump the fluid out and the diuretics only seem to prevent it from gathering in my ankles and legs. On the positive side, the gout has left me and I'm walking freely and without pain. If I turn quickly (thereby causing an inertia effect) or if the car goes over a bump in the road, the fluid in my stomach area causes me pain. The worst part though, is the swelling. I look down and it appears I'm pregnant.

Nicola and I attended a family wedding celebration last Saturday night. Several relatives had heard for the first time of my need for a transplant. It was an odd series of conversations, ranging from one who dropped the subject and walked off as soon as she saw other guests, to an in-depth analysis from a lovely couple who seemed genuinely concerned about me. Of course, it's impossible to explain to numerous people that for me, these conversations are repetitive, and particularly draining when held with loud disco-music in the foreground. I can't explain this terribly well, and I'm sorry for that, but I saw the worry and concern for me in my brother's eyes. I appreciate the fact that he does as I've asked and treats me as a normal person. By this I mean that I don't want this illness to become so big it takes over my life: I want it to stay in perspective, and I don't want to explain it over and over 'ad nauseum.' We laughed about old times - our childhoods and the funny ways of our parents - and I love that he always seems to tell me stories I've not heard before. He's four years my elder and can remember lots more than me.

When Nicola and I arrived home, we lay in bed talking in the dark for a time as we often do before we go to sleep, and I wept at my predicament. I wept because I have a tremendously strong urge to apologise to my wife, my brother, my sons and others for causing them to worry. I consciously try to follow Morrie's advice ('Tuesdays With Morrie' by Mitch Albom) and allow my sorrow free reign for a limited time only, and then it's important to climb out of the 'pit of wallow' and get on with living my wonderful life. I feel so incredibly attached to Nicola on a psychological, intellectual and emotional level that I hardly dare imagine my life - my predicament - without her.

If I Can Stop One Heart from Breaking (Emily Dickinson – 1830-1886)

We've just returned from our mini-break in London where we had some welcome respite from 'waiting.' An uneventful train journey, followed by a taxi ride to the hotel, ensured we avoided stairs and/or bag carrying. And - more importantly - arguing about stairs and/or bag carrying. The Amba is in a great location: close to many theatres and within walking distance of Trafalgar Square. After checking-in, we spent some time in our room so Trevor could rest. He's increasingly tired and seems to fall asleep as soon as he sits down. We walked down to Leicester Square a little later and booked tickets for an evening performance of 'The Lion King,' and a matinee of 'Les Miserables.' To end the day, we had a relaxing evening trying out the Nespresso machine, the iPad, and sharing some of the indulgences from the complimentary mini-bar.

Since breakfast was available in the Executive Lounge, we decided to take advantage and avoid any potential for queues and noise. Having said that, a couple of minor irritations did occur. Consequently, when a manager happened to ask if everything was okay as we were leaving the hotel to go for a walk, we decided to bring these to his attention. The carton of milk in our fridge was out of date (I only discovered this after I'd poured it into my coffee); also, in our view, the Executive Lounge was a less relaxing environment than the Amba's website claims as one of the hotel's managers had chosen to hold interviews there while we ate breakfast. Awkward. He even asked the waitress to turn down the piped music so he could concentrate on the applicants' responses!

After bringing these concerns to the attention of the manager, we began to wonder whether we'd accidentally stumbled onto a stage on which a farce was being played out. In the manner of a well-constructed practical joke, the events which unfolded began in a fairly low-key way. The manager apologised profusely and asked if we'd accept a drink in the cocktail lounge that evening. We explained that we had a reservation at the theatre but if we could have a drink before this, we would appreciate the gesture. Feeling that we'd shared our concerns and these had been dealt with to our satisfaction, we spent the day taking gentle walks and generally relaxing.

Mid-afternoon, we returned to our room where Trevor decided to rest on the bed and have a nap before our visit to the cocktail lounge. Just after he'd nodded off, the room doorbell rang and I jumped up to answer, trying to avoid disturbing Trevor. A member of staff ceremoniously entered the room and deposited a bottle of wine and basket of fruit on the dressing table. Before leaving, he handed me an envelope. Trevor was still asleep. I opened the envelope to reveal a card which expressed the management's sincere apologies for Trevor's and my dissatisfaction. Although unnecessary, I thought this was a nice touch and sat back down to continue my book.

The doorbell rang again. I jumped up. This time, a female member of staff politely handed me a large paper carrier bag, inscribed 'Hotel Chocolat' together with another envelope. This card explained that the management deeply regretted the milk was out of date and asked us to accept the chocolates by way of an apology. I thought this a little over the top, but am seriously addicted to Hotel Chocolat so was taking a peek inside the bag when the doorbell rang again. This time, a male member of staff handed me an envelope. He left and I read a letter from the General Manager who asked us to phone him about the reservation for cocktails. Presumably, the proposed cocktails had been superseded by the other gifts.

As I returned to my seat, the phone rang, this time waking Trevor who answered it. I could make out from one side of the conversation that the arrangement for cocktails was being changed which I thought was fair enough. The hotel staff had really gone to a lot of trouble for just some sour milk and a sour manager. But, when Trevor finished the call, he explained the General Manager was very apologetic and felt that the cocktails weren't enough; he would like us to have a complimentary dinner, as well as cocktails, before we left for the theatre. We discussed this and agreed we could manage a light, early dinner and then go to the theatre. Trevor called the Manager who dashed off to reserve our table.

And, it didn't end there. When we arrived in the cocktail lounge, it was full except for one table on which there was a reserved sign and some leaflets. Assuming this table was taken, we opted to stand at the bar. But, when we explained to the barman that we had been invited for cocktails by the Manager, he directed us to the reserved table, where we noticed the leaflets were in fact programmes for 'The Lion King.'

And, it didn't end there either. We ordered cocktails and a main course each; the waitress was keen for us to choose wine, but we were reluctant to drink much before the show. She urged us to return after the show when we could have a dessert as well as more complimentary cocktails, a liqueur and coffee.

And, even more bizarrely, when we'd entered the restaurant, there was a wedding breakfast taking place in a stunning balconied area. This wasn't a concern since our table was out of the way in the main restaurant. But, before our meals arrived, the members of the wedding party were ushered out of the balconied area, a table was reset and we were invited to relocate to this 'more pleasant environment' to eat our meal.

After the theatre, we went to the cocktail lounge, where a table had been reserved for us. It looked like this had been reserved – and empty – all evening, as groups of other customers were glancing enviously at the vacant chairs. We ordered a coffee and a liqueur and tried really hard to pay, but the barman said it was more than his job was worth.

It's funny, but Trevor and I seem to be magnets for this type of thing. When we tell people the story of our trip to London, they say, "Oh, you two; these things always happen to you." We have such fun together. I try not to let myself linger on thoughts of the future too much because a future without Trevor is too dreadful to contemplate. You know the part of your brain that plays tricks with you and sows seeds of foreboding doom? Mine's on overdrive. I know it's stupid, but I can't help wondering if I'm experiencing such happiness because then the awfulness of loss will hit me more acutely.

CHAPTER FOUR

With a Heavy Heart

5th September 2015

We went to the Freeman Hospital for a planned three days this week, though I was 'released' after all tests and meetings had been conducted inside two. If the hospital could organise in a smarter way, I'm pretty sure we could easily have done the necessary within a day. I met with my Cardiologist, Dr MacGowan, had a lung function test, a CT thorax scan, and a meeting with the lung specialist, Dr Lordon. My Transplant Coordinator, who comes across as light-hearted, even flippant at times, seemed to be responsible for pulling everything together. Dr MacGowan explained that I would not be given an admission date yet; he wants to wait and see if an improvement in my kidney function is sustained. I think this is the first bit of good news I've had on any of my organs in quite some time. He said that he didn't want to start my 'prison sentence' - his words - earlier than absolutely necessary. There's a part of me that feels as though this 'stay of execution' - my words - gives me a chance to put my affairs in order prior to a long stay in hospital; but, there's also a part of me that just wants to get on with it. Dr MacGowan reduced the Candesartan dosage from 24mg daily to 12mg in an effort to help my kidney performance further, and the Transplant Coordinator said she'd call me on Wednesday when the blood test results are available for the period after this dosage reduction.

Nicola and I had a huge argument soon after we arrived at the hotel, again over something trivial. We were waiting to be served in the restaurant and Nicola turned on her mobile phone. I'm fairly intolerant of people who use mobile phones in social settings, especially restaurants, and it irked me that we were seated opposite each other and I could see only the top of Nicola's head while she looked at her screen. I didn't handle my objection well. It was a mess of an evening after that: Nicola lost her cool with me and, I felt, raised her voice in the restaurant. Afterwards, I went for a walk alone to gather my thoughts, doing about two miles in half an hour which in retrospect wasn't smart. I'm genuinely saddened at how my heart condition puts a strain on our relationship on occasions. We have to find a way to overcome this and avoid these spats, as they upset both of us.

I'm finding Max Crompton's book, 'A Change Of Heart,' quite useful. Max had a heart transplant at The Freeman Hospital and eventually took the bold decision to publish the journal he kept throughout. I think he'd be pleased he's helping me through the recording of his experiences. There are things I have in common with him that resonate very strongly, such as my healthy appearance when I'm supposedly very ill with a heart that can give way at any moment. However, there are differences too, such as his ability to be on 'day release' from his hospital cubicle, allowing him to spend time with his wife and infant at their nearby rented accommodation. The Transplant Coordinator told me that when I'm admitted I'll be connected to a drip so inotropes can be fed into my body. Apparently, I need these to strengthen the contractions of my heart muscle which will hopefully keep me alive until a heart becomes available. Max was in hospital with congenital heart disease for which the process seems different when compared with cardiomyopathy. A pre-requisite of being on the waiting list for an urgent heart transplant is that patients are in hospital and undergoing some form of active treatment.

During the most recent 'stay' at The Freeman, albeit as an outpatient, I was allocated a bed on Ward 27 and allowed to return with Nicola to our hotel each evening, exactly the same as my last visit. I have to confess that I don't relish the prospect of being an in-patient and in a bay, sharing with five other men. I notice that I must come across as an unsociable character; I'm not at all extrovert in these circumstances. I just want to read the newspaper or my book, or talk in hushed tones with Nicola. Most of the other guys are shouting across the ward to each other, sharing their life histories or discussing the state of the English Premier League. I just don't have the personality for that kind of thing, plus I find it a bit disturbing when I'm trying to read, sleep or otherwise occupy myself. Honestly, the thought of a stay of twelve months or so in these conditions fills me with dread. But I do know I'll buckle down and do it. I'd never be rude or unpleasant towards other patients; I just don't want to have to socialise.

We drove home on Thursday morning, 3rd September, and chose a pleasant route via the A19. More scenic - not as busy as the A1 - and we stopped for breakfast at a lovely little café run by a pair of middle-aged women, cooking and baking everything they sold. I had poached eggs on toast and Nic her usual, a toasted teacake. Obviously, we've a lot to digest again, not least of which is the search for an apartment or house for Nicola during my stay.

Once home, we unpacked and headed straight off to see Nicola's Dad, who's not in a good way. He's 84 and has had a resurgence of the lung cancer he was diagnosed with seven years ago. His breathing is extremely laboured and my heart goes out to him as he seems to have to suck in hard at almost every breath. Much as I want to visit with Nicola, I find it difficult because it's like watching my biggest fear being played out: dying of breathlessness.

Our latest visit to The Freeman was difficult for several reasons. It begins to feel a little like we are being pulled one way and then in the diametric opposite direction in terms of the management of Trevor's case. Dr MacGowan did confirm that Trevor will need to be admitted to hospital to wait for a heart, but he wants to wait a while as Trevor's kidneys appear to have improved a little. It seems that the measurement of kidney function in terms of heart transplant readiness is serum creatinine; whereas, renal specialists generally talk about eGFR (estimated glomerular filtration rate which takes into account creatinine, age, sex and race). This time, we'd been asked to go to The Freeman for three days, but were done in two. To be honest, we spent most of the two days waiting. Waiting for tests. Waiting for results. Waiting for nurses. Waiting to be allowed out. I guess waiting is something I'm going to need to get used to.

Since nothing much was happening while Trevor was waiting on Ward 27, I decided to leave him to sleep for a while in the afternoon and walk in to Jesmond to locate and register with some letting agents. It's difficult as I can't commit to precisely when I'll need a property, but at least I'd have an opportunity to get some idea of the area. At first, I walked on the path alongside the main road. We've driven that way a few times when we've travelled towards the centre of Newcastle. After a while, I came to a bridge, preceded by a public footpath that ran alongside a small river. Since the traffic bridge was very narrow, I decided that the footpath looked more inviting so took a detour, expecting it to be a short cut. It was a beautiful walk but there weren't many people around and I felt a bit jumpy which made me feel sad as it reinforced how alone I feel without Trevor. Finding a property to rent by myself and going ahead with a rental feels quite daunting. I've never done that before. But I guess this is what the foreseeable future looks like, so I'd better get used to it!

Continuing the walk along the riverbank, I came across a picturesque scene of a waterfall. Wanting to share the view with Trevor, I took a photo on my phone to show him when I got back to the hospital. I also made a promise to myself that one day, when he has a new heart, we will walk along this path together.

Continuing my walk, I eventually found a bridge across the river and a route through a pleasant housing area that led me to the centre of Jesmond. I registered with a couple of letting agents which seemed to boost my self-esteem and walked back to the hospital a little more in control and a little less intimidated.

When we came up to Newcastle, we weren't entirely sure what the plan was in terms of Trevor's admission to wait for a heart, and I seem to have been left with mixed feelings about Dr MacGowan's decision not to admit him immediately. It does give us some time to get ourselves organised, and of course I'm delighted that we can spend time together out and about, but I'm also anxious because I fear a heart not being found in time. Spending 24-hours each day with Trevor means that I'm the one person who experiences the real him, and I'm not convinced that a slight improvement in kidney function is an accurate reflection of his condition. The deterioration over the last few months seems palpable to me. He denied for ages that his condition was worsening, but a few times, I went out into the garden and found him prostrate on the path. He told me he'd needed to lie down because he felt breathless and dizzy after doing a relatively light activity in the garden.

Eventually, on election night and with Trevor's agreement, I emailed Rob Bain, my Cardiologist friend, and asked for some advice. When I explained Trevor's condition, Rob replied immediately and arranged to see him in clinic the next day. I certainly count our blessings: if we'd had to convince a GP that although Trevor looks ok, he's actually worsening and needs to be reviewed by a Cardiologist, I fear we would still be waiting for a referral.

When we saw Rob in clinic, he arranged a variety of tests, observed Trevor on a treadmill, then sat us down and delivered the news. It was a shock to learn just how much Trevor's heart has deteriorated: I'd expected his drugs to just need adjusting a bit. Rob told us as gently as he could that Trevor needed to be referred for transplant assessment, but I knew from how serious he looked that things were pretty dreadful. That was a few weeks before our wedding. Of course, we talked about postponing it, but decided to go ahead; whatever time we have together, we plan to enjoy every moment.

Our wedding was sooner than we'd originally intended because of my Dad's health. In his dry way, last January Dad told us he'd received an appointment from Grimsby Hospital for June 2015 and was delighted to announce that this obviously means he's guaranteed another six months of life – on the basis they wouldn't send an appointment so far in advance if they thought he'd be dead! Trevor and I had planned to marry in a few years, but it was important to me that my Dad could be there so, with an element of irony, we opted for this June.

Absurdly, whilst a part of me feels enormously lucky that Trevor's case has been taken on by a heart transplant centre, another part feels utterly wretched. My mind keeps playing through the darkest scenario of admission to The Freeman, a heart not becoming available, and the final weeks or months or however long he has being spent confined to hospital. Selfishly, I want it all. I want Trevor to have the opportunity of life that only a heart transplant can offer, but I also want assurances. And there are none. It feels like a massive gamble with incredibly high stakes: Trevor can go into hospital and forego whatever life he has left in the hope a heart will become available before his condition worsens and he dies. Or he can stay home, get progressively more ill and die. We have no choice. I know that. But in this situation, our time and how we spend it takes on a much greater significance.

Another recurring thought is although our situation seems desperate, we are entirely dependent on a person we don't know suddenly becoming brain dead. Somebody who today is living an ostensibly healthy life needs to die in order for us to resume living. That situation is far more desperate than the one we find ourselves in. For me, it all centres on that word, 'hope.' Whereas we have hope, the partner, parent, child, loved one, of the donor will have no hope. And they don't even know that yet. How can I possibly wish for that? It feels like I'm hoping for somebody's loved ones to go through the hell that we went through when Kevin died. Except they won't have eighteen months to prepare themselves for it. The rational part of my brain recognizes that this person will die anyway and they will no longer need their organs. They're not dying so Trevor can live. They are dying anyway. But that's the rational part. And pure emotion is stimulating my brain; especially at night when the hours until dawn seem very far away.

In the depths of darkness, it feels as though my mind works against me, exploring in detail every negative scenario. One illogical fear is that Trevor will miss out on a heart if he doesn't get into hospital soon. Almost like the sooner he gets started, the sooner he'll finish. But that doesn't make any sense at all. There's no starting gun. I panic that something will happen before he even gets into hospital - Dr MacGowan stressed just how ill Trevor is and that he could deteriorate at any moment.

While he sleeps, I listen to him breathe. Periodically, his limbs jerk. Restless legs caused by failing kidneys. Noisy breathing. Sometimes it stops altogether and I count the seconds. Elephants. I remember somebody once said you can count seconds by saying aloud the word 'elephant.' One elephant, two elephants, three elephants. Occasionally, it's twenty. Sleep evades me. What if Trevor's limbs stop jerking and his breathing ceases?

Tonight, my insomnia and I lie in a Premier Inn bed. Funny, part of their marketing campaign is their 'Good Night Guarantee' which promises a great night's sleep or they'll refund your money. I'm not sure this qualifies. We'd booked to stay for three nights, but Trevor was discharged sooner than expected so we decided not to make the journey home immediately, but have a more gentle drive home in the morning. Yesterday evening, we ate at the Brewers' Fayre next to the hotel, where I'm sad to say we ended up having a humongous row. I suggested we check our calendars to see what we have planned over the next few months since inevitably we're going to have to cancel some things, or at least give tickets away. We'd ordered and were waiting for our meals, so I looked at the calendar on my phone. Trevor went ape. Allegedly because I was on my phone while we were in a restaurant, but I think my mentioning the need to cancel our plans really touched a nerve. He readily admits he's never good at changes to plans. He's not recovered from being grounded over Italy. So I guess it was fairly insensitive of me to drop something else into the mix, but the emotional aspect hadn't occurred to me. I was focused on the practical. It's beginning to feel like everything I plan to say needs to be pre-analysed for its potential to cause turbulence.

When we returned to our room after dinner, Trevor went out for a walk. A long walk it turns out: I spent forty minutes worrying about him. Trying to figure how I could explain to The Freeman that he'd gone out rambling and keeled over so thank you for your interest but he won't be needing a heart transplant. Under the circumstances, they might think I was a tad irresponsible for letting him go. But, boy, he can be stubborn.

After what seemed like forever, Trevor returned. We managed to talk a bit and smooth a few of the rough edges. I suppose we're both feeling fairly frazzled. It's difficult for Trevor. I know it is. He has a huge amount to come to terms with. But it's not easy for me either.

This morning, we had a slow amble home, choosing the A19 which seemed to offer a less frenetic route. Just after we arrived home, my Dad phoned. This in itself is unusual since he rarely phones, but he sounded confused and asked when I would be going to see him. This was strange as I'd explained we'd be away all week so he shouldn't have expected us home until the next day. I explained to Trevor that I needed to go to Dad's. I felt torn, as though I shouldn't leave him alone, but at the same time Dad needed me. Trevor insisted on coming with me. When we arrived, Dad was in a terrible state gasping for each breath which was making him extremely anxious which in turn was making his breathing worse. I really didn't know what to do.

A couple of weeks ago, I thought Dad needed oxygen therapy so contacted the Out of Hours service to enquire about oxygen at home. This wasn't very successful. After a long wait, the 'Rapid Response Team' - comprising two people wearing white polo shirts emblazoned 'RAPID RESPONSE' – turned up, took a brief look at Dad and announced that he didn't need oxygen. So that was it. He was left gasping for breath. I find it's like talking to a wall when attempting to have any form of dialogue with the type of healthcare staff who aren't necessarily well qualified but have been given surprising levels of autonomy. They seem to become intimidated when asked a question they're unable to answer, and have a preference for sticking rigidly to some kind of one-size-fits-all decision matrix for delivering healthcare. As a doctor once pointed out to me, it's only dead patients who fit into boxes!

Anyway, Dad wouldn't let me stay with him overnight, so I insisted I'd return first thing in the morning. He can't go on like this. I really believe the best place for him at the moment is the Hospice where his symptoms can be controlled and he has a much better chance of being given treatment to help his breathing. Looking after terminally patients in their own home sounds very appealing, but unless there's a spouse or other family member present 24/7, it's very difficult.

Even with a family member present, it's fraught with problems. Before my late husband was admitted to the Hospice, I struggled enormously to look after him at home. He was a large-framed man, over six feet tall and had lost the use of the left side of his body. We were entitled to up to four care visit per day. However, despite the terminal nature of his illness being clearly understood for more than a year before his condition deteriorated to end-stage, there was no care available. Although not intended to fill the gap in homecare delivery, the local hospice community nurses kindly attended at around ten o'clock each morning to help me wash Kevin and take him to the toilet. I then had to cope until the next morning. After a few days, a hospital bed and commode were delivered to our house and paramedics helped to relocate Kevin downstairs. My daughter lent me a baby monitor which included a camera so allowed me to try to get some sleep each night while keeping an eye on Kevin. If I needed any help, I either had to request help from Marie Curie nurses or call an ambulance. Marie Curie is a charity which again appears to be providing a service to plug a gap in resources; the nurses did their absolute best but it wasn't ideal: when a patient needs to use the toilet, they can't generally wait for up to two hours. On one occasion, Kevin had insisted on using the downstairs toilet, rather than the commode. The only way I could get him there was to somehow transfer him to the commode chair, and then wheel it into the cloakroom. I'm five foot four inches tall, and around nine stone so transferring him from bed to commode by myself was almost impossible. Somehow I managed it, and pushed him to the cloakroom. By this stage of his illness, the brain tumour had made him aggressive and irrational so when he insisted on standing and walking to the toilet, it all went wrong. He ended up on the floor, trapped between the sink and toilet, covered in faeces, and completely stuck. I called an ambulance.

Similar experience ensued in respect of access to analgesia when the pain in Kevin's head became severe. The immediate response that's needed in this situation, at the end of somebody's life, simply isn't there. Although we'd intended that he should die at home, when a bed became available at the local hospice I felt enormous relief that Kevin accepted. I remember watching as five nurses and an ambulift transferred him onto a commode in the hospice. I also recall that when he was begging for pain relief at the end of his life, the hospice nurses administered this within minutes.

My Dad's end of life care has to be the best we can manage.

Losing My Religion (R.E.M. 1991)

I'm told to pray, by well-meaning individuals with honest hearts and genuine intent. I don't believe in God, but I have respect for the faith of others, whether they are Christian, Muslim, Taoist, Buddhist, Hindu. I have friends who follow these and we occasionally have meaningful conversations about the power of their own faith, and the rights and wrongs of religion. I was baptised a Christian in the Church of England but lost my religion when in my mid-20's. That sounds uncomfortably like losing my virginity, but I just grew disillusioned with going to church and the 'holier than thou' attitude of many parishioners. Since then, I've always been irritated by people who attempt to convince me to follow their faith. Having said that, if people say they are praying for me then I feel humble and honoured. But, I don't appreciate people who say that Nicola and I should pray because I need a heart transplant. I've never perceived myself as a victim and I've never felt sorry for myself when it comes to my condition.

The beliefs I hold are relatively straightforward, I think. I believe that every living entity on this planet is 'in relationship' with others within the natural world around it. Although it's not a religion *per se*, the belief is founded in what is known as Gaia Theory, developed by a scientist called James Lovelock around 1970. Lovelock postulates that the Earth and its atmosphere is a single living entity that's capable of self-adjustment and self-regulation. For example, a tree is in relationship with the air around it, the soil in which it grows, the birds, plants and animals that live in, on and around it and that rely on it - as it does on them. The reliance is mutual. The same for humans and all other living organisms. Each one is dependent on the others for existence, growth and development. For me, there is no God within this but Lovelock named the single entity, Gaia. When I have discussed this concept with religious friends, they tend to tell me that we're pretty much talking about the same thing, meaning what for them is God, for me is Gaia. It's only my opinion (which I stress because I do accept that I may be wrong), but I don't buy the notion that there is a divine being making decisions about humanity: our lives and our tribulations; who has a heart attack; who dies in a motorbike accident; who recovers from cancer; and so on. And there is no divine being deciding whether or not we get a bumper harvest this year.

I studied this subject during my MSc. in Organisation Consulting at Ashridge Business School between 2004 and 2006. I can honestly say Lovelock's was the first and only book I've read that has resonated with me so strongly that I've thought, 'Wow! This makes sense to me - it accurately describes my paradigm, my view of the world. At last an explanation of the world in which I live.' It was as if the author had articulated my beliefs in a way I've never been able to. My view of life and death on Earth fits with this theory - each human being has a brain which is regularly generating electrical impulses. At death, I believe that this 'life force' leaves the body and is absorbed into the ether, the atmosphere surrounding the planet. I don't believe I'll go somewhere (heaven) as a thinking human being in spirit form to watch over others. I'll be remembered by a few people for a couple of generations, after which, nothing. That's how it is and how it should be.

If I believe in anything, with regard to me, my life, my possible death, it's the sheer randomness of it all. This 'thing' known as me: my mind, body and spirit, changes every day. Certain parts die off, certain ones replenish, others simply age. I lean toward the machine metaphor and with mine there's a part, a pump, that's faulty and needs replacing if the whole is to continue.

I happen to live in an age and society when this pump replacement is scientifically, medically and ethically achievable, so this makes it a possibility for me. The professionalism of the highly qualified and experienced physicians at The Freeman leads me to believe it might happen ... if the right replacement pump comes along at the right time. Whether this happens or not is, I believe, based entirely on luck as opposed to the judgement of some divine entity.

Of course, I'm aware that such a pump is likely to come from a man roughly my age and size but I know not what kind of man he will have been, what kind of life he will have led. And neither do I believe how he has lived his life or how I have lived mine have any bearing on our outcomes. It becomes less an issue of religion for me and more an issue of philosophy. I know that I don't ever long for another to die to allow me to live – I could never think like that. I feel much more comfortable in the mindset of 'whatever will be, will be.' There's not a jot I can do to influence matters one way or another. In fact, I am but a jot on this planet and for me it's randomness - for others fate or God - that determines the outcome.

10th September 2015

My Transplant Coordinator at The Freeman, called on Monday to notify me of a suggestion Dr MacGowan and the team have made. They will not admit me to hospital and instead will place me on what they call 'watchful waiting.' This means that as a result of the improvement in my kidney performance, I'm on the cusp of the 'window of opportunity.' I will still definitely need a heart transplant, but she reiterated that 'incarcerating' an apparently healthy patient in hospital is very different from admitting an ill person. Dr MacGowan will see me again on 16th October and we'll take things from there. In the meantime, we need to get all the administrative 'ducks' lined up and orderly; such as consent forms, donor organ choice forms, dental check, vaccinations etc. I drew a graph of what I believe to be the 'window of opportunity,' adapting that which Dr MacGowan had drawn for me, and placing real timeline data into it. It was a great way to practice with Apple's Keynote presentation software! (See figure below).

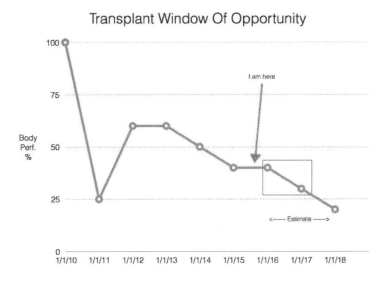

The estimate must include, of course, my deteriorating kidney performance because if they leave my heart alone and continue treatment as medication-based, it's only a matter of time before I need dialysis permanently. I understand they won't do a heart transplant on someone having kidney dialysis because the kidneys 'take a hit' during, and immediately after the transplant. Chronic kidney disease of a serious nature would disqualify me from the heart transplant waiting list so I need my kidneys performing satisfactorily in order to proceed.

I attended an appointment with my Renal Consultant, Dr Helen Collinson, and found that a little frustrating. I'm trying to persuade her that she must concede my overall treatment to Dr MacGowan and the staff of The Freeman Hospital. Now that I'm under that hospital's control, any treatment of my kidneys will be done by them as part of the treatment of my heart condition. She seems reluctant to let go.

I arranged for a dental check-up and also to see my GP for vaccination assessment. I'd really like to return to The Freeman on 16th October having done all of my 'action points.'

Having almost finished Max Crompton's book, I have to confess it leaves me with a range of emotions. I don't regret reading it for a minute, but knowing I will (hopefully) go through a similar experience fills me with dread at times, and joy at others. The recovery process appears to be complex, exhausting and frustrating, as well as having elements unique to each patient. But it's a mountain I'm willing to climb. It reminds me of the praise I receive from people who say I'm coping so well with my condition and the prospect of a heart transplant. It's not a case of coping because in my view I have no choice: it's either a transplant or death from organ failure. What I do try hard with, however, and believe I have choice in is how I respond to suggestions, proposals, assessment and treatment. I'm resigned to the need for a transplant, so either I go through it with a smile on my face, or crying, 'Poor me!'

Will You Still Love Me Tomorrow? (The Shirelles 1963)

It's true to say that I want to have a successful heart transplant so I can continue to live, and enjoy a fuller, richer life. Key to that enjoyment is the relationships I have with family and friends. When Nicola and I started living together in October 2013, I started to have a relationship with her son, Sam, and daughter, Amy. Despite having lost their step-father a short time before, they welcomed me into their lives with such heartfelt warmth, openness and friendship. When we married in June 2015, I 'inherited' Nicola's four grandchildren and one 'step-grandchild.' Sam has twin boys aged 8 years, and Amy has two daughters, Millie, aged 6, and Elodie, aged 3. The girls are without a father (or father figure) in their lives and I'm determined not to become yet another mature male in their lives who they love and then lose. When I arrived on the scene, Millie asked her mum when Grandma's friend, 'Treasure' would visit. She'd misheard my name, but her version stuck and I was 'baptised' Treasure. To the delight of many members of Nicola's family, this seemed to catch on, meaning I'm sometimes in a department store with one of the girls who will yell 'Treasure!' when she wants my attention. Shoppers stare.

One of Sam's twins, Corey, asked his father if, after I have a heart transplant, I'll still love their Grandma, Nicola. I thought that was so sweet, and at first that it showed us the way in which children think. But that's not entirely accurate. I've since read that the adult relatives of heart transplant patients often fear the recipient will lose their love for them. It made me start to think about the words, phrases and metaphors in the English language referring to the heart as the centre of the emotional being. I guess the boys wondered if, at the changing of my heart, I'll have to start again with an emotional blank sheet!

It has been easy to fall in love with all five of these children, the fifth being Ollie, the grandson of Nicola's late husband. Ollie's parents, Stuart and Laura, also welcomed me warmly into the family.

I know it's hard for my sons to come to terms with the possibility of losing their father. Both live in Oslo and we see each other only once a year on average. Christopher is 29, and Daniel is 17 months younger, at 27. To my great sadness, I seem to have a stronger relationship with Christopher as, so far as I can understand, Daniel struggles to come to terms with my divorcing his mother despite this being more than ten years ago.

In 2011, my only sibling, Robert, and I lost both our parents in a car crash. The post-mortem indicated that our father may have had a heart attack (myocardial infarction) at the wheel. His heart condition has no relationship to mine; to my knowledge, cardiomyopathy is not something that has previously occurred in our family, to anyone.

23rd September 2015

My big news came yesterday when the Transplant Coordinator called me from The Freeman to say that on 22nd September 2015, I officially joined the heart transplant waiting list for the UK. It was an odd feeling. I felt happy to hear the news, even a little euphoric, because it's another step forward toward my goal of being fixed and leaving The Freeman a free man with as clean a bill-of-health as possible.

I was waiting in the car while Nicola and her brother, Andrew, were in the Funeral Directors' making arrangements for her Dad, who died the day before. As if we haven't seen enough of hospitals and medical staff lately. Still, I'm relieved for her Dad that it's all over, and his suffering at the end was managed carefully by the hospice staff under the watchful eyes of Nicola and her GP sister-in-law, Anne. They represented him when he was no longer capable of representing himself and they did it in such a stalwart way. He had asked them to do their best to make sure he didn't suffer unnecessarily and this they did impeccably. Don't we all hope for dignity when death finally comes to us? I'm glad that in the almost two years that have passed since his wife died, we took him out on many occasions to restaurants, cinema, theatre, and so on. Best of all, he attended our wedding three months ago and loved the day. I'll miss his making my days warmer with interesting conversation, and I'll even miss his occasional grumpiness. So it's understandable that on returning to the car, Nicola's response to my news was a bit 'flat' as her head was filled with funeral arrangements. We talked about it and didn't argue - we are getting better and better at knowing each other.

Today, I attended Grimsby Hospital for an appointment with Drs Collinson and Imran, Renal Consultants, and kidney transplant nurse, Michele. Both consultants are based at Hull Royal Infirmary but undertake outreach clinics at Grimsby. To cut a long story short, the renal team seem keen to prepare me for dialysis and/or put me in the line for a kidney transplant, leaving me in this weird situation of two medical teams wanting to 'crack on' with two different organ transplants at two different hospitals. You have to love the NHS. Anyway, I again made it clear, politely, that my wish and intention is that my one body, containing heart, kidneys and all other organs is under the jurisdiction of Dr MacGowan at The Freeman Hospital; that we'll be starting with a heart transplant and if thereafter, my kidneys need some form of treatment or replacement, we'll cross that bridge. Dr Collinson suggested I reduce my Allopurinol dosage gradually from 300mg daily to 100mg. Subsequently, I contacted The Freeman and Dr MacGowan approved the change as it's simply an effort to help my kidneys perform better.

These days, I'm carrying three litres of fluid around my stomach and heart, which makes any form of exercise or exertion laborious, and characterised by breathlessness. My stomach is bloated and solid to the touch. I keep telling myself that I know the fluid will leave me at some stage. But, will it? If it does, when will it return and what will be the cause?

The Broken Heart (John Donne, 1573-1631)

It's been a difficult few days. Trevor and I have spent the time since his last trip to Newcastle, catching up on jobs around our home, and visiting my Dad in the Hospice. Dad wasn't keen to go into the Hospice but acknowledged he needed some help. Initially, he seemed to improve a bit after he'd been given oxygen and at least everything was within easy reach for him. I don't think the meals or care at St Andrews' Hospice in Grimsby are a patch on those I experienced with Kevin at St Barnabas' in Lincoln, but at least Dad was safe. He made progress, and plans were made for him to be discharged home, with a 'maximum care package.' Looking after him properly, with just four visits by carers each day was certainly going to be a challenge. I struggle to understand how somebody so frail can be safely looked after in this way. If he happens to want to use the toilet when a carer happens to be present, that would be helpful. In truth, carers don't seem to be allowed to do an awful lot – lifting a patient is out of the question so I'm not convinced it would have worked.

It's sad but you seem to be required to die in a reasonable space of time if you're to occupy a hospice bed. Anyway, a hospital bed had been ordered and Dad had reluctantly agreed this could be sited in his lounge. My brother arranged movement of furniture so the bed could be accommodated together with a commode. And after some confusion, arrangements were made for oxygen cylinders and equipment to also be delivered.

Everything was in place for Dad to be brought home on Friday. But, on Thursday evening his condition worsened and it was decided that he should remain in the hospice over the weekend.

On Saturday morning, Trevor and I called in to see Dad who told me that the doctor had visited and said there was nothing more that could be done. A difficult conversation ensued. Dad told me that he wanted to die and for it to be over with. Since being diagnosed with lung cancer in 2007, he had been anxious about dying through extreme breathlessness and he once again spoke to me about his fear. It was a strange conversation: an intense mix of wanting to say the right thing, not knowing what to say, not really wanting to put thoughts I was having into words, but conscious that time was running out. I don't think anything can prepare you for saying a final goodbye to someone you love. And I'm not sure any of us really feel grown up enough in that moment to have that conversation with a parent. I remember Amy and me teaching Millie that when Elodie was born she would need to say, 'Pleased to meet you.' So, maybe the reverse is, 'It was nice knowing you.'

I don't recall our exact words. Dad was as sharp as ever and we were able to have an authentic conversation. I thanked him for being a great Dad and we talked about a few memories. Dad apologised for ever having smoked, and I reminded him that the world was a very different place when he was a young man. I think I said something about if it hadn't been lung cancer it would have been something else as we can't live forever. Then, we said, 'goodbye.' It was the most emotionally unemotional conversation I have ever had.

After that, we turned to practical matters that are so much easier to discuss. I asked Dad if the doctor had prescribed anything to further relieve his symptoms. Dad said the doctor had, but he didn't hold out much hope of being given them. He'd previously described the nursing as a bit 'hit and miss.' Nurses frequently coming into his room and promising to do something 'in a minute,' but that minute rarely came.

We talked about what Dad wanted. I explained that it was likely he would have been written up for more frequent Diamorphine and possibly other drugs to help calm his breathing. Then I explained it was likely if he was given the dose of drugs prescribed, he would go to sleep and not wake up again so he wouldn't be aware of his breathing. Dad wanted the breathlessness to end. He looked at me with such hope in his eyes and begged me to make sure he got the medication he'd been written up for.

By now, Dad was exhausted and we said a final, 'Goodbye.'

Before I left the hospice, I stopped at the nurses' station and asked what Dad had been prescribed. The nurse explained that although the doctor had written him up for additional Diamorphine and a drug to relax him, he hadn't received these because the details hadn't yet been 'transferred to the nursing notes.' I asked if this could be done and explained Dad's wishes.

When I phoned later that night, the nurse said that Dad was reading his Kindle and had asked her to tell me he was feeling a little better. It didn't wash. I knew he just didn't want me to worry about him.

The next morning, we were called in to the Hospice because Dad's condition had deteriorated further and he had fallen into a coma. When I arrived, my brother and niece were already there. I noticed Dad's shoulders seemed to be heaving each time he took a breath, so I went to the nurses' station to ask what medication Dad had been given that morning. 'Nothing,' was the response, 'because he can't swallow.'

And there began twelve hours of negotiating, pleading, and challenging to secure Dad the death he wanted. It was an emotionally draining experience that I fear will remain with me for a long time. Emotional not just because I lost my Dad, but also because on this occasion end of life care in the Hospice fell short of the standards I would expect.

In the end, we made certain my Dad had a peaceful and comfortable death. We were with him and could reassure him he could let go. I read that somewhere when I was preparing for my late husband's death: sometimes, people who are dying try to hold on, and they can be helped to relax by their loved ones reassuring them that it's fine and they can let go.

After Dad's breathing stopped, I went to find a nurse so that they could record a reasonably accurate time. Then I went to find Trevor. He'd remained in the Visitors' Room because I think he was finding it hard enough to come to terms with his own mortality without experiencing someone else's. Trevor came back to Dad's room with me and we said a respectful goodbye to Dad together.

I believe that everybody deserves as dignified, peaceful and respectful death as possible. And it's important for all healthcare practitioners to remember that those who love the dying person are suffering too. Maybe some day death will cease to be a taboo subject and families will have the conversations that need to happen. How else can we know our loves ones' wishes, especially in respect of organ donation?

Saying goodbye to Dad was especially difficult because I felt anxious his condition has worsened since he knew I would need to spend a lot of time away in Newcastle with Trevor over the coming months. Part of me wondered whether he'd wanted to avoid being one more thing for me to worry about. But I think I also went through the range of emotions most people experience when they lose their last parent. The recognition there has been a shift in the generations and you're now the 'oldest.' The sense of not having a senior person – a proper grown-up - to seek advice from. But most of all, that empty feeling of intense loss and sadness.

Of course, for me, that was all competing for head room with the still vivid memories of Kevin's death, and fear of the future if a heart didn't come available for Trevor.

So, unfortunately, when I came out of the Funeral Directors' and Trevor told me he'd been placed on the waiting list for a heart transplant, I think my response could reasonably be described as impassive. We both knew it was the next step, so - for me at least - it did feel like more of a formality. I was about to go with my brother to register Dad's death and it felt at that moment as though Trevor and I were once again oceans apart.

As I mentioned before, in November 2010, as preparation for my discharge from St Vincent's Hospital, I was fitted with an Implantable Cardioverter Defibrillator (ICD). Professor Macdonald explained he wanted me to accept this equipment mainly because I lived alone and he would feel happier if I had a 'back-up' in case of emergency. In short, an ICD is a pacemaker, a defibrillator and a computer in one, measuring about 4cm x 3cm, designed to monitor and control the heart's performance in terms of rate and rhythm. Leads are connected from the ICD and into the heart's chambers - see figure below. If the ICD detects an abnormality (called an arrhythmia), it will give the heart a gentle nudge and put it back into normal (or sinus) rhythm. If, on the other hand, it figures that a gentle nudge is insufficient, then it will deliver a very firm 'kick up the arse,' exactly the same as a defibrillator applied externally to a patient whose heart has stopped. I felt such trust in the Professor that I signed the acceptance forms and was subsequently taken down for fitting. I remember thinking that anaesthetists are very cool people because mine was giving me a *local* anaesthetic just large enough to tip me over the line into unconsciousness. How do they do that?!

My first recollection was an odd feeling just under my left clavicle that caused me to change my sleeping position from face down to lying on my back. After the stitches were removed, the wound was checked and the small operation was declared a success. However, the surgeon had been unable to check the machine's defibrillator so a few days later I was put to sleep again while the equivalent of a kick in the chest by a horse was delivered. All was found to be working well.

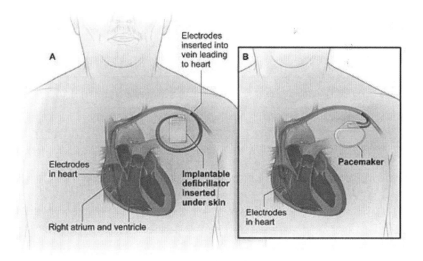

After being discharged, I was scared to death of this machine inside me. It felt like what it was: a foreign body, inserted under my skin and sewn in. It didn't give me any pain at all, but felt alien and somehow, wrong. I'd be so ultra-careful in showering - dab it dry rather than rub it - and generally treat it with tender kid gloves. I went to a support group for ICD ... wearers? owners? customers? and met with many people who were in the same boat. Almost all were older than me by a good ten years. After a presentation, the questions to the technician and the manufacturer's rep. came mainly from women. These fell into two categories: the wives and daughters of men who'd had an ICD fitted, and women with ICDs. Most of the men seemed to be silent recipients, 'wrapped in cotton wool' by their wives and daughters who were the main seekers of information. Just a few anecdotes from these meetings: most women wore a piece of home-made padding (such as a thin sponge) under their bra strap; one woman asked if it was ok to have an argument with her husband as she was frightened that she'd set it off; another worried that the ICD would somehow burst through her skin as it seemed to be so close to the surface. All of the issues were of a psychological nature, rather than physical, but still very real to the people involved.

Following one of these meetings, I decided to do something psychologists call 'reframing.' Cognitive reframing is a psychological technique that consists of identifying and then disputing irrational or maladaptive thoughts: a way of viewing and experiencing events, ideas, concepts and emotions to find more positive alternatives. I decided rather than hold thoughts of an alien being sewn inside me, to 'reframe' the ICD as a friend and ally, a supporter of my heart and a safeguard of my life. Something that had hold of my heart and was helping to keep it safe. I began to appreciate it and at night, before falling asleep, would think thoughts of gratitude, good fortune and well-being as a result of having it. Similarly, I've never entertained thoughts of anger and frustration with my heart, and have never ventured down the path of 'Why me?'

The reframing included silent words of encouragement to my heart for its partial recovery and its performance, fighting back to help me return to the underwater world. I remember having an epiphany moment, a break-through of sorts, when at the home of a dive friend, Dave Harasti and his wife, Suz. Their eldest boy, Will, had some kind of super-hero costume on - I think it was Spiderman - and as usual with three-year olds, his imagination began to take over. I was lying on the ground outside on a warm, summer day playfully wrestling with Will, as Spiderman defeated whichever arch enemy I was supposed to be. Suddenly, Will threw himself onto my chest, wrestled and then stood on me in victory. His right foot was on my ICD and remarkably, I'd not noticed for quite a few seconds. Dave was occupied painting a window frame and Suz was horrified at what she saw, reminding Will of the need to go easy with me. A complete release washed over me - my ICD had finally been given some rough treatment and I hadn't felt a thing. I told Suz I was good, and Will and I continued the game. Driving home with a big smile on my face, it felt as if I'd exorcised a bit of a demon. I'd determined to make my ICD my friend and ally and here it was, happy to take part in some joyful 'rough and tumble' with a three-year old. Just like me. Just like it was a part of me.

25th September 2015

Bigger news still came through yesterday when a voicemail was left on my mobile phone. (Yes, yes, I really must get back into the habit of carrying it around with me.) It was a straightforward message - as a result of a letter received from Dr Collinson, Dr MacGowan would like me to be admitted to The Freeman on Tuesday next week, the 29th September. This is my call for an indefinite stay, the commencement of my 'prison sentence.' I was stunned, and I do know why - one of my personality traits is that I don't react well to late and sudden changes of plan, which is exactly what this is. The appointment, scheduled at Newcastle on 16th October is cancelled and I'm on my bike. A'way the lads, indeed. I was a little upset, knowing that the day is finally here when massive change is being introduced to my life. It means giving up my residence, significant parts of my relationship with Nicola (by that I mean living together, being together, doing things together), and the same for family and friends, too. My independence. Nicola and I watched most of Mary Shelley's Frankenstein and then went to bed to read a little. We cuddled like never before.

29th September 2015

We drove to The Freeman this morning and I took a bay on Ward 27, as usual. After a while my Transplant Coordinator swung by and had a chat with us. As a result of her shift roster, I'd been unable to speak to her on the phone so there was some information missing between us; especially around a) details of the bone marrow issue, and b) Nicola's Dad's death and funeral. The Transplant Coordinator was in good spirits and we had a few laughs, which always feels good, and I noticed that she said something that gave me a eureka moment. I explained I'd struggled a lot with bloating and fluid retention, and Nicola and I have experimented until we're blue in the face to try to find the triggers (specific causes). The Transplant Coordinator shrugged and told us to stop wasting our time because there's only one trigger and that's my 'rubbish' heart. She emphasised the critical need for me to try and maintain a positive mental health in the face of waiting for a heart transplant.

Subsequently, Dr MacGowan arrived and talked to us briefly about a further investigation he wants to do regarding my bone marrow sample results from earlier in the year. He needs to speak with the Haematologist at The Freeman, as well as Dr Bain in Grimsby. In view of this, and also taking into consideration that I look so well, he was quite relaxed about my being admitted a few days after the funeral. Reassuringly, he said we should call or just go to The Freeman if my condition deteriorates or we have any worries between now and then. Of course, it would be remiss of him to see me and fail to have a good stare at the vein in my neck, so he did this and left. Such a nice bloke, I feel privileged and reassured to be treated by him.

So, we left the hospital and drove off to check out some suburbs for a possible apartment location. We established quickly that Jesmond is a serious student area, with most of the properties being former large residences converted to several apartments. We moved on to Gosforth and felt much more comfortable with the 'vibe' there. We called in to an agent's office - Rook, Matthews, Sayer - and looked at photos of what appeared to be a lovely place in a quiet, secure area. The landlord is a doctor and we were so keen on the property that we placed a deposit there and then, without a physical inspection. It will set us back £950 per month and we committed for the minimum 6 months.

I had really mixed feelings about this visit. On the one hand, I'd worked hard to take on board the notion I was being admitted to hospital for an indefinite period, whilst on the other, I was delighted to have been given a few days' postponement. More time with Nicola, a chance to spend some quality time with my son Chris who is visiting the UK, and more of Nicola's home cooking! At least I'd been given a definite date of 13th October 2015 for admission to The Freeman so I can develop my attitude and mental approach. Having had this 'taster,' I know I must stay positive regardless of the challenge of waiting on a six-bedded bay, attached to a drip. I can see I must stay busy, I must develop a routine, and I must look upon my body and mind as one entity that needs to be healthy in the face of a massive operation. Most of all, I *must* believe a donor organ will come available for me.

When at Heart You Should be Sad (Sir Walter Raleigh, 1554-1618)

The recent visit to The Freeman was another test of our mettle. We arrive believing this is it: Trevor will now be a permanent inpatient until a suitable heart becomes available. Or doesn't. A couple of hours later, we're looking at rental properties around Jesmond before once again driving home.

It's difficult. I've been trying to prepare myself for attending Dad's funeral on my own while Trevor is in hospital in Newcastle. Trying to figure what I'll do if a heart becomes available on the same day as the funeral. Trying to figure how I'm going to search for somewhere to live. There seem so many things to sort out that at times I've felt completely overwhelmed. I must admit to also feeling frustrated that Trevor didn't mention Dad's death to the Transplant Coordinator when she phoned, while he was waiting outside the Funeral Directors', to let him know he'd been added to the Transplant Waiting List. I know he's the patient, but at times it feels as though he's living on a parallel planet where only his needs count. I firmly believe if Trevor had explained the situation, Dr MacGowan would have suggested they wait and admit him after Dad's funeral. It's entirely understandable that Trevor's keen to move forward with the heart transplant and wants to feel like he's making progress, but sometimes I don't think he gives much thought to how I'm feeling.

Before we left Newcastle, we looked at one property in Jesmond. It was on the third floor of an old terraced building and had on-road parking. I don't think the area was right for me as it's predominantly student digs. I also think secure parking is important in helping me to feel safe. We called in to an estate agent in Gosforth and liked the look of a property nearby. Viewing wasn't possible, but it looks ideal from the photos: a modern open-plan apartment with two bedrooms and two bathrooms. It's in a small complex and has allocated parking. Since it will be difficult for us to get back to view before we need to take over the tenancy, we drove to the complex and took a look from the outside. We've decided to take the risk. The landlord wasn't keen to let it for just six months, but we offered to pay the full rent in advance and she agreed on this basis. So at least that's sorted.

I really shouldn't be around people at the moment. For the first time in our adult lives, my brother and I have managed to fall out. It's over my Dad's funeral – I didn't mind so much about my Mum's funeral as she and I weren't that close. Curry seemed a somewhat unusual choice for a funeral reception, but not wanting to make a fuss Dad decided to let my sister-in-law have her own way on the proviso that he could also have scones with jam and cream. However, my Dad's funeral is different as I was very close to him and want it to be how he would want. Admittedly, he wouldn't have wanted Andrew and me to fall out about it! I think I'm so focused on trying to get my ducks in a row, I completely forget to have empathy for people outside my immediate sphere. Maybe that's how Trevor's feeling too.

As I dealt with the probate after my Mum died a couple of years ago, as well as for Kevin, initially it seemed to make sense for me to deal with the bulk of work associated with Dad's estate too. Aware that time will be limited, I made a start on it straight away, but the added pressure of Trevor's immediate admission wasn't something I'd foreseen. The list of tasks seems never-ending: as well as the funeral arrangements, there's the issue of the various agencies that need to be informed, the house to be cleared, estate agents appointed. As luck would have it, owing to a computer fault, the 'tell us once' service wasn't working when Andrew and I registered Dad's death. Whilst initially the Registrar assured us it would be up and running in a few days, it's now been decided that the service will not run for the foreseeable future. This means instead of telling one body once, I have to tell everybody individually. My best friend, Christine, came over to help with this; we wrote a list of people we needed to inform and shared the calls between us. I was immensely glad of Christine's support - it's pretty unpleasant explaining to one anonymous person after another that my Dad has died: Department of Work and Pensions; Local Authority; Library; Water Board; DVLA; Passport Office; banks; building societies ... why do old people have so many bank accounts??

Having collected Dad's expanding file from his house, I'd envisaged that his alphabetical filing system would make it straightforward to identify who I needed to contact. I was wrong. Evidently, he'd given up filing anything in any sort of order around 1978. And also retained every bank statement, council tax bill, and any other piece of paper since around that time. I have various piles of paper stacked around the sitting room all waiting for action. As well as the phone calls Christine and I made, I've written a heap of letters and completed numerous forms. Andrew and I have made appointments at most of the banks and building societies in Grimsby. And we've made some progress on clearing Dad's house.

Inevitably, the funeral itself was tough. To add to this, Andrew and I had chosen to hold the funeral reception at a local hotel, but the service was considerably below expectation. Although the food was just about adequate, the requested drinks weren't forthcoming and it was necessary for people who'd attended the funeral to queue to buy drinks from the bar. I felt crushed when a family member admonished me loudly in front of a large group. Oh well, as my Dad would undoubtedly have said, "It's all part of life's rich tapestry."

Young Hearts Run Free (Candi Staton 1976)

After our return home, Nicola and I were being dutiful grandparents when we collected Millie (6) from school and delivered her to her friend Lily's 7th birthday party. En route, she asked me whether it's the red side of my heart that's the problem, or the blue side. 'Whaaaat?' I thought. Nicola explained that Millie has been researching the heart on the internet, and pictures typically present the right side of the heart coloured red – obviously, in the human body this represents the left side of the heart which is responsible for pumping oxygenated blood around the body. Millie also had some other questions, viz:

- What do they do with your old heart after they've put in a new one?
- Is it burned in a box (cremated) like Great-Grandad was?
- Or is it just thrown in the bin?
- Do they sew up your chest after they're finished?
- Is this all done while you're asleep and how do they make sure you don't wake up?

It was moving, refreshing and liberating all at the same time. Moving, because it shows she cares for me and has taken an interest; refreshing because it's rare at my age to witness the beautiful naivety and curiosity of years as tender as hers; and liberating because it forced me into speaking the words, listening to them and being comfortable with them.

The Heart Wants What It Wants (Selena Gomez 2014)

Coping with my gradual deterioration, especially over the last year, has been hard. Far too often I wake in the night and suffer insomnia, itching, restless legs and more. Some are the result of the medications I take, while others are the result of chronic kidney disease (CKD) brought on by my cardiomyopathy. It's not unusual for me to have very dark thoughts at say 4am, after an hour or two of the most uncomfortable tossing and turning in bed. Sometimes, I just want to drive to The Freeman right there and then, and sometimes I just want it all to end. I feel exhausted from lack of sleep, and driven to distraction by the CKD symptoms.

- Walk and/or jog for a mile or two
- Swim 1km as I often did during rehab.
- Run across the road
- Go up stairs two-at-a-time
- Carry a picnic and walk in the countryside
- Bend down and tie my shoelaces effortlessly
- Do small jobs in the garden
- Go on a bike ride
- Shower and dry myself vigorously with a towel
- Sign up with a 'walking football' club
- Wash and polish the cars
- Travel internationally
- Walk up slight incline after having eaten a meal
- Walk up a hill
- Dump indifference and regain enthusiasm for life
- Have a good night's sleep
- Live an active and intimate life
- Play with Nicola's grandchildren

    I lie awake and think of what my heart wants. To some, I think the list will appear uninspiring – there are no marathons, no Tough-Mudders, no Channel swims, triathlons and the like. Instead, I want to be able to return to my version of living life to the full with Nicola, without having the awful anxiety that is associated with so many routine tasks and activities. I've written my 'shopping list' (above) so that I can return to it after my transplant rehabilitation and see what I'm capable of doing.

CHAPTER FIVE

Follow the Heart

Two Hearts (Phil Collins 1989)

I met Nicola at Hydro Fertilisers in 1989. She'd left nursing and having a secretarial qualification was putting that to use in working for the Production Planning Manager while figuring what career path she did want to follow. I needed to liaise with her manager and his staff from time to time. We would chat and sometimes exchange emails through which we discovered a similar sense of humour, wit, and interest in language, literature and the arts.

One Saturday afternoon, we bumped into each other in a local park - Nic had her children with her, and I had my sons with me. We sat on a bench and chatted while the children enjoyed themselves playing on the equipment and then in the circular bandstand. We walked to the aviary and the children were fascinated that I could make Dougal the Parrot speak.

We connected in many ways and somehow progressed to meeting occasionally for a drink in an evening. Through our conversations, it was clear that we shared a common view: we would always make life decisions based on the best interests of our respective children. For me, this meant being a good father to my sons whilst trying to work through the dissatisfaction I felt with my marriage. Fatherhood brought me enormous enjoyment and I wanted to ensure my sons were provided with the childhood they deserved. Similarly, Nicola wanted to persevere at her marriage in the belief that this was best for her children.

In 1990, I was offered a promotion and a move into the sales force, and three years later this involved moving my home and family to Cambridge. My new role required that I attend meetings at the Immingham Fertiliser Plant I'd moved away from which meant Nicola and I could continue to meet socially from time to time when I was in the area. I was disillusioned with my marriage and Nicola was unhappily married to Adrian. It was as if we both needed these infrequent interludes of intelligent conversation and fun to be able to bear the grind of monotonous marriage. For some years, I'd thrown myself at my work in order to distract me from a relationship in which I was unhappy. The business meetings in Immingham were not that frequent, probably just once a month or so, but often enough to continue to spend a little time together. In early 1995, Nicola began divorce proceedings against Adrian, and I moved to a position in Brussels. We decided our circumstances were no longer compatible and we shouldn't see each other anymore. To begin with, we stayed in touch but my career was becoming more international and Nicola had taken a management position at a local hospital.

In August 1995, I received a phone call to say Nicola had fallen from a horse and broken her spine. Not too long after this, I heard on the Hydro grapevine that she had become engaged while in hospital, and later married. Thereafter, we lost contact and probably both thought 'that was the end of that.' Eventually, and maybe inevitably, my marriage to Monica ended and we divorced in 2003.

Nicola and I got back in contact around 2006 with the advent of a website called 'Friends Reunited,' and emailed perhaps once or twice a year; you know the kind of thing, life updates, children's progress and the like. The past stayed in the past.

After I completed my MSc. at Ashridge Management College, I did a post-grad qualification in Executive Coaching. This coincided with Nicola's husband, Kevin, being diagnosed with an aggressive brain tumour. At this time, we began to write more often, maybe once a month. I was learning how to help managers make sense of their working lives, while Nicola was desperately trying to make sense of her personal life. The techniques and methods are very similar.

Kevin passed away in May 2013 and Nicola's children encouraged her to take a holiday – she'd previously given up work as an English teacher while she cared for her dying husband. We agreed that she would come over to Australia where I was living and spend a month with me. When she arrived in September 2013, I'd recently agreed a redundancy package with Hydro and had been searching for an HR position in Australia. Apart from one very quick coffee together in January 2013, when I visited the UK as part of my 'farewell tour,' we hadn't seen each other for over twenty years, but when we met in Australia as widow and divorcee, it was as though time had stood still. Maybe it was the maturity brought on by the passing years, or maybe it was my imagination, but the world for us both felt less pressured, less intense and somehow, calmer. We were in love and the rest, as they say, is history.

My Heart and I (Elizabeth Barrett Browning – 1806-1861)

Trevor and I met in late 1989 when we both worked for Hydro Fertilisers based on Immingham Dock. I worked in Production Planning, and Trevor in Distribution. He'd recently completed his degree in Business Studies and his career at Hydro was beginning to take off. I'd taken a secretarial job while I decided what I wanted to do having given up a career in nursing when I married and had children.

It was strange, certainly not a case of 'love at first sight,' but there was definitely something that attracted us to one another. We exchanged emails, chatted on the phone and became aware we were in similar situations: both, for entirely different reasons, in unfulfilling marriages. And we both felt the same sense of responsibility for maintaining stability for our children.

As our friendship developed, we discovered an outlet from the mundanity of our marriages: snapshots of intelligent conversation, humour, and sensitivity. I thought these fleeting episodes of sanctuary would enable me to continue in my marriage. And I think Trevor felt similarly in terms of his marriage. When Trevor was promoted and moved to Cambridge in 1993, we continued to see each other on the odd occasion he was in Immingham for meetings. Our stolen moments averaged around one evening a month, which was more or less the same as when he'd lived locally. We emailed each other lots; that was always part of our connection, the joy of words.

Eventually, my marriage came to an end when it dawned on me that continuing was more psychologically damaging to my children than splitting up could ever be. By this time, I'd reignited my NHS career with a management role and felt prepared for independence. In late 1994, I began divorce proceedings, and early in 1995 I met Trevor for lunch and explained I couldn't see him anymore. I needed to move on with my life. We did exchange a few emails and Trevor sent me a postcard from Brussels where he was working. He'd borrowed the words from a Beautiful South track: 'I love you from the bottom of my pencil case.' I kept it. I'm not sure why. I remember it was in a basket in my kitchen.

Later in 1995, just after I'd started dating Kevin, I had a horse-riding accident and broke my spine. It was a bad break, not that I imagine there's a good one. I asked my friend, Christine, to phone Trevor, tell him about my accident and ask him not to contact me. No more emails. No more cards. The next few months involved a lot of surgery and rehabilitation. And a lot of pain. Kevin moved in, our relationship flourished and we went on to marry.

It wasn't until around ten years later, with the advent of Friends Reunited, that Trevor and I resumed some contact, just emailing a couple of times a year with updates on family and career.

And then in October 2011, my world turned upside down when Kevin was diagnosed with a devastating brain tumour. The worst kind: glioblastoma. It was a death sentence and I struggled enormously to come to terms with the brick wall I was facing. By now, Trevor was living in Australia, and when I told him of Kevin's diagnosis, and prognosis, he offered a shoulder. Sometimes, I would email him when I was confused or frustrated with events. Sometimes, he could help me to make sense of what was happening. Sometimes, he was just a person far away from my dark world who wrote to me about books, music, films ... anything that wasn't terminal illness.

Early in 2013, having decided to take a redundancy package from Hydro and settle in Australia, Trevor visited the UK on his 'farewell tour.' We met for a coffee and fell into our trademark banter. It was a brief, light-hearted respite from the brutal reality of terminal cancer.

When Kevin passed away in May 2013, Trevor and I agreed I should take a holiday in Australia. A month on the other side of the world to have a complete break from ... well, from being Nicola, really. I guess it was an opportunity to rediscover myself. To discover what next. But, as we exchanged emails and planned the holiday, we began to realise that instead of a whole bunch of reasons we couldn't be together, there was just half a world standing between us. It was now or never. And neither of us saw never as an option.

A month after my trip to Australia, Trevor moved back to the UK and we settled into living together. I was conscious how fortunate I felt of this second chance of happiness. There was just one blot on our horizon. While I was in Australia, Trevor had an out-patient appointment with his Cardiologist who delivered the blow that, in his opinion, Trevor's prognosis was five-ten years as long as he didn't get flu or something. That was difficult, but if anything strengthened our resolve to be together and made us commit to having the best possible five-ten years.

And now, just two years in and we're forced into separate lives as Trevor is admitted to The Freeman Hospital. Facing turbulence in our relationship as we learn to live under an entirely new set of circumstances. Facing a future devoid of certainty.

PART II

A Change of Heart

CHAPTER SIX

The Heart Misses a Beat

15th October 2015

I was admitted to The Freeman Hospital two days ago for an indefinite period. As we left, we said goodbye to the landscape gardeners working at our home - it will be an exciting sight to return to: a completely rebuilt front and rear garden based around low maintenance principles. En route to the hospital, we stopped by at Gosforth and were shown around the property we plan to rent for Nicola. We're both very happy with it; it's relatively new, modern, two bedrooms, a beautiful shared garden and in a safe and secure setting.

We arrived at the hospital and reported to Ward 27 as usual. There, I was shown into a cubicle, rather than placed on a shared, six-bed bay, which in itself lifted my spirits substantially. It was a strange feeling. After several visits to The Freeman over the last three months, this time I'm here to stay until the most important event of my life takes place. I struggle with fully appreciating the enormity of the situation. How many people do you know who've had a heart transplant? Do you even know anyone who knows someone who's had one? As I unpacked, these were the thoughts going through my mind. Nicola was still trying to find a parking space so it was a lonely, empty few minutes as I went about the task.

Quite quickly, a nurse arrived to take my bloods and soon after that, Dr MacGowan stopped by. He explained that he was still working on tying up the loose ends associated with my haematology results - the various tests I'd had at The Royal Free Hospital in London earlier in the year. Two junior doctors arrived separately over the next few hours; I've often been a fascination, something of a puzzle for the medical profession so it's not unusual for me to be quizzed about my history. Around 6pm, Nicola left me to go to the Premier Inn she was staying at, and we spoke with tenderness, love and affection at the challenging prospect of spending our first ever night apart. New territory for the both of us.

Later, a dapper and articulate Dr Wallace, the Freeman's Consultant Haematologist, arrived and together we went through the history of the investigations into various blood disorders that the Royal Free had looked at. It was a bit of a 'downer' when he explained that the presence of rogue 'kappa' proteins in my blood may be a block to my being entered on the 'urgent' heart transplant list. There is a 5-10% chance of my contracting cancer of the blood - myeloma - after a transplant, and as the chemotherapy treatment would be quite severe on my system, it's possible that my body wouldn't be able to cope. A multi-disciplinary team (MDT) meeting will take place at noon on Friday and a decision will be taken. After he left, a range of turbulent emotions tore through me. Having been told repeatedly that I've been admitted for a heart transplant, it's clear now that this might not be the case. We've just signed a six month lease on an apartment and now we might not need it. I've just prepared my life in such a way as to allow a 6-12 month period 'out,' readied myself for the long haul, informed families, friends, financial adviser and his faithful dog, and now I mightn't get out of the starting blocks. I accept these things are complex but the pendulum swings between 'Yes, we can save your life,' and 'Hmm, now we're not so sure.' How do I deal with that level of uncertainty?

Yesterday, 14th October, Dr MacGowan returned and informed me that in his opinion, it's worth taking that risk and though he can't make any promises, he expects to recommend I be listed as urgent. That picked me up somewhat. There's something about his matter-of-factness, his clarity and brevity. Without the words being said, I sense he believes it's going to happen and that transmits to me, filling me with optimism. Some doctors have the ability to do that.

The reason for delaying my journal until today, my third day of 'incarceration,' is that I wanted to give my reflections on what for me is a very interesting subject - the degree to which I succumb to 'institutionalisation' at the hospital. The comparison with a prison term is, I'd imagine, both relevant and appropriate but I plan to let the reader decide. The task I have set myself is to observe, notice and describe.

On arrival, I spread out my possessions in the room and waited for someone to visit me to explain the routine of the ward; for example, meal times, drink times, visiting times, lights out, and so on - the general protocol, or as we used to say at work to new employees, the way things get done around here. No-one came to do this - I had to figure them out for myself, through observation and inquiry. I'm not a very outgoing type as the 'new boy on his first day at school' and I noticed that I was extremely reluctant to approach the nurses' station. It seems as though many staff are there, and if I can't find the nurse allocated to me, others haven't much of a clue who I am. Most appear to avoid making eye-contact in case I become a task, one more little job to do. Even after three days, I'm not sure to whom I need give notice that I want to go for a walk around the main hospital corridors, because the nurse allocated to me doesn't make themselves known. I guess this is what 'going stir crazy' means - I honestly don't know how I'll cope with an extended period of time either in one room, or worse, on a bed in a bay of six.

My Transplant Coordinator called in to say that if I move to the urgent transplant list, which is likely, then I'll move to the Coronary Care Unit (CCU) and share a ward with four other men who're also waiting; two of them on VAD pumps and two of them like I'll be, on inotropes. I don't relish the thought of being connected to a drip permanently, but hey, I guess that's going to be the least of my challenges when things get underway.

I've really had to insist that my diet be controlled according to the needs of my kidneys. Again, no-one it seems, except myself and Nicola, thinks it important, but I know I need to do whatever I can to protect my kidneys. Nicola knows this dietary stuff better than me, even down to ingredients level, but I have learned the basics of what I need to avoid; high salt and potassium foods being just two. Certain fruits, cheeses, meats, vegetables needing to be cooked in a certain way, and so on. My kidneys are critically important in the big scheme of things - I know that much - and as my weak heart has supplied them with a poor pump performance for five years, they need all the TLC they can get.

Eventually, and at our request, a lovely woman called Kerry made enquiries and came up with a menu for renal patients. I have to say, the choices seem to be the same as the general menu but with restrictions on potatoes. The odd thing is, there appears to be less correlation than you would expect between what I order and what I receive. I find it a wee bit sad that Kerry, who delivers my meals so cheerily, has had no training in dietary control and didn't know that a banana is high in potassium, for example. It's not Kerry's fault, rather the NHS for failing to develop competence in *everyone*.

After two nights, I've hardly slept a wink. I'm on a single bed, with a mattress and two pillows covered in plastic. The sheets are like cardboard so I can seek no comfort from them, and similarly blankets have been washed and cleaned a thousand times. When bed-making, the healthcare assistants often have to reject sheets as they've not been adequately cleaned and are still soiled. But there appears to be no quality-control system, or process for providing feedback to the laundry service. It seems like a lot of wasted effort.

In my efforts to achieve sleep, I lie inside, I lie on top, I sweat, I shiver, I try face down, on my side, bed flat, bed tilted. I try every combination and when I've exhausted them, I begin again. I'm suffering a heightened level of restless leg syndrome as well as uncontrollable itching, but it's the noise that wears me down more than anything else. Layer by layer the sounds build - nurses shouting, from bed to bed patients calling, cleaners cheerfully chatting, mops and buckets clanging, blood pressure machines buzzing, monitors beeping, tea ladies' 'Milk and Sugar?' trilling, ambulance sirens wailing, paramedics delivery announcing, porters whistling, fire alarms testing, visitors laughing, the lost directions-seeking, the doctors' phones ringing, staff gossiping, the urgent footsteps striding, the television game show hosts guffawing, and different radios tuned to different stations playing. I use toilets and showers that others use, and I never cease to be amazed at what patients think is acceptable to leave behind. Many leave towels lying on the floor, much as you might in a hotel. Occasionally, it's faeces, urine, blood or vomit that greets me when I walk in. It's not the nurses' fault, they clean up as soon as they're made aware of it. 'Don't let the bastard system grind you down,' I tell myself, but it does; it wears away at my spirit inexorably, like the tide against the coastline. There are no rules, everyone wants to be kind and tolerant, but the fact is members of the public have different personal standards, and some are way below reasonable. I just don't function well in a system like this.

I've decided not to ask for medication to help me sleep as I want to give it time to see if I can adjust without. Nicola asks me not to discount sleeping tablets entirely, even if this is just to offer me the sanctuary, and sanity, of an occasional night's sleep. I know she's right, and they have now been prescribed, but the fear of dependence is currently greater than the exhaustion through lack of sleep. At times I'm shocked by the behaviour, noise and general lack of supervision in and around the nurses' station. Afternoons, especially during visiting hours, are much worse than mornings when nurses seem to be at their most industrious. I'm all for people enjoying their work and having fun, but there are limits. Management should be hell bent on greater gender diversity - the ratio here is about 14:1 of women over men - as this would undoubtedly bring greater efficiency.

An alarming and amusingly worrying aspect of being placed in an institution is the way I have started to look forward to meal times and drink breaks. Today, the serving staff failed to offer me afternoon tea, so half an hour later, I found myself striding down the corridor to get what's rightfully mine! There is an element of humour here but seriously, I notice I start to time my day according to events like food and drink. The day seems so much longer if even a most trivial event is missed. I did it politely and kindly, of course. The food so far has been extremely average to say the least, serving to remind me of the way I'm spoiled by Nicola's home cooking and baking. Psychologically, I think there's also an element of a friendly face breaking up the monotony in something as simple as serving me a cup of tea. As at home, I try to make sure I savour each mouthful of food, so that I focus on taste and texture, and despite its mediocrity, strive to enjoy it.

    Nicola and I walked to the hospital restaurant so she could have some lunch. It's interesting to observe the food choices of the cross-section of society dining here. I commented to Nicola that the restaurant offers healthy and non-healthy choices; it seems, though, that many overweight people choose not only unhealthy, but huge portion sizes. (They're allowed to serve themselves.) Looking at the level of obesity on display at this hospital - patients, visitors and staff alike - it's difficult to understand how people's hearts can possibly keep on distributing blood around their vast bodies. Nicola chose soup for lunch and smiled when I explained that when it's served to 'us,' it comes in a mug. That small pronoun 'us' has significant connotations in terms of institutionalisation: I see myself as belonging to a defined group, of which Nicola is not a part. She pointed this out and though my response was a little grumpy, she's absolutely right. Nicola can eat her soup from a bowl, with a spoon, wherever she wants. I am served mine in a mug, by a nurse. My choices, and with them my identity, appear to be shrinking already; I have a wristband - a tag - with my name and number on.

My Heart and I (Elizabeth Barrett Browning 1806-1861)

And so it begins: today, Trevor was admitted to The Freeman and I'm now sitting in a room at the Holystone Premier Inn, on my own. It seems strange being alone at the hotel we've stayed in together so many times over the last few months. As regulars, we've got to know some of the ladies on reception here quite well; they ask about Trevor and seem genuinely concerned. It's kind of reassuring to see a friendly face and not be surrounded by strangers all of the time.

I'm not sure exactly how I feel. Frightened. I worry about how I'll cope, but I'm not even sure what I'm coping with. Lonely. Since we began living together, Trevor and I have rarely been apart; I'd never have believed it possible to spend the amount of time together that we do, but somehow it works. Now, I feel uncertain about what to do or how to spend the time. I did go to the restaurant for something to eat, but it was weird being in there without Trevor. I wasn't really hungry so found it difficult to eat.

There's also something about having felt responsible for Trevor for so long now that I'm reluctant to let go. It sounds like I'm building my part up, but I worry that nobody else will look after him as well as I would. In contrast, I also feel a sense of relief - I know there will be a lot more waiting, but at least we're no longer waiting for Trevor to be admitted to hospital.

We've both been feeling the stress in recent days and yesterday evening the tension boiled over. We were finishing our packing – a task that, if he were honest, involved more physical exertion than Trevor was really capable of - and once done, we'd planned to sit down together for our last evening. But before we'd finished the packing, Trevor's youngest son, Daniel, phoned. After the call, Trevor was upset and tearful. I tried to console him: told him that Daniel would be fine, other people would support him, and Trevor needed to focus on himself. Platitudes, mainly. In essence, Daniel's call had brought Trevor face-to-face with his own mortality and his own fears. My words simply made a difficult situation worse.

Sadly, some tension remained this morning, and I'm not sure the issue was resolved by the time we arrived in Newcastle.

Pondering on this in my hotel room, and in the absence of any obvious alternatives, I shed a few tears in the hope that might make me feel better. It didn't! So, I opted for a soak in the bath with a cup of tea. Amy always laughs that a bath is my guaranteed cure-all!

Later, I phoned Christine; we talked a bit about Trevor and the hospital, but also about teaching and other stuff. It felt good to chat and to laugh a little. It has begun to feel as though Trevor and I are living in a bubble from which we can see the outside world, but not touch it. I think it's tempting in this type of situation to begin to believe that you are the only ones facing any challenges, but it's all relative really. After listening to Christine's stories of recent classroom histrionics – pupils' not Christine's – I did reach one conclusion: I'd rather be in this hotel, with Trevor in hospital waiting for a heart transplant, than trying to teach 8JBL, my worst ever class!

I made another cup of tea and Trevor sent me a text about his visit from a Haematologist. It's frustrating that only now has anybody at The Freeman decided to look at Trevor's dodgy blood results which I tried to share with them back in July. The Renal Department at Grimsby Hospital referred Trevor to Haematology last year when they noticed that he has a high level of kappa protein cells in his blood. After a bone marrow biopsy and skeletal survey at Grimsby, he was referred to the Royal Free in London where he underwent extensive investigations to test for amyloidosis, and then for light chain deposition disease. Both of which were eliminated. I'd felt frustrated when I tried to explain this aspect of Trevor's medical history and hand a copy of the blood and bone marrow results to the Transplant Coordinator after the initial transplant assessment. I was more or less told 'not to worry my pretty little head about it.' Perhaps Trevor and I are more switched-on than other patients, but it would be helpful if clinicians wouldn't treat everybody as though they're entirely clueless. Ironically, the NICE guidelines require clinicians to 'involve' patients in decisions about their health. Ha! That's not going to happen unless and until some clinical staff improve their skills in listening.

16th October 2015

Ouch! It came like a kick in the stomach, hitting me totally 'out of left field' as the Americans say. Dr Wallace and Dr MacGowan came to visit me after the MDT meeting today. This was the meeting at which it would be agreed I'd join the urgent list forthwith. The Transplant Coordinator had told me earlier that she would be the one handling the associated administrative tasks. Dr Wallace explained that the blood test he'd requested had been done and the results were worrying. The level of the rogue 'kappa' protein in my blood has increased from around 300 to 750 since it was tested by The Royal Free Hospital in London. He had discussed my case with my Haematologist in Grimsby, Dr Levison-Keating, and with Dr MacGowan. The fact is that such a high 'kappa' count, if it continues at such a growth rate, would give me a 30% chance of developing myeloma, or cancer of the blood, at some stage in the future. More worryingly, the other blood protein measured, lambda, has not increased; the ratio between these two proteins is what concerns Dr Wallace the most. Apparently, the increase in this ratio may be an indication that there has already been some progress in any blood disease. If treatment of this condition is required, it tends to be a combination of medication and chemotherapy, and as such I would not be allowed onto the heart transplant waiting list. If I were to have a heart transplant, there could subsequently be an unacceptably high risk of my developing cancer of the blood. Treatment of the cancer would then risk harming the transplanted organ and challenging my immune system. They can't risk wasting an organ on a person who might die from something else within a short period of the transplant. The doctors are of the opinion that I may be suffering from two serious, and unrelated conditions - a heart and kidney problem, and a likely cancer of the blood problem. Now that's what I call bad luck!

I feel immensely frustrated by all of this. The medical profession has brought me so very far down the transplant track - I've actually been admitted to hospital on the basis of an indefinite stay - only to do a 'U-turn' because what was originally described as a formality has become a 'deal breaker.' When we first came to The Freeman, and were told the world-rocking news that I need a heart transplant, Nicola offered to one of the Transplant Coordinators a detailed report by The Royal Free on my blood condition. Nicola had brought a spare copy with us just in case. This was declined and we were told that The Freeman itself would do all the necessary transplant tests when assessing my suitability. We were not to worry and should leave everything to them. That same report was the one that piqued Dr Wallace's interest when I gave it to him earlier this week. He could have had it two months ago.

Dr Wallace seemed keen to discharge me back to the care of Grimsby Hospital, but Nicola intervened and suggested it would be both preferable to us and speedier in terms of their reaching any decision, for the bone marrow biopsy which is now deemed necessary, to be undertaken at The Freeman. This would avoid any conflicting priorities between different hospitals, and also ensure that a single laboratory is responsible for analysing the tests. (Where would I be without my wife, who seems so 'on the ball' when my head is spinning, frantically trying to take it all in?) Dr MacGowan supported this proposal and it was arranged for me to have another bone marrow biopsy at The Freeman, on Monday next week. Both Nicola and I had the distinct impression that Dr MacGowan wished to proceed with listing me, while Dr Wallace was caution personified. If the risk of myeloma was 5-10%, Dr MacGowan said that's a risk he was prepared to take, but Dr Wallace puts the figure at closer to 30%.

My biggest challenge now is my psychological state. The Transplant Coordinators and various other staff have emphasised since the beginning the huge importance of a) positively wanting a transplant, and b) maintaining a positive attitude throughout an indefinite stay. When this was explained, I could see the sense and set about the process of moving from a stance of absolute abhorrence to the notion of transplant, to welcoming and hoping for it. I had reached the point of wanting to get on with it, even to the point of enthusiastic anticipation. To do this is no mean feat; it takes an awful lot of reflection and a deep look into my own psyche. Do I feel I'm in competent hands? Yes! Do I accept that without a transplant, my life is considerably shortened? Yes! Do I want to be around for my wife, family and friends? Of course! Do I want my life back? Certainly. Am I prepared to go through the incarceration, sacrifices and pain? I am. Do I have any choice? No!! Now, it seems, there's a considerable chance that The Freeman will be sending me on my way having said that there's nothing they can do for me. The future once more looks very bleak. The pendulum has swung again. A Paul Simon lyric runs through my head, "I want a shot at redemption. Don't want to end up a cartoon in a cartoon graveyard." (You Can Call Me Al – 1986.)

19th October 2015

I shudder to think of the cost of the waste. The deficits that almost all NHS Trusts are facing, along with hospital performance are in the news every single week. £2 billion is the shortfall for 2015, yet I repeatedly see waste, inefficiency and delay through my patient eyes. My experience here suggests that the doctors and consultants are exceptional - highly competent, professional, and articulate with a great bedside manner. The staff supporting these people are a different matter altogether. The work environment is akin to a social club with work periodically interrupting group gossip; miscommunication and misunderstanding is the norm rather than the exception; and standards generally – from dress to safety – are low. Without question, the ward is overmanned because people are asked to work according to the division of labour rather than process.

Let me describe this morning's experience: I was allowed to leave on Friday evening on condition that I returned on Monday morning for the bone marrow biopsy. This will ensure Dr Wallace has access to more and better information regarding the kappa levels in my blood, and will enable a definitive decision regarding my suitability for transplant. When this was agreed on Friday evening, the staff nurse asked that we arrive between 8.30am and 9am for the procedure to be carried out at 11am.

We arrived today at 8am and I was shown to the same cubicle I occupied last week. We had some breakfast in the canteen and returned around 8.30am. At 10am, no-one had spoken to me or visited me, so Nicola suggested I go and ask when the procedure will be carried out, where and by whom. I was reluctant to do so because my preference is simply to register my arrival and sit and wait. I conform to the hospital's (inadequate) system. Nicola's, in contrast, is to question, clarify and liaise with nursing staff so as to ensure they are 'on my case.' In hindsight, I am glad I followed Nicola's advice if only for the fact that she knows hospitals and how they work, and I don't. At 10am I approached the nurse responsible for me, a lovely woman named Rosie, only to discover she had no idea what was supposed to be happening. She couldn't answer any of my questions and promised to get on the case immediately. A short time later, Rosie came into my cubicle to say that there had been some confusion, but a doctor would come to my room to carry out the procedure within the next hour or two. Nicola was right – if I hadn't pursued my case, I think I'd still be waiting three days later. Golly, I hate saying 'You were right and I was wrong,' to my wife!

The doctor arrived, Nicola left, and part of the bone marrow biopsy was done. I say 'part' because it's in two sections: the 'lower pain' bit and the 'high pain' bit. The doctor could only do the first as I bled more than she liked and she didn't fancy doing the second based on what she saw. (I had the strong sense that she wasn't at all confident in what she was doing; she seemed really scared of hurting me.) My attitude is that it's impossible to do a bone marrow biopsy that doesn't hurt the patient, so let's bloody well get on and get it over with. She said she'll give the samples she has taken to Dr Wallace and he'll decide if he has what he needs for analysis and data. She dressed the wound and told me to remain on my back to help stop the bleeding. She said she'd tell the nurse to check after fifteen minutes that the bleeding had stopped. Forty minutes later no-one had arrived to do the check. I called to Rosie, as she went by, but she didn't hear me. A few minutes later I called another nurse who went by my door, and I explained the situation. I asked her if she'd just take a look and confirm it had stopped. It was then that the 'ikke mit bord' happened, to quote some Norwegian. Translated, it's a saying that describes a restaurant waiter if you stop them and ask for something and they reply - 'you're not my table.' In other words, I wasn't her patient. The nurse told me she'd have to get Rosie to check it as she is my nurse. Seeing the amazed and disgruntled look on my face, and at my encouragement she came closer to the bed and confirmed the bleeding had stopped. All she had to do was look at it!

I know it's only a small example, but many Organisation Consultants will say that this picture tells a thousand words; about empowerment, decision making, leadership, teamwork, and the way work gets done. A hospital is task and specialism oriented rather than process and flow. It's vertical rather than horizontal.

After lunch, Dr MacGowan swung by, and later my Transplant Coordinator As far as they're concerned, one situation they must avoid is giving me a new heart, which involves medication that suppresses my body's immune system (to avoid rejection of the new organ), then finding that I need chemotherapy to fight cancer of the blood. This would drive my body's immune system in the other direction. It makes sense and there's nothing personal in it. I know it's for my own good, and hey, they can't risk wasting a heart, but I'm rapidly approaching the end of my rope. If I didn't know better, I'd believe it was all part of some huge sick joke, to mercilessly play with my emotions - we swing from hope, optimism and positivity to despair, pessimism and negativity, and back again, on and on. Each time - and I think this is inevitable - I begin to adjust my psychological state, my mindset to coping with the predicted outcome. I can't take much more. Just tell me definitively, please, yes or no, live or die, thumb up or down.

Nicola returned after a while - she'd spent some time sitting in the sunshine outside, keeping out of my way, reflecting on the tense conversation we'd had earlier about the benefits, or not, of being an "active participant" in my healthcare, as opposed to a "passive recipient" (her words). We talked about this a little and Nicola asserted that although in many ways she would prefer to have 'blind faith' in the system and simply assume that everybody is working to a clearly defined process - tests will be done and results made available in a timely manner - she has experienced the NHS as a nurse, a manager, a patient, and a carer. That makes it very difficult for her not to spot gaps in service and question assurances that 'everything is in hand.' We have been assured that a decision on my suitability for heart transplant will be made at the MDT on Friday. Dr Wallace needs to provide input, and to enable this, he explained to us last Friday, he requires a number of complementary investigations to be carried out and reported.

So far, I have had part of a bone marrow biopsy; the full procedure was aborted because I bled a lot. Nobody has discussed any other investigation. Nicola obviously felt anxious about encouraging me to follow this up with my named nurse, but still chose to risk having the discussion with me. This time, I obligingly spoke with my named nurse. She agreed to contact my Transplant Coordinator who, a little later, came to my room. When I asked about other procedures, she said nothing else was scheduled, but as I'd had a bone marrow biopsy, clearly Dr Wallace was on the case and discussing it with his team. Nicola was less than convinced.

Towards the end of the afternoon, the doctor who had performed the procedure returned and explained that the results so far showed no changes from the previous bone marrow biopsy done in March at Grimsby. She hadn't been able to discuss this with Dr Wallace as he was away for the day, but she would catch him before clinic tomorrow and find out whether he wanted her to perform a complete biopsy. She also told me not to take warfarin tonight, just in case she needs to dive into my bone and suck out some more marrow. My words, not hers!

Nicola and I asked about the other tests and the doctor said that she wasn't aware of these. She looked at the notes I carry, and asked about previous tests I'd had. She made some notes and said she would also discuss with Dr Wallace the further tests he would like arranged. We explained that whilst we didn't want to appear demanding, we are keen to ensure that all information is available on Friday to enable a decision to be made. Since I'm in hospital all week, it seemed reasonable to suggest that the tests could be done at any time.

So, that's day one. Nothing much achieved. A life or death decision for me, but that doesn't change anything in the way the system creaks on at its own pace.

AMY: *Are you okay? Went to hairdresser and then swimming with Ella x*

NICOLA: *I'm fine. Was just fed up and was going to bore you with it. Difficult. But I am fine. Xx*

AMY: *Have they done bone marrow? X*

NICOLA: *Yes, but only part of it cos bled cos of warfarin!! X*

AMY: *Oh God. So do they have to do it again? X*

NICOLA: *We'll find out tomorrow. It's so disorganised. The Haematologist definitely said he needed several tests to make a definitive diagnosis – CT, bloods, bone marrow. Just bone marrow half done and everybody telling me not to worry my pretty little head about anything else. I just know we'll get to Friday and they'll realise don't have all info they need. It's like Chinese water torture for me!!!!! X*

AMY: *What a nightmare ☹ Are you staying there in the meantime? X*

NICOLA: *Yep. All freaking week!! I think Trevor's allowed out at night. Need to get here between eight and nine each day. Parking a nightmare. No decision on anything until Friday!! X*

AMY: *Not surprised, it sounds like torture. Can you plan some meals out or anything? Is Trevor up for it? X*

NICOLA: *I think we just need to get through the next week and try to 'go with the flow.' I'm very bad at that! X*

Unsurprisingly, it wasn't possible for the MDT to make a decision on Friday about whether Trevor should be added to the urgent waiting list. The results of tests weren't available – inertia reigns supreme!

So, we're back home. Waiting. Again! Oh, and, just for good measure, various key people aren't available this week, and it's half term next week, so no decision will be made for a few weeks. Still think I should write to Jeremy Hunt and suggest he rethinks his whole '7-day NHS' thing. I remember my frustration while working in the NHS where it was entirely implausible to expect to get anything done during sizeable chunks of the year: ski-ing holidays during February/March; Easter holidays; Whitsun half term; six weeks summer holidays; October half term; and you really could forget about anything from 1st December because staff were winding down for Christmas and New Year! During each of these periods, staff absence meant serious reductions in theatres and clinics, and progress was severely restricted on any service developments or plans. The problem is compounded by the absence of any real flexibility between staff. The NHS is excellent at specifying precisely how many additional hours will be required and how much it will cost to carry out an additional theatre list or clinic: ward/clinic clerk time, secretarial, clinic/theatre/ward nurses, porters, theatre technicians ... the list is infinite. By contrast, in my twelve years as an NHS manager, I never once heard anybody say, 'This clinic/theatre is cancelled today so what should we do with the freed-up resources?'

Meanwhile, Trevor's struggling a lot. He is managing virtually no sleep and lies awake for hours each night with restless legs and ceaseless itching. I wish so much that there was something I could do to help him. He's determined that he won't take sleeping tablets; it's almost as though even considering it is somehow giving in. During the day, he is surprisingly perky. For someone who needs an urgent heart transplant, he looks remarkably well.

4th November 2015

Today, the awaited phone call from my Transplant Coordinator finally came: "We've done the bone marrow tests, Trevor, and Drs Wallace and MacGowan have decided that you are transplantable."

The wave of relief was palpable. I thought I'd prepared myself for the possibility of bad news - to hear that there's no more they can do for me - but in that moment, I realised I hadn't. Breathe, process the information, relax.

In just a few weeks, I'd moved emotionally from finding the word 'transplant' truly abhorrent, to loving it, savouring it, practising how it sounded, rolling it around my mouth. I'm suitable for a transplant. When you are dying, and you receive good news like this, you don't jump around for joy, elated. The context doesn't allow it. It's good news. No, great news. But I'm still dying, still slowly deteriorating, and a whole lot more good news is needed before I can even contemplate celebration. I raised a smile - grateful, humble, satisfied and happy for now.

By coincidence, my brother arrived when I was on the telephone and it felt good to share the news with both him and Nicola together. Though we've never lived in each other's pockets, the bond between us is strong. The deaths of our parents in 2011 inevitably brought us closer together. I feel a responsibility to come through this for him, and for others of course, so they don't have to deal with loss. It's strange, imagining what their lives will be like without me in them. We're a very small family and somehow it felt reassuring and comfortable to have a 'blood connection' in this moment. I shed a few tears, perhaps not as many as if I'd been alone with Nicola. The additional news was that there are two patients - we have to assume of my general size and blood type - who are now in The Freeman, awaiting donor organs.

Reflecting on the conversation with my Transplant Coordinator, I notice I feel a little outrun as I register that two guys are now ahead of me in the queue. It's not a competition, I know that. In some ways, though, it feels like a race, not against others, but against my own body. In fact, if there are three of us waiting to be transplanted, once body size, blood type and antibodies are taken into account, the chances of more than one of us being a perfect match is extremely remote. I'm philosophical about what comes available, when and for whom. If ever 'que sera, sera' applied, it's here. Not for a moment could I be envious of a person receiving 'perfect compatibility' news. To him, as the Aussies would say, 'Good on yer, mate!'

The choice offered to me was between being admitted to the hospital to start the wait, or to wait at home, for maybe a couple of months. I felt nervous about making that choice, fearful of 'out of sight, out of mind,' until the transplant coordinator reassured me she'd keep an eye on my condition through weekly emails. If

I deteriorate, then I'll be admitted immediately. Based on this, I chose to wait from home. It's difficult, because if I'm honest I do feel that my condition is making life tough for Nicola, and I just want to get on with the transplant. But, in reality, being admitted to hospital right now is unlikely to bring a transplant closer. For me, the window hasn't opened yet.

Nicola and I talked about the apartment we've found in Gosforth, which is still being held for us. Despite the probability that the apartment will stand empty until after Christmas, we decided fairly quickly to contact the letting agent and commit to a six month lease. Yes, there's a cost to that, but we felt the peace of mind of having an apartment for Nicola to move directly into is well worth it. We just have to hope the doctors don't change their mind, after we've spent over £6000 on a property rental.

All of My Heart (ABC 1982)

In the end, we waited ten days for the results of the investigations. It was a relief when the Transplant Coordinator finally phoned and we learnt that Trevor is still transplantable. But, they'd decided to defer his admission because, apparently, another patient has been admitted in the meantime. It's not ideal as Trevor is really not well. And, as if he didn't have enough to contend with, he also has all the symptoms of a cold this morning. I worry it will develop into another chest infection. We're supposed to be driving to Sheffield this afternoon to see ABC - a band popular in the '80s - at The City Hall this evening. I happened to speak with my sister-in-law this morning and she suggested I phone our GP and ask for some prophylactic antibiotics.

That sounds fairly simple, but these things are never as straightforward as Anne suggests. I guess if you attempt to communicate via a GP's receptionist and happen to be able to use the title 'Dr' in front of your own name, you'll have more success. In my experience, there's quite an art in getting past the receptionist to speak to a GP. With this in mind, I circumnavigated the receptionist and went straight to the reasonable lady who works in the dispensary. She's more helpful and will at least put herself out a bit, which is a refreshing change from the 'resolutely cannot do' attitude displayed by most of the admin staff at the Practice. Fortunately, I've had lots of interactions with our GP, so when Dr Backhouse returned my call, I explained the situation and she was happy to prescribe antibiotics. I collected them before we set off to Sheffield.

We had an early meal at Marco Pierre White's restaurant next door to the hotel. At my insistence, we then used a taxi to get up the hill to the City Hall and back to the hotel afterwards. Trevor can be remarkably stubborn if he feels I'm treating him in any way like an invalid. The ABC gig wasn't that good. An audience, largely made up of overweight women who were presumably massive fans (albeit not so massive as they are now!) 'back in the day', screamed a lot. And videoed large chunks of the performance on mobile phones. I absolutely don't get that. Why spend an entire concert looking at a small screen in front of you and then watch a poor quality video of a concert at home later? It seems to be part of the current 'post-your-life-on-Facebook-for-friends-to-envy' society. But I can't help thinking that while constructing a video of it, these people are missing their actual life. And they're certainly spoiling mine: I don't want to be distracted by dozens of lights between me and a band.

To cap it all, Trevor had a rotten night in the hotel. Which means neither of us got much sleep. It's so difficult for him especially now he has a full-blown cold. His weight seems to be rising exponentially - maybe something to do with ceasing Candesartan. Dr MacGowan advised him to cut back the dose and then stop taking it, in the hope that this would help to protect Trevor's kidneys. But I'm not sure how long he can carry on like this. Or me! I'm permanently set on a state of high alert: surreptitiously watching for any indications that Trevor is about to collapse, while attempting to ensure he sees no sign of my anxiety.

Once back home, the realisation that life is going on for other people hit me again when I had a terribly sad phone call from my aunt. My cousin, Lesley, who is just a few years younger than me, was diagnosed with breast cancer a couple of years ago. Actually, her diagnosis was the day after Kevin's funeral. Lesley underwent gruelling treatment involving chemotherapy and radiotherapy as well as surgery. But her cancer was an aggressive form and the recurrence was detected almost immediately that treatment for the primary cancer ended. This time, with secondary bone metastases. My aunt called to let me know that on Sunday morning, Lesley passed away. She was 48. While Lesley was in a hospice in Warwick and Trevor was undergoing transplant assessment in Newcastle, we'd exchanged frequent text messages. Remarkably, Lesley maintained her sense of humour throughout her illness. I never will forget her tales of hospice meals; including cheese and potato pie ... with gravy. It sounds trite to say that deaths of young people put life into perspective. But I know how much Kevin wanted to live, and how much life Lesley still had to live.

I thank God that if nothing else, Trevor has hope.

I Lift My Heavy Heart up Solemnly (Elizabeth Barrett Browning 1806-1861)

> AMY: How's Trevor tonight?
>
> NICOLA: He seems a bit better. He wanted to die this morning, but seems less glum tonight. His ascites still growing though. X
>
> AMY: That's awful ☹ He doesn't show how low he is to anyone else. X
>
> NICOLA: I'd better turn iPad off as he's settling back down. Hopefully, giving him a slug of whisky in his hot toddy every three hours will keep him cheerful. ;-) xx
>
> AMY: Haha. Night night. Xx

> NICOLA: Good night. Try to sleep now. Xx

CHAPTER SEVEN

A Heart Stopping Moment

11th November 2015

Nicola and I co-created a weekly update to send to The Freeman, the first of which read like this:

> "Current daily medication: 40mg Pantoprazole, 2x25mg Carvedilol, 40mg Furosemide, 12.5mg Eplerenone, 200mg Amioderone, 100mg Allopurinol, 3mg Warfarin.
> Weight/Fluid Retention: Little or no fluid on ankles, but abdomen continues to be distended – this seems to link with the cessation of Candesartan (24mg daily). Normal dry weight is around 90.5kg; this has increased to 92.5kg over recent months and is currently 94.5kg. Abdomen becomes bloated on exertion which causes discomfort. Physical activity appears increasingly limited as tolerance to exercise has reduced – routine tasks such as carrying shopping, towelling dry after a shower, walking upstairs, have become more difficult over the last six weeks.
> Blood Pressure: Generally around 105/70 since stopping Candesartan (previously around 90/65).
> Other: Began symptoms of a cold virus last Thursday (4/11/15) – we contacted GP on Friday to request antibiotics in case these were required over the weekend (experienced significant chest infection following previous colds). Began coughing up green phlegm and spiked

> *a temperature on Sunday so commenced 500mg Amoxicillin tds. Still has a cough and some wheezing. Insomnia, restless legs, and itching remain unchanged.*
> *Bloods: Having blood test today - we'll provide results within next few days.*
> *I hope that all makes sense. We are taking ownership of the apartment in Gosforth on 17th November so if you'd like to review Trevor on 18th, please let us know."*

Within an hour or so, my Transplant Coordinator replied with:

> *"Thanks for the update. Dr MacGowan would like to admit you to ward 27 next Wednesday the 18th – the time has come. If you could arrive before lunch on Wednesday please that would be great. Thanks."*

So, it's happening, and this time there will be no further tests or doubts. It's the real McCoy. As before, my feelings are mixed: on the one hand, a sense of relief that we're getting on with it, that is the process of getting better will commence; while on the other hand, I am struck by the enormity of it all. I concede that the performance of my heart has deteriorated again, and that it's struggling to pump at a rate that provides me with a semblance of normal existence. In terms of the graph that Dr MacGowan drew for me some months ago (see below), I acknowledge that the window has opened and I need professional help.

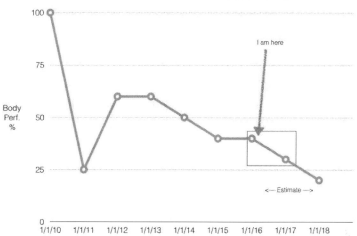

CHAPTER EIGHT

After My Own Heart

18th November 2015

After two days of settling in to the Gosforth apartment, the time arrived for Nicola to bring me in to The Freeman. Within five minutes of my arrival, Dr MacGowan saw me, listened to a synopsis of my condition and prescribed a quadruple daily dose of the diuretic Furosemide, from 40mg to 160mg. This will be delivered intravenously rather than in tablet form. At check-in, my weight was 96.4kg, around 6kg more than what I imagine to be my dry weight. This first day was filled with new tests and arrival procedures and to be honest, it felt good to be under the attention of so many medical professionals.

    Nicola and I have spoken about the way we plan to deal with visiting, access to each other and the importance of the need to realise that the process of keeping our spirits up is a two-way street. For my part, I've explained that I need some time on my own here and we've agreed that the first attempt will be for her to visit me once per day, either morning or afternoon. On her part, Nicola needs to get used to the area she's living in, find shops and supermarkets, and best of all, cosy up in a nice, plush apartment during the evenings. Smothering each other is something we must avoid.

20th November 2015

I've continued to have difficulty sleeping and last night was no different. It was Friday night/Saturday morning and the five-day ward I'm on was almost empty. The ward was manned by two Filipino nurses, one of whom served the evening hot chocolate drink a full hour earlier than the usual time. I noticed how this irritated me. I'd been thinking again of the similarities between an indefinite stay in hospital and a prison sentence, and here was a great example. I'd started to schedule my day around certain events that occur reliably on a routine basis. The ire of prison inmates is caused when a person in authority changes that routine without proper consultation with those on the receiving end of it. I'm sure that to most people this seems the most trivial of things – a hot drink at 9.15pm rather than 10.15pm, but to the incarcerated it's extremely important. This is institutionalisation and it happens so quickly.

    I was struggling to sleep and the main reason was the noise the two nurses were making at the nurses' station. It was loud conversation and on many occasions I could hear both parties speaking at the same time without listening. My ear plugs normally solve the problem but in this case the noise was loud enough to render them useless. At 12.30am, I took my blankets, left my room and informed them, "I'm going to seek another bed in a quieter place." I was quite 'ratty' by now and made a couple of pertinent points, one of which was to ask them why they don't bring in a book to read, because that would advance their intellect much more than 'bullshit talk,' or 'pissprat' as it's known in Norway. I returned to my cubicle around 6am and by the time Nurse Nicola arrived to do my obs at 9am, the news of my 'dummy spit' was all over the ward. The staff were supportive to me as it seems these nurses had previously had feedback as to the volume at which they speak.

    Another example of institutionalisation: fluids in and out of my body are measured daily so as to closely follow the effect of the intravenous diuretic being administered. When I hand over a bottle of urine to Nurse Nicola, she asks me to wait until she retrieves a glove before she touches the bottle. Perfectly logical and hygienic. I stand there like a dummy, holding a bottle of my own wee, until she returns, having snapped a glove on one hand. So, I thought, why don't I take a glove from the box and present to her both the glove and the bottle? It just seemed logical to me, that's all. So I did this the next time I had a bottle to hand over, and on presenting both to Nurse Nicola, she burst out laughing! She snapped on the glove, took the bottle and returned, still grinning and shaking her head, some minutes later with the reading for my charts. She told me that no patient has ever done that, and we laughed at how institutionalisation disrupts normal behaviour patterns which then in turn, subsequently become normal. Children, dogs, and some adults clearly want to conform and be obedient!

21st November 2015

Farewell to Ward 27 and hello to Ward 24a, which is the Coronary Care Unit (CCU). I was transferred because Ward 27 is a five-day ward and a home was needed for me for two nights. My weight has continued to fall, and stands now at 92.4kg. I'm so happy with that and still feel I have plenty of fluid at my stomach and ankles to rid myself of. Excited to see what my true 'dry' weight really is!

The big change for me is the move from a cubicle to a bay with six beds, five of them holding other male patients. Only one of these, a guy called David from Harrogate, is in the same position as me - waiting for a heart transplant. We're not competitors as it were, because he weighs in at 115kg compared to my 90kg, so a heart suitable for me won't fit him and vice versa.

I was awake at 6am today, having accepted a sedative for the first time in my life last night. Both Nicola and the doctors suggested it would be an intelligent thing to do, and it was - I didn't even manage to see the end of Match Of The Day!

A Heavy Heart Belovéd (Elizabeth Barrett Browning 1806-1861)

> NICOLA: Wot you up to?
>
> AMY: Lol just saw you were up. It's hammering down here and I'm worrying about the trampoline as don't think it's fixed down. You? X
>
> NICOLA: Just stuff in my head. The anaesthetist came to see Trevor yesterday – that was scary stuff. He'll be sedated after the op and that can be anything from a few hours to weeks or months!! The psychologist also came and she was asking what support I have. I think Trevor forgets sometimes it's not just him. Maybe that's natural when you're faced with own mortality. Psych said I will need other people who can visit him instead of me. I said geography makes that difficult! X
>
> AMY: Huge change of life for you both plus the worry. X

I've been trying to get used to living in an apartment by myself and acquaint myself with the local area. Almost every road seems unfamiliar; it's strange having to rely on a satnav to get home even from the local shops. Having said that, I'm glad that we chose this apartment – I like the modern layout and furnishings and am enjoying this uncluttered living. It seems curious that owning a reasonably large house full of chattels I've discovered I can live without ever seemed important. I wonder whether I'll want to maintain this minimalism when I return home.

On Thursday afternoon, I decided to walk to The Freeman and back. The walk there wasn't too bad; I stuck to the footpaths and it took about three quarters of an hour, which was okay. On the way back it wasn't so good. At this time of year, it gets dark around 4.30pm so was very dark by the time I left the Freeman at 7pm. It was about 8.15pm before I got back to the apartment. The route I'd cheerfully walked during daylight seemed so much more intimidating in the dark. Achy and a bit fed up when I got back to the apartment, I didn't feel much like making anything to eat so settled for a cup of tea.

Parking at the hospital is tricky, but I'm going to have to find some way round it as I'm not sure walking each day is going to happen.

It's weird but the days seem to be beginning to merge into one as my new version of 'normal' takes hold. Usually, I drive to the hospital around lunchtime, which is when it's generally easiest to find a parking space. After a bowl of soup and cup of tea in the canteen – to be fair, it's labelled 'restaurant' but that's a bit of a stretch - I go up to Ward 27 around 1.30pm. Trevor and I sit and talk for a while over a cup of tea, and then go for a walk round the hospital, often ending up in the canteen where I drink yet more tea. Sometimes we go and sit in the Chapel - it's peaceful there, and doesn't smell quite so much of hospitals. When we return to the ward, I sit with Trevor while he has his evening meal at around 5pm, and then come back to the apartment between 6.30 and 7pm.

Trevor and I had a couple of days apart when I drove home for a night, and then to Birmingham for my cousin's funeral and a night in a hotel in Warwick. The evening before Lesley's funeral, I spent some time with Marion, Barry and Lloyd, my aunt, uncle and cousin, as I'd decided not to go to the reception after the funeral. Although, it would have been good to catch up with family and friends, it's difficult being so far away from Trevor. It was a case of 'standing room only' at the crematorium: Lesley was a popular lady and many, many people wanted to pay their respects. Despite having attended far too many funerals over the last few years, I still struggle with the entire concept. It seems like a lot of people cheerfully make the effort to go to a funeral but fail to visit a person while they're alive. Why is that? And why does it bother me?

Maybe, for me, it's all part of an eternal quest for the meaning of life, but I find myself at this time repeatedly deliberating on the point of so many of life's social constructs. Funerals seem bizarre. Some seem personal and a genuine tribute to a loved one's life. Others more of a tick-box exercise. I recall a few years ago, Sam asking me after Kevin's mum's funeral, "Is that it? A person has ceased to exist and that's all that happens?!" Sam felt alienated from the entire process and his words made me question what we consider 'paying respect.' Is it about recognising the part someone played in our life and the loss we feel? Or do we seek reassurance that we are good people since we stand in a room and listen to somebody say some words about a person in a box?

I struggle enormously with actions that come across as phony. When Kevin died, I vividly recall people who weren't that close to us crying when they were told he'd passed away. This felt anachronistic. It wasn't as though it was a surprise. We all knew he was going to die. He'd been heaving an increasingly discernible death sentence round for over a year. With a long slow death like his, surely the grieving takes place over many months. Absolutely, the news of his terminal illness hit me with the force of an articulated lorry. His pain ... and my pain, sucked the oxygen out of both of us. And coming to terms with the end of his life seemed insurmountable. But, as the months passed and Kevin deteriorated, death's inevitability tightened its grip. His suffering became progressively worse than continued life at any cost. His death became something that was entirely expected. His dying was harrowing, but in accordance with his wishes, I was the only one who witnessed this, so that couldn't be the catalyst for anyone else's tears. But for some people it seemed that death and crying were some kind of reflex: smile at humour; flinch at pain; cry at death. Attend another funeral. Carry on with life. Learn nothing whatsoever.

Surely, the only point of death can be the reminder that time is the most precious commodity we have. Life is for living. Death is final. Ironically, that is, unless you happen to be an organ donor.

22nd November 2015

There was hustle and bustle of medical staff around David's bed, which woke me early this morning. It transpired he'd been informed around 3am there's a heart available for him, and that he is now 'nil by mouth' with the exception of a few sips of water. Apparently Dave had called his wife and son who set off immediately from their homes in Harrogate to be with him, his operation being scheduled for 8.30am. I congratulated him, and noticed that I had never seen a face like his before - a person who has been given the gift of life. His situation is all the more poignant because hearts for a guy his size are few and far between. He said he was both scared and excited, but honestly, his smile was something to behold. As staff left their night shift, they came in to congratulate him and wish him well. The curtains were drawn so David could be shaved by staff, and subsequently he headed off to the shower to finish the job. His wife and son arrived with happiness and relief etched on their faces.

8.30am came and went and the joy started to gradually slip away and be replaced by anxiety and concern. Around 9.30am David's Transplant Coordinator arrived to explain to him and his family that there is now a question as to suitability, in other words, the 'match' between the new heart and his body. Half an hour later, news came through that the surgeons had decided not to proceed, so the heart presumably goes to another patient somewhere in the UK. What a terrible roller-coaster ride David and his family experienced! On my first full day on the ward, I witnessed first-hand what might happen to me and I learned some salutary lessons from it. I felt so upset for him. He just seemed to withdraw into a shell and I thought the best thing to do was respect what appeared to be his wish to be left alone.

Later in the day, Christopher called me and my spirits rose from an enjoyable forty-five minute chat with him. Towards the end of the day, I wrote a mail to him and his brother Daniel in an effort to manage their expectations over the coming months. Here's what I wrote:

> *Hi.*
>
> *I want to write this in advance so you both understand what is likely to happen and when, and so you know what to expect.*

There is one other waiting for a heart transplant, a guy called David who's been here eight weeks, and who weighs 115kg, which is considerably more than me. So we are not competitors for one heart that comes available, and in truth, the bigger you are, the harder it is to get one. At 3am today, David was woken and told not to eat or drink anything as a heart has come available for him. He called his wife and son (they all live in Harrogate) and he was told to be ready to go to theatre at 8.30am. Staff hugged him, we congratulated him, and he smiled the smile of a person given the gift of life. They shaved him and his relatives arrived. 8.30am came and went and then his Transplant Coordinator came to tell him the match between the new heart and his body is not good enough, and so he can't have the op. He and his wife had already called their friends and relatives and as the time passed, their phones rang and rang with people asking for updates. He looked totally gutted. He hasn't spoken all day and has just watched tv with empty eyes, or slept.

I don't want this to happen to me, or to us. I don't want to make 'goodbye and good luck' calls to you before I go down, and if I were to get similar news, have to call you again to say 'it's all off.' I will only know it's happening 100% for sure when the operating theatre doors open and I'm wheeled in. I also think if I make the calls to you, they might be too emotional and that's not good before I go down.

So I've asked Nicola to make three phone calls to my side of the family after I go down. Those will be to you two, and Uncle Robert. If for any reason she can only reach one of you, then she'll call that one back and ask you to tell your brother. This is a 'cascade' for communication and it saves Nicola from dozens of phone calls. When there are updates, the three of you will be the first to know. It'll just be a case of waiting by the phone.

After the operation, which lasts about eight hours, I'll be sent to the Intensive Care Unit (ICU) where I'll remain sedated until the doctors decide I'm stable and can wake up. If there are complications, the time

> spent sedated will be longer. At best, it'll be two days, at worst, a month. I may need kidney dialysis during or after the op., or both. That might be short-term or it might be permanent. During my time in ICU, only two people may visit me, and they have to be nominated beforehand. Obviously, they will be Nicola and Uncle Robert. After ICU, I'll be in hospital for about a month if all goes well, and may have visitors as normal. If we live close by the hospital, as we do at Gosforth, I'll be allowed to go home earlier because if anything goes wrong, such as rejection signs or infection, I can be brought in within ten minutes.
>
> The thing is, it's impossible to know when all this will happen; it could be tomorrow, it could be next March. I just want you to know how things work when I get the call.
>
> Love you both, Dad.

23rd November 2015

After just two nights in a bay on Ward 24a, I was moved back to Ward 27, my home for all of last week. I packed, said my farewells and was brought upstairs. I've noticed that my spirits fall quite markedly each time the hospital changes my bed location. It seems I just get used to a set of circumstances, become content with them, and I'm asked to uproot and head off. The next time I see my Transplant Coordinator, I'll mention to her that on the one hand she reminds me of the importance of staying positive, but on the other hand, the system is not exactly conducive to supporting this effort. Packing, transferring wards, unpacking, trying to get a tv, securing blankets and towels, helping staff understand the changeover in terms of procedures and medications, receiving new procedural instructions, adapting to a new team of nursing staff - it's all pretty draining stuff.

Nicola called me from Brigg Garden Centre and we video-connected while she had afternoon tea with Amy and Elodie. To be honest, that was the last thing I needed. I'm stuck in this place, unhappy with my lot, and asked to connect with the three of them having a ball. Nicola wasn't to know, so I don't write this in criticism; it's just an observation of the effect on my spirits. I'm told I'll move from Cubicle 1 to Cubicle 3, which has a tv, around 8pm tonight when the current occupant is discharged. Great. Another move.

30th November 2015

I returned to The Freeman first thing this morning, after having received a lovely boost to my spirits when Dr MacGowan suggested Saturday that I be allowed 'home' for the weekend - so long as that home was in Gosforth, two miles from the hospital. I was thrilled at the prospect of spending some time with Nicola outside of the hospital environment. We could cuddle, hold hands and just be ourselves during this temporary reprieve. A funny and remarkable thing to notice was the anxiety I felt at having been released from the rigours and routines of 'prison.' I even started to stress over whether or not the hospital was trying to contact me with an available heart, so I found myself checking my phone dozens of times. It was just so odd to be able to make decisions about mealtimes, to drive to the supermarket, have a glass of excellent Riesling, and not have to wee into a cardboard bottle! There's a serious point here, and that's the speed at which institutionalisation begins to affect our minds. It's easy for me to see why some offenders stick with a life of crime, thus ensuring they spend most of their lives within the penal system: three meals a day, warmth, security, friendly faces, routine. There's a familiarity with routine that, despite the arduous circumstances, is unnervingly reassuring.

The efforts with the quadrupling of my daily Furosemide dose from 40 to 160mg, and the switch of taking this intravenously rather than orally, is having a definite effect. Ten days ago, I weighed 96.4kg, yet today I weigh 88.6kg. I'm more mobile, much less breathless and happier, mostly because I can do more. For the last few days, I've even spurned the elevator a few times and chosen to walk upstairs.

Lonesome Heart (Bill Simmons 1969-)

> AMY: How's Trevor doing? xx
>
> NICOLA: Much the same – less fluid, but itching is driving him mad. xx
>
> AMY: Just been to double check at the house and nothing that looked like a bus lane ticket. Bless him with the itching. I don't know whether it's worth trying to Facetime him again tonight? Or call?
>
> NICOLA: Thanks for checking. I've stopped driving in bus lanes now I've given up trusting the Satnav. Trevor was talking about calling you today while you're off. I'm going in later today. Think he might sleep this morning cos didn't sleep last night.
>
> AMY: Because itching worse at night? X
>
> NICOLA: Yes, he just feels like skin on fire. X
>
> AMY: That must be awful. Anything they can do for it? X
>
> NICOLA: They're trying various things – creams and stuff, but nothing really works. I'm just making some soup. Don't have food processor here so will have to sieve it, I think. Bit sick of paying £1.20 at hospital for a bowl of something that resembles dishwater. Xx
>
> AMY: Guess that is quite expensive every day. Sieve will be interesting. Xx
>
> NICOLA: I wouldn't mind paying if it was worth it, but it's truly dreadful. Not sure the kitchen staff at The Freeman have cooking qualifications – or if they do, it's in how to open a packet and put in microwave. I'm looking forward to Christine's visit next week. Xx

> AMY: I bet you are, it will be good for you to have some company. Xx

3rd December 2015

My third week in hospital began yesterday. My weight this morning was 88.3kg, a total loss of 8.1kg over two weeks. My exertion capability is greater and my breathlessness much less, and still I think there may be a kilo/litre of fluid still to be removed. On the whole, I manage to stay within my fluid intake limit of 1.5 litres per day, and when that's hard, I suck ice cubes or boiled sweets.

Nicola and I are in the midst of a terrible misunderstanding, which I find very sad. While watching tv last night, I fell asleep on my bed, around 8.15pm. I planned to watch The Apprentice at 9pm so I certainly hadn't turned in for the night. Through text messages, I discovered that Nicola and her friend Christine had visited me last night at the time I'd dozed off. She chose not to wake me, and instead leave some mints on my bed-table to let me know she'd been. On waking to discover this, I was absolutely distraught. I just can't understand her logic - she surely must know that I'd prefer to be gently woken to her smiling face than left napping. She wrote to say that she thought she'd let me sleep, as that would be more beneficial for me. I can't get my head around her logic. Every day my spirits are raised by seeing her, by sharing a conversation, the reassurance of her touch and presence. I know for sure there was no intent on her part to hurt me, but to misjudge my sentiments in this way seems impossible for me to fathom.

I'm settling into a daily routine that is still in development. There's no design behind it - it has simply emerged. I'm woken at 6.30am, weighed and my observations done. I'm served breakfast of Rice Krispies and milk, yoghurt, a piece of fresh fruit and tea. The diuretic drug Furosemide is injected intravenously, a blood sample is taken and my medications are dispensed. My water is replaced, my bed made and my room cleaned. Typically, I take my breakfast dishes back to the kitchen, partly for the exercise but mainly because I hate being waited on hand and foot. I shave and clean my teeth in my room and then walk over to the Bay for a shower.

Today, I told Nurse Nicola that I was going to the Newsagent to buy a newspaper and she asked if I'd take an order for papers from the guys on the ward who're not allowed to go. So maybe I've got the beginnings of a little job starting up. After half an hour of either watching or reading the lunchtime news, if I'm feeling tired from lack of sleep, I take a nap. Nicola comes to visit in the afternoon and usually stays until around 7pm, after which I watch tv or a movie.

4th December 2015

Nicola and I talked through our thoughts and intent about her visit last night, and we made up. It was difficult because neither of us could see the other's point of view. My Transplant Coordinator happened to be in my room when Nicola arrived and saw from Nic's face that there was something wrong. She sided with Nicola and told me to grow up. It's strange, when I was first admitted, I thought Nicola and I would need to be careful to give each other space and yet I felt devastated that she didn't wake me. She's my contact with the real world. I think I need to keep confirming that I do have a life outside of the hospital.

Meanwhile, in here, my newspaper round has extended to confectionery sales – I do a round of the ward to take orders and then wander to the shop. It's nice to take some exercise and help the bed-bound at the same time. Today, Friday, was another routine day for me; the reason I'm not journaling every day is that it'll just bore the reader. The monotony is bad enough for me, let alone sharing it with others. I do feel though, that I'm coping with it pretty well.

We had a lovely bit of fun on the ward this afternoon, typical I guess, of the lightheartedness prevalent in many workplaces on a Friday. I passed urine into the usual vessel, a grey, non-transparent cardboard bottle and took it to the nurses' station. Normally, I hand it over, a nurse takes it to the sluice room, measures it and reports the data for me to record. The competition to 'guess the weight of Trevor's pee' has now got a little out of hand. No less than five nurses passed the bottle to each other and declared their guess. "Wait for me, wait for me!" shrieked Surfer Girl (aka Nicola1), as she ran down the corridor, keen on having her bid registered before the betting closed. It was a close run thing, and I was a little bit out for the first time. I'd pee'd 290ml and Nicola2 was spot on. The prize was a choice between two Hotel Chocolat chocolates: minced pie brownie or mulled wine. Nicola2 started her bragging and strutting, much to the chagrin of the other competitors, before eventually choosing the little brownie. "I want you to watch me eat it!" she crowed to the Surfer Girl as she popped it in, 'oohing and aahing' as she savoured it. "Ah, I hope it gives you diabetes!" retorted Surfer, at which everyone burst out laughing. There's nothing like black humour in the nursing profession - you gotta love it.

My Transplant Coordinator swung by to tell me that I was being granted weekend leave again, though the description of Saturday 2pm until Monday morning 9am as a weekend is stretching it a little. Still, I mustn't complain and the fact that she said this looks like being a regular thing lifted my spirits. There are many benefits, such as having quality time with Nicola, breathing outside air, looking out to sea, going for a drive and so on; the only downside being the disruption of packing and unpacking.

All But Death can be Adjusted (Emily Dickinson 1830-1886)

Trevor and I agreed that I should come home again for a couple of nights this week. I needed to tie up a few things with Dad's Estate, including going to his house to take readings from his gas and electricity meters. It's not ideal, but it was easier to transfer his utility accounts to my name until the house is sold - I'd looked after these for him over the last few years anyway as he didn't have internet access, so it was straightforward to change the name on the account. It will be a relief when the house is sold and there's one less thing to worry about.

It seemed really odd that just after I arrived home, the phone rang and it was a lady from the hospice asking whether I would like bereavement counselling after the loss of my Dad. That made me realise that I've not really had sufficient time to think about it. That worries me. I know Dad died. I know the last few days of his life were very difficult. And of course I know he's not here any longer. But I don't think I've processed those thoughts. Sometimes, I think, 'I must remember to tell Dad that,' when something funny or ironic happens. And then I remember. But I think that's fairly normal. I've heard people say that they've had similar thoughts about people who've died, and it takes a long time for those thoughts to stop coming. It's this idea that I'm never, ever, ever going to be able to speak to Dad again that I'm struggling with. His death felt so hurried. Squeezed in amongst the pressure of other worries. And because I'm living in Gosforth for the most part, my life doesn't follow its usual patterns – I don't shop in Grimsby, or go to the cinema at the Whitgift, or do any of the other routine things that would lead to the thought that I'll pop into Dad's on the way home. I guess I'm experiencing fewer of the memory jolts that remind people that a loved one is no longer there. I worry that at some point it will hit me. Another articulated lorry.

It sounds obvious, but I truly don't know how I'll cope if Trevor doesn't come through this. He says I'm stupid to think that I'm jinxed in some way - but sense-making is arguably part of the human condition so it seems natural to try to understand reasons for what happens. The only plausible reason I can ever come up with is that it must be my fault that bad things happen to people around me since I'm the common denominator. Or does that make me narcissistic and potentially psychotic? The rational part of my brain recognises there aren't always reasons, but the emotional part frequently seems to take command and switch into overdrive. I guess religion must fill the gap for some people and provide answers to life's conundrums – is it too blasphemous to suggest that pre-Enlightenment, it must have been incredibly simple to convince people there is a God? And then use that to control them. God works in mysterious ways, eh?

I know there are lots of people in worse situations than me and feel guilty that I'm feeling sorry for myself and becoming self-absorbed. But death is such a taboo subject in our culture that I don't think any of us are prepared for it. I can remember worrying when Kevin was terminally ill about how I would cope with his death. At that time, thoughts I had about Dad and his lung cancer seemed too dreadful to contemplate. So, I didn't. Similarly, I couldn't allow myself to give more than fleeting thought to Charlie's demise as he was lurching towards the dreaded twelve years' life-expectancy of a Labrador. But now, and over a relatively short period, they're all gone. Have died, I mean. Are dead. And Trevor needs a heart transplant. And even if a heart becomes available, he might not survive the surgery. The Transplant Coordinator spouts survival statistics at us fairly regularly: 20%, we're told - 1 in 5 - don't come through a heart transplant.

Does death consume everybody's living? Or is it just mine?

11th December 2015

Poking a hornets' nest with a stick is never really advisable, and it feels as though that's exactly what I've done. Having said that, the metaphor is a bit unfair as no-one really became angry. I guess the final straw came in the middle of the night. I'd endured an awful 3.5 hours during visiting time when my Romanian neighbour had four visitors around his bed for that period, talking loudly across each other, frequently on their mobile phones, then swapping places with extended family. They pushed their chairs so far back they were sitting in my bay! For goodness' sake, he was in for two nights for a minor procedure, a pacemaker implantation. He then woke me at 3am as he started to watch television. In addition to this, two male patients had cried and whimpered themselves to sleep; the sound of this is so draining of my energy. I felt exhausted by the time my weigh-in came at 6.30am: deprived of sleep, my morale at its lowest since I arrived almost four weeks ago. Regretfully, I was very short with the night nurses, Clive and Nicola1 (aka Surfer Girl), though it was Clive who took the brunt of it. I left the curtains pulled around my bed for the day, and sat on my bed, miserable and sulking. As the morning passed, a number of people came to see me to try to get an understanding of why I felt the way I did. These included Emma, the Social Worker; Healthcare Assistants Nicola2 and Victoria; Transplant Coordinator; Psychologist, Lucy - all of the persons closest to me, really.

My unhappiness centered around two main issues: the inappropriateness of a long-term patient such as me being placed in a six-bed bay populated by patients staying in hospital for 48 hours or less; and the fact that in a cubicle I had enjoyed a set of privileges which were now taken from me. In terms of the first, the six-bed bay is absolutely manic at times, catering for a high volume of patients turned over at a rapid rate. At one point, a bed was being stripped and washed by two Healthcare Assistants, a patient fresh from theatre was being placed in another, a third had two Boston Scientific guys explaining a newly implanted ICD to a patient, and a fourth had a doctor explaining a prognosis to a patient and his wife. In the fifth, a guy was dressed in his 'civvies' trying to sort out discharge papers with a nurse so he could go home, and in the midst of all this I sit on my bed with head in hands. Stop the world, I want to get off!

During my first ten days on Ward 27, I occupied Cubicle 2, which contained one bed, plus overhead tv and free telephone to BT landlines. Nicola and I could close the door to the said chaos and gain some privacy. Most days for about 20 minutes, she'd sit on my bed and I'd curl up behind her with my arms around her waist. Intimacy such as this was the main highlight of my day and meant so much to us both. When I'd slept badly, after observations, bloods and doctors' rounds were finished, I'd close the cubicle door and sleep for about two hours, sometime between 9am and 12pm. Healthcare Assistants Nicola2, Victoria, and Domestic, Kerry, would 'protect' me from outside incursions such as the ward cleaner. "Don't go in there, he's sleeping!" I heard one of them call. Kerry knows my preferences for lunch and dinner are sandwich and salad respectively, so she'd take care of all that. Sometimes I'd receive a dish I named 'Kerry's Surprise' which could take all manner of appearance, texture and taste. Golly, those two hours of sleep were so precious to me. I'd wake feeling refreshed and with my sense of humour intact. Seemingly silly things were important - the cubicle offered sufficient space for Nicola to sit facing me in comfort, whereas in a bay bed she'd have to sit parallel to me, twisted at a ninety degree angle. Another big deal for me is that I'd call our grandchildren, Millie and Elodie, when they were home from school. As anyone who has children knows, phone calls with them are a little chaotic as they have an under-developed sense of the 'rhythm' of a conversation. Volume is required! I tried, but just couldn't manage these calls knowing I was overheard by as many as ten people. On losing the precious privacy for these calls - I sometimes say the most ridiculous things to them - it struck me how these calls were another big highlight of my day. Losing them hurt. Occasionally, Dr Lord would bring students in to examine me, or learn the history of my illness. Events like this were intellectually stimulating, as well as time-consuming. They helped me to use up my day and keep my brain alive, but of course, they're impossible to conduct on a six-bed bay.

These were the sources of my frustration and misery - the chaos of a busy high-turnover ward, together with my loss of privileges. Meetings were arranged for early next week to try to resolve the problem, or at least alleviate it. Then Rachel intervened. Rachel is in charge when the Ward Sister isn't working. She came to my bedside and told me she'd looked at the plans and had managed to engineer a return to Cubicle 2. I could have kissed her. With three to help, the move was over in a jiffy, and walking into the cubicle felt like arriving home from work on a Friday evening. Nicola2 gave me a massive hug and I shed a few tears at the relief of my nightmare being over. I'm not overstating that, it really was a nightmare; whilst reminding me regularly of the importance of staying positive, the system seems to do everything in its power to erode my spirit. Nicola2 commented that my situation had prompted a discussion amongst the nursing team, that in a way it was a wake-up call for them to differentiate long-term patients where possible.

Social Worker, Emma, called by to check on me about 7pm - she's such a lovely person with fantastic listening and empathy skills and I go home to Nicola this weekend with a renewed sense of determination that I can come through this open-ended wait comfortably.

It would be remiss of me not to mention a task that Nicola2 set for me - to decorate Ward 27's Christmas tree (see below). I had a ball, or should that be bauble? Staff were amazed to see a patient set to work and the novelty of it caused many comments and laughs a-plenty. There's a serious point here though. Nicola2's social antenna is open to receiving signals that tell her I'm sometimes bored and need things to do. In my view, her giving me that job is 100% a part of nursing and caring for me, preparing me for a heart transplant by introducing variety into my day, and thereby keeping up my spirits. I had a fantastic conversation with a junior doctor, Jonny, on this subject - how the softer, emotional, psychological side of nursing care is accepted in the professional ranks, but is often squeezed out at the expense of other duties, some of them administrative. However, it's a bit like leadership - you need a natural, innate ability at people skills in order to excel at it. Some nurses here will dispense your medication but never ask how you are. Some ask, but are clearly not interested in your response; it's just that they've been trained to 'tick the box.' Others seem to have an intrinsic sense of compassion and genuinely care.

I'm looking forward to the weekend immensely. I just can't wait for it to come. With her new partner, Luke, Amy will bring Millie and Elodie. Luke and Amy will stay in a hotel in Gateshead, and the girls will have a sleepover with Nicola and me. I love their company and cuddles, the control and discipline that Grandma doles out, plus their fascinating questions about my heart. Ella normally wants to look under my shirt to see if the damaged one has been taken away yet. Millie is a bit more intellectual, wanting to look at medical diagrams to understand the procedure. The innocence and naivety of children never fails to amuse and amaze.

16th December 2015

We all enjoyed a lovely weekend and I noticed how little my brain had been devoted to transplant issues. The girls had their sleepover with us and were as good as gold, sleeping pretty much from 7pm through to 7am in their new inflatable beds. On arrival, Ella leapt on my knee and pulled up my shirt and jumper to reveal my bare chest. She let out a sigh of disappointment on not finding anything new and asked if, when the operation is done, I'll have a neat zipper in the heart area. She's pure gold. When they left, she gave me a long cuddle, lying on my chest and stomach, her head positioned across my heart. Craftily, I told her that if she were to lay her head against me and cuddle me, she'd help my ailing heart to mend. She fell for it and lay there for ages, her love warming me through - the best raising of my spirits imaginable.

Today sees the commencement of week number 5, most of it having been spent on Ward 27. A nurse, Andrea, agreed to spend some time with me as I wanted to talk about the post-operative phase of a heart transplant. It was probably one of the most valuable forty minutes I could have spent, with Andrea patient and informative even about my 'stupid questions.' Nicola pointed out to me later that she notices I'm more courageous with my questioning now, hungrier for information. I'd not realised this but I think she's probably right – I covered subjects with Andrea that previously I've cowered from. How soon after the operation do they bring me round? When does Dr MacGowan hand off my case to another professional and how is that done? How do the surgeons deal with the difficult-to-move fluid that is still around my stomach area? How soon after the operation do the ICU nurses have me back on my feet? What are the tubes connected to me after the operation and over what period are they removed? What's the most painful part of recovery for patients? Andrea handled all of these with candour and honesty, having nursed heart-transplantees for over twenty years. I know I'll be in safe hands.

Dr MacGowan sees me daily and suggested I try a two-day leave of absence this coming weekend. That means my final intravenous injection of Furosemide will be around 1pm on Friday 18th December; I'll switch to tablets for two days and return to my cubicle on Ward 27 on Monday morning. Several people this week were involved in a nurse-initiated discussion about the degree to which I need to be on the Ward at all. I stayed calm and I did participate, but all the while was thinking 'surely this is Dr MacGowan's call?' In the end I let the discussion ride, and believed that Transplant Coordinator, Neil, was probably right – again, my physical appearance belies the seriousness of my heart condition and interested parties must be careful not to fall into that trap. In any case, I can't imagine for one minute that I'd feel comfortable waiting at home for a heart; psychologically, I feel stronger if I'm close to the action, visible and permanently on hand. I know that's only my state of mind – if a heart came available for me, wheels would roll quickly – but that's how it is, how I feel. I know that means I turn down the chance to be in a home environment with Nicola, but what would be our quality of life if I'm permanently on edge? In such a kind and understanding way, Nicola supported my decision.

O Christmas Tree (Ernst Anschutz)

AMY: Hello

NICOLA: Hello

AMY: We were wondering about coming to see you Boxing Day for the day? Xx

NICOLA: It's a long way to drive for a day. If you want to stay over, we can fit you in. xx

AMY: We don't want to put you out. Luke has offered to drive. We can set off early and leave once the girls are tired. Put them in pjs. Xx

NICOLA: Trevor says you should stay over. Xx

AMY: We could but we don't want to be hard work. Just thought it won't be Christmas without seeing you. Was sad when I saw Sam earlier and thought that it will be different this year, and Luke suggested we come up. Xx

NICOLA: Then come. You're welcome to come when you want to and stay as long as you like. Stay or not. Up to you. Only condition is Elodie is only allowed to cuddle Treasure ☹xx

AMY: Luke says no deal on the only cuddling Treasure as the cuddles are the only thing that stops him throttling her :-P

NICOLA: He's caught on quickly there! Xx

It was great to see Amy and the girls, and meet Luke, at the weekend. Even better that the girls stayed with us at the apartment while their mum and Luke had a night in a hotel. We had lovely cuddles in bed on Sunday morning and it was truly relaxing. It's amazing the capacity to which small children have the ability to force you to 'live in the moment.' There is no way to stew on doubts and fears when Elodie wants to play. I think children are the best respite.

Millie brought me a fir cone that she'd made into a miniature Christmas Tree; strangely, for someone who purports not to enjoy Christmas, I'd felt surprisingly disappointed that I had no decorations at all. So Millie's tree felt really special. It's funny, the extent to which we enjoy small tokens when life feels devoid of enjoyment and light-hearted moments.

The cloud hanging over us can feel so dark at times, and I feel under such pressure to keep my fears to myself. If a heart isn't found; if Trevor becomes too ill for a transplant; if Trevor doesn't survive surgery ... then these are unequivocally the last months, days, hours of his life. It would be unfair of me to fill them with my worries. I try so hard to inject fun and pleasure into our days. His days. But when I'm on my own in the evenings, images of the future taunt me until I give them my attention. It's then that I'm most frightened. How could I cope with this loss? The loss of Trevor. Even typing those words feels dangerous, as though I'm testing them out so I get used to them. I have a tremendous sense of guilt at what must sound like self-pity, or self-absorption. Firstly, it's Trevor who is suffering. Not me. And also there are so many people facing much worse situations than mine. And am I really wishing for somebody to lose their life? For someone to have to live through bereavement and pain so that mine is relieved? It feels selfish on so many levels to wish for a life that's carefree.

Trevor says that if he gets a heart, he'll never ever lose sight of how lucky he is and will always be appreciative of every experience because he will be lucky to be alive. We disagree about this. I'm far too cynical and think that humans are quick to move on and take life for granted. I'd like to be able to pray to someone for a heart for Trevor and promise in some kind of *quid pro quo* deal that I'll be a better person who's more philanthropic and far kinder. But I'm human. And humanist.

It will be good to see Amy and the girls again over Christmas. It would have seemed too strange not to see either of my children over the holiday. Paradoxically, I hope wholeheartedly that it's not convenient for them to come. But a heart comes instead.

23rd December 2015

If things go on the way they are, I'll write my journal once a week, for two reasons; first, I found Max Crompton's account of the pre-operation period to be repetitive and boring after a while, and second, life is tending to be a bit same-ish for me, week in, week out. That doesn't mean for a moment that I'm finding life tedious, rather, I think I'm managing myself and my psychological state extremely well. I'm doing my best to stay active, with plenty of corridor walking, returning plates and dishes to the kitchen myself, and a trip to buy an ice-pop from the newsagent's a couple of times per day.

Nicola and I saw my Transplant Coordinator in the canteen, where she told me that I was considered for an available organ this week, but it was deemed not a good enough 'match'. I'd like to describe a transformation in my thinking that I noticed. Compton had described a similar conversation in his book, and on reading it I was convinced that if this occurred with me, I just didn't want to know. I just wanted the call for the real McCoy, not any ifs, buts and maybes. Five weeks later, I noticed that my emotions were not irritation or annoyance, but instead appreciation. Confirmation that experts are searching for an appropriate organ, that I'm being analysed and considered, felt good. I didn't feel let down or disappointed, just reassured. Again, I think this shows how my thoughts around transplantation are developing.

My sons, Christopher and Daniel, came to visit on Monday, together with Christopher's partner, Ann-Cecilie. I'd given some thought to the format of the day because I didn't want to get into a sour discussion with Daniel, or great sadness with either of them. We spent half an hour in the day room and then I asked if I could speak with the boys in my cubicle individually. I wanted to tell them that whatever happens, I love them, but I wanted to do this without breaking down. I'm not afraid of showing emotion I just feel that it's not in anyone's interests to break down in tears. What's to be gained from a discussion about their lives in the event of my death? I just asked them to read the two documents I've written so far, so they develop an understanding of me, my thoughts and my history.

Tomorrow is my 56th birthday, and it would be so good to receive a new heart on that day. As the daytime goes by, I feel more confident and relaxed about the preparation. The nighttime however, is a different kettle of fish. When I wake during the night, I have the most ludicrous thoughts coursing through my mind. What if we're sleeping and don't hear the phones? What do I write to the donor's family to thank them? How will Nicola manage if I don't come through the operation? How will my sons and my brother take such bad news? And then there are the dreams. I dreamt that the Transplant Coordinator couldn't be bothered to call me but sent a telegram instead. By the time I arrived at The Freeman, I'd missed the heart. In the same evening, I dreamt that James Corden from Gavin & Stacy fame kidnapped me with a friend of his. Either awake or asleep, my mind is a wreck at night. When the sun rises, everything melts away like snowflakes warmed by the sun.

I'll close with a funny story from today. Healthcare Assistants, Victoria and Nikki, arrived at my cubicle with new bed linen. Victoria asked if I'd like to have my bed linen changed. I couldn't be bothered to climb off the bed, and in any case, I don't sleep in it, but on it. She said in a more than stern tone that I should get the hell off that bed because, "It's 'minging' in here and needs a fresh change." I jumped off the bed and fell into the chair laughing. Happy moments like this really keep me going, and when Nicola arrives, they side with her and get stuck into me. It's a lovely 'craic' we have going (as the Irish say) and it makes me feel human, feel myself.

30th December 2015

On my return to the ward to begin week number 7, I'm asked of course, how my Christmas was. I smile and say it was great, and in some ways it was, but I think few people can empathise with how I feel, and what I experience. Christmas was wonderful for being alone with Nicola, for being able to catch up on sleep, and for rebuilding and reconnecting our relationship that inevitably dips a little when we're apart. The high point for Christmas was two things: first, Millie and Elodie climbed into bed in between me and Nicola, and that was pure heaven. Now, don't get me wrong, I wouldn't want it every day (ha ha) but once a year is just perfect. Second, Amy gave me a birthday card that said 'You're Like A Dad To Me' on the front, and that made me feel warm, loved and appreciated by her. I'll always be grateful for the way in which Amy and Sam have welcomed me into their family and their lives.

Dear Heart, Why Will You Use Me So? (James Joyce)

> NICOLA: Trevor had a bad night – was bloated, retaining water on his stomach, etc etc. He's quite high-maintenance. XX
>
> AMY: Must be difficult. Xx
>
> NICOLA: It's afterwards I dread!! He's forgotten how to make a cup of tea and leaves his pots exactly where he used them. I keep asking Kerry, the ward domestic, if she's free at weekends. Xx
>
> AMY: Haha. Have you discussed it with him? Xx
>
> NICOLA: Yep!! Every weekend. xx

Christmas and New Year were pleasant in some ways and difficult in others. It was good to spend a significant time with Trevor in the apartment. But sometimes it feels as though we're treading water. We're not making progress in any way, because there's nothing we can actually do. The only practical contribution I can make is to provide food which is nutritious, pleasant and low in salt. I know that Trevor manages to pass more urine if he remains horizontal, so we often lie on the bed and talk, or he naps and I stay with him. We sometimes go out in the car for a drive, or to sit by the sea; he especially enjoys watching the waves break onto the beach at Tynemouth.

    I think Trevor feels like the apartment is mine and he's just a visitor, which is unfortunate. It's true to say that I live in it by myself for the majority of the time, and when he's here with me, for obvious reasons, I prepare food and do most of the chores. It's difficult to avoid the absolute 'patient/carer' roles that seem to have evolved. In a strange way, that's more possible in The Freeman where Trevor's a patient and there is transparency regarding the responsibility of staff who look after his needs. There, my role is Trevor's wife who's visiting him in his room which is full of his belongings. During my visits, he contributes to discussions about what we should do to fill the time; when we should take a walk, or drink tea. And, he returns our cups to the kitchen. But in the apartment, where it's just Trevor and me, it's more complicated. I want to feel like I'm spending time with Trevor, my husband, but I'm struggling to know how to communicate that.

6th January 2016

We spent New Year's Day 2016 lying in bed listening to the cricket from Cape Town. Sometimes, when I'm witnessing something as special as Ben Stokes smashing world records with impunity, while Nicola and I are drinking tea, chatting and lying in the warmth with the rain drilling away at the window panes, my heart condition fades into the background. It was remarkable - as if every ball Stokes hit flew for a four or a six, and when he was done at 250-ish, Jonny Bairstow took up the cudgel and reached 150 not out. Utter cricket heaven ... if you're English.

The switch from intravenous to oral diuretic had gone reasonably well over a ten day period; my weight had not increased much at all, staying always between 88.5 and 89kg. However, on my return Dr MacGowan took one look at the artery in my neck and placed me straight back onto IV, so the obvious conclusion is that fluid had accumulated over the break. This bore out Nicola's suspicion as she said she'd noticed a change in my physical condition, in terms of the ascites (swelling) in my midriff region.

I've noticed that each return to hospital on a Monday morning is characterised by a fairly significant dip in my spirits. I should count myself fortunate that I'm given three nights at home with Nicola and to be fair, I don't know what I'd do without that, but the return to hospital each week is like a spiritual kick in the stomach. Still, it's fairly temporary and I'm soon back into the swing of hospital life.

My Transplant Coordinator gave me some news that lifted me enormously. She told me that when it comes to the UK list of urgent heart transplants, for my blood type and size, I'm next on the list. Wow. The whole country and I'm next in line. All I feel is humility and gratitude. Sometimes it's hard to come to terms with the fact that an ordinary-Joe like me is being cared for and prepared for a major life-changing operation by so, so many people. How will I thank them when the time comes? How will I be able to hold it together to show my gratitude? I am more convinced than ever that Dr Bain in Grimsby will have saved my life. Until he took me on as a patient, I'd spent a whole year trying to see an experienced cardiologist, and all Hull Royal Infirmary and Leeds Teaching Hospital had provided were a GP, a trainee cardiologist and a locum. The moment I walked into Dr Bain's office I felt I was in safe, capable and professional hands, being treated by a kind and compassionate doctor who'd seen it all before.

Here at The Freeman, Dr Lord swung by for a chat. I am conscious of the psychology of the physician/patient relationship, and wish to avoid the adoration that comes with that, but I'm very impressed with Drs. MacGowan and Lord. The latter is not treating me at all but occasionally stops by for a chat, which lifts my spirits no end, and increases my understanding of what's to come. I shoot questions at him like a manic machine gunner and listen attentively to his patient replies. I'm now brave enough to ask about the operation itself. Who does it? How long does it last? Does the team take a break? Does it take long to remove my ICD? How do they get the new heart to start beating? And much more. The summary of his responses is that it's much more of a routine operation at The Freeman these days, simply because they have done so many. If I've never had heart surgery, then it's more likely to be a trouble-free operation. Stitching blood vessels together is not a time consuming task, and removal of the donor organ isn't always conducted by the implanting surgeon. The heart will be 'kick started' either by drugs or by a defibrillator and it's OK for it not to be beating for a few hours, so long as blood is pumped through it. Most important, when the 'go' is given, heaven and earth are moved to make everything happen smoothly, the biggest challenge being to make sure that the steps of the process occur in the correct order whilst under time pressure.

13th January 2016

Goodbye week eight, hello week nine. Nicola bumped into my Transplant Coordinator on the stairs at The Freeman; she reiterated that I'm number one on the list for a donor organ in the UK, and that they've had several offers of blood group type 'A' organs but none of them suitable. I guess that means size. So I wait. People tell me to be patient (a patient patient?) and that it'll come, no doubt in their minds. I think this is one of those situations in which friends and relatives think they can imagine what this is like, but I doubt they truly can. It's the open ended nature of the wait that feels so strange. As I've written before, someone could walk through the door as I sit and type this, or they could come in the middle of the night tonight, or in nine days, or nine weeks. I notice that I tend to push away the event in my mind, always imagining that I have a couple more weeks to wait. So when it comes, I think it will be something of an unexpected shock; I imagine I'll feel a mixture of fear and excitement.

Today is Amy's birthday, 31 years old, and the happiest I've ever seen her. That warms my heart. I spoke only with Millie and Elodie, and Millie passed on the birthday greetings to her Mum while I listened. I asked Millie if she has been helping her Mum open her presents. I was tickled by her reply of "Nah, she hasn't got much really."

I'm terribly saddened by the lack of contact I've had with my sons. I wrote to Daniel to thank him for visiting me and he has not responded. I wrote a long mail to Chris a couple of weeks ago and haven't received a reply. It's sad but I must endeavour to make sure this issue doesn't sap my spirits. Perhaps it's just a phase

I'm in, but I'm finding it more and more difficult to keep my spirits up. My days are the same, and so are my weeks. I think being granted weekend leave, to sleep and relax with Nicola, is keeping me sane. The bloating of my stomach, and the discomfort associated with that – caused by moving from intravenous to oral diuretics – seems a small price to pay for the freedom, silence and company of the weekend. Books, movies, documentaries, 'confectionery tv' and the Internet can only stretch you so far and without doubt, the key to getting through this is the establishment of a routine.

You Fill My Heart (Rachel Brewer 1991-)

> NICOLA: We're having a picnic in the day room for lunch tomorrow. Xx
>
> AMY: Sounds nice. Must be getting fed up though. When I went to the house, I thought you must be missing creature comforts. Xx
>
> NICOLA: Yes, it's strange. Trying to sort things like annual tax assessment via email and phone never easy. Xx

Thinking of ways to make a difference to the day is becoming increasingly challenging. Whilst I've always encouraged Trevor to try to stick to some sort of structure during his time in hospital, I also believe it's important to have something to look forward to. He's really tried hard to follow my suggestion that he gets up each day, washes, shaves and dresses in daytime clothes. I think this is important in maintaining dignity and a sense of being human. When we go down to the hospital canteen, although Trevor has a cannula *in situ*, he's far less obviously a patient than so many people we come across. It feels as though some people have no dignity at all: we even saw a woman come in wearing just a theatre gown, TED stockings and slippers. I didn't allow myself to look at where the gown would have been tied up across her back so can't honestly recount whether or not she was wearing underwear. But it absolutely wouldn't surprise me if she wasn't!

We often see the same people in the restaurant so clearly Trevor isn't the only long-term resident in The Freeman. I think it's another of the changes that I've noticed in the role of the nurse: when I trained, we were required to encourage patients who were mobile to get up and dressed during the day, so that they could undress at bedtime. As well as retaining some dignity, this also helps patients mentally prepare for bedtime, and assists in them getting some sleep. Now, it seems as though nurses have no input into patient behaviour. Patients seem to be largely left to navigate their own way through the system. Perhaps that's linked to a reduction in the average length-of-stay, and maybe it's not the end of the world if people don't have a wash or shower for a few days. But I think we all feel better when we've freshened up. And it's far easier to actively participate in dialogue with medical professionals when you're not in your night clothes. I think that anything that encourages people to be involved in their own health has to be of benefit. I wonder whether doctors have the same view, or whether they prefer patients who feel vulnerable and don't question anything.

20th January 2016

We made huge progress at home over the weekend in terms of trying to solve the bloating I suffer from time to time. We switched to small meals on a little and often basis, we eradicated alcohol completely (it was only a couple of glasses of wine in a whole weekend, but still) and we took great care with exercise, also doing that on a little and often basis. The additional point was that I must dry myself after a shower more slowly and with fewer vigorous or 'high hand' movements. I arrived home on Friday afternoon last week with no bloating, and returned Monday morning in the same state, with my weight having stayed constant. Success! Our conclusions sound obvious: any effort that puts my heart under strain - a big meal, a brisk or long walk, climbing stairs, or any form of vigorous activity (even if it is only for a few seconds) - has to be avoided. I felt great to return to The Freeman in good condition after the weekend, for the first time, and perhaps this is an example of how the management of my condition is shared between me, Nicola and the professional staff here.

Some of my days are not without lower-than-usual spirits, and I've noticed that Mondays are particularly hard. I try not to beat myself up about this, recalling the words of Max Crompton 'you can't stay 100% positive 100% of the time.' As Dr MacGowan put it, Mondays for me feature the feeling of returning to boarding school after the summer holidays. Nicely put, summing it up perfectly. I receive regular reminders from the professional staff that 'it *will* happen,' which I find hugely reassuring. Several times per week I try to 'forward visualise' the image of being woken and told to prepare for the operation. The reason I do this is that the greater the time I spend confined here, the more 'routinised' or institutionalised I become, so the more likely it is to shock me when someone actually does come to break my routine. In fact, that routine has become a way of life for me now; it's literally my existence and has been for nine full weeks.

Today, Nicola will arrive around lunchtime with a platter that we'll share together in one of the day rooms. Can't wait! After this hospital and heart experience, I'm not sure I'll ever again take the small stuff for granted. Week number ten begins today.

27th January 2016

Farewell week ten, greetings week eleven. Another week in the same routine, so nothing much to report. Dr MacGowan asked me this week how I was feeling and I replied that I actually feel I'm in the best condition since I came into The Freeman. In fact, tip-top and ready for a transplant, just bring it on. My fluid level is fairly low and under control, my weight is stable and I described my mood as 'cheerfully fed-up,' meaning sad at not having received a call, but happy that I'm number one on the UK 'urgent' list for my size and blood type. Though I feel down on some days, I realise I have much to be thankful for: a low level of antibodies reduces the risk of rejection; both Nicola and I being retired and able to afford an apartment that keeps us together; normal level risks of myeloma and kidney failure; a passionate belief amongst staff that the operation will happen.

CHAPTER NINE

Have a Heart

29th January 2016

Nurse Andrea, experienced in both pre- and post-transplant nursing, woke me with a start at 1.20am stating that she needed blood from me. When I asked for what reason, she explained that a heart my size and blood type had been offered to The Freeman and I was to be the intended recipient. To my surprise, I felt only excitement and relief - no fear. Andrea took about a dozen ampules of blood and had them taken away immediately for testing. I sent Nicola a text message saying that the process had begun and as is the norm, the wheels take a long time to turn. To my relief, Nicola replied to say she'd try to get some more rest and that she'd be in early morning. She was a model of calmness and had a great effect on keeping me calm, unhurried and patient. I'd been warned many times that the process can be halted as late as the patient being made ready for transport to the operating theatre. Visits by a doctor to give me a general health check, transplant coordinators, anaesthetists and a surgeon led me to believe more and more that this is it, it's happening. To be fair, each of the professionals visiting reminded me of the risk of a 'no go' decision at the final stage.

Both Nurse, Andrea, and Healthcare Assistant, Victoria, came by: Andrea mostly to check on the next step of the preparation process, Victoria to offer spiritual support through distracting conversation. Victoria accompanied me for a chest x-Ray, and on my return Andrea set about me with a clipper/shaver. I can't explain why - perhaps it was fear of the unknown - but I was really quite anxious about the shaving part. No need, as Andrea set about me as if she'd done a hundred sheep in her time, and I was no more than a triviality. I showered and 'gowned up' and returned to my room to find that Victoria had stripped my bed of the hair laden linen and made a brand new bed for me. What amazing kindness and efficiency.

Nicola arrived in time for visits by the senior anaesthetist and the surgeon, Mr Shah. Both were models of politeness and answered my questions fully. A final check on my identity and I was good to go. Nicola's presence was a big deal to me. It was as if Victoria had helped me make it through the night, and then handed me over to Nicola. She remained calmness personified and again it transmitted itself to me. The Transplant Coordinator popped in to say that she expects a decision mid-morning, so around 10am. I had asked Andrea to ask the ward staff at shift changeover to avoid any celebrations, congratulations, 'high fives' and that kind of nonsense. What on earth is the point of celebrating something that might not happen? The staff respected my wishes and were as good as gold.

At 11.20, Transplant Coordinators, Hazel and Jill, called in to break the news that the surgical team had decided it's a 'no go.' I didn't feel anywhere near as disappointed as I expected to. Hazel and Jill were genuinely saddened at the news, that much was clear. Hazel explained that the decision had been made because the heart was slightly diseased. Again, it's impossible to be anything but grateful for the massive amount of effort, energy and cost that's expended, and of course for the fact that I'm not in receipt of a diseased organ. It might sound obvious, but these people love nothing more than helping to give the gift of life to a person, so they're terribly disappointed when it doesn't come off. I even had to console two of the Healthcare Assistants who I've come to know so well, which was a surreal experience.

Apparently, when most of the boxes have been ticked, a surgical team travels to the donor's hospital and conducts a series of tests. At first, these are external to the body which is normally on a life-support machine, but then the chest is opened and the organ checked both visually and manually. Yes, you're reading that correctly: while it is still beating, the surgeon looks at the heart, manually feels the valves and arteries (because disease can be felt) and will then hold it to complete the check. When the heart itself is rejected as a whole transplant organ, the healthy parts such as valves are removed and subsequently other organs.

Some months ago, I'm quite sure I'd have fainted halfway through writing that paragraph, but the closer I come to the transplant, the more interest I have in the two processes that bring the patient and the donor organ together. My admiration for a deceased donor and his grieving family is immense. What a massive, massive gesture the gift of life is.

Having been 'stood down' at 11.20am on a Friday and as my cannula had been removed Hazel confirmed I was free to go on weekend leave as usual. It was fantastic timing that an hour later I was sitting in comfortable surroundings with Nicola discussing the experience, albeit through gulps of cold drink after ten hours of 'nil by mouth.'

Why Art Thou Thus Cast Down, My Heart? (Hans Sachs 1494-1576)

On the bedside table, my mobile pinged; I'd only just dropped to sleep so was immediately awake reading the text from Trevor. At first it seemed odd that he'd texted to say that a potential donor heart had been found. This was something we'd spent the last three months living for and we'd discussed to the last detail how this situation would be handled. Trevor was supposed to phone me and I was supposed to go straight there. But he didn't and I didn't. Somehow, it seemed less urgent than I'd expected so I replied and said since it would undoubtedly be a lengthy process, I would get a little more sleep and go to the hospital early the following morning.

 I managed to get a couple of hours' sleep. Then, I showered, dried my hair, put on some make-up and went in to face the day. Trevor was lying on his bed, wearing his hospital gown and looking very much like a patient waiting to go to theatre. An anaesthetist came to see Trevor and went through the risks with us - it's not what I'd call 'easy-listening'! The risks, ranging from it being necessary to keep the patient anaesthetised for a significant period, to the patient dying - and everything in between - are explained in great detail. Part of me thinks that anyone who cheerfully agrees to that and willingly signs a consent form must be bonkers. But I also understand that when there is no option, you will sign anything that offers a sliver of hope. Nurses drifted in and out of the room. At some point I had a cup of tea.

 Conversation between Trevor and I felt stilted. When there's really only one conceivable topic and you've exhausted that, it becomes grim. I think there are some occasions in life when there is just nothing to talk about. And when someone is looking down the barrel of a gun which has a twenty percent chance of blowing their head off, it's difficult to find anything you might want to talk about. Holidays you'd like to go on; restaurants you'd like to visit; sports teams you'd like to win future tournaments; television dramas you haven't finished watching, are all fairly insignificant.

 At around 10am, the Transplant Coordinator came to tell us that the transplant wouldn't be going ahead. The heart was diseased and not suitable for transplant. In some ways, I think we were almost relieved. This was how it's supposed to be: most experience at least one 'no-go' before they get a transplant, so this is all part of the process. We must be getting closer because we'd now done our 'no-go.'

 Since it was Friday, we got Trevor's things together and transferred to the apartment. It was a weird feeling: perhaps the ultimate anti-climax. As I'd driven to The Freeman that morning, I'd felt quite high on anticipation, but by lunchtime the world was dead flat. I'm not sure how you are supposed to cope with the thoughts that inevitably begin to circulate in your grey matter. Fear that this was the one chance and it's fizzled before it even flickered. What if another heart doesn't come up? And, are we any closer? Not really, it could still be tonight, tomorrow, next week, next month, never.

Trevor and I talked a while and shared how we felt: primarily, our relief that Trevor's bad heart hadn't been replaced with another unreliable one. Better to have one in good working order that's had only one careful owner; ideally a vicar's wife! We consciously decided to make the most of the weekend and open a bottle of wine to celebrate being alive. Being cared for by professionals who were looking out for Trevor.

When I delivered Trevor back to Ward 27 on Monday morning, I couldn't help thinking that we should have been three days post-transplant; through the most hazardous period, hopefully no longer ventilated, able to communicate. Instead, we've picked up one 'chance,' not passed go, and certainly not collected anything.

I've read somewhere that as soon as a transplant takes place all thoughts of the waiting become nothing more than a distant memory. But it's hard to imagine that. Our lives at this time are entirely defined by waiting; at least eighty percent of my waking day is spent wondering when a heart will become available. It's impossible to conjure up any image where that's gone and all I focus on is Trevor's recovery.

1st February 2016

I suspected that the Monday after Friday's episode would be hard; walking onto Ward 27 as if it was a completely normal day was a bitter pill to swallow. There's no one at fault, just a bit of bad luck that couldn't be helped. Now, the situation is the same - I don't know if another organ will come available in a few days, or another eleven weeks... or beyond.

My Transplant Coordinator came to see me this morning and I asked if we could have what I term 'a difficult conversation'. I described how unhappy I feel at the service she provides, or more accurately, the lack of it. I see her infrequently and then only for a couple of minutes at a time. I also explained I'm unhappy at some of what she says to me; for example, she recently tormented me by saying I'd likely be jealous of another person (smaller than me) who was getting a heart transplant; and she has reiterated ad nauseum that I have to remember there's a twenty percent chance I won't come through this at all. She apologised for the first and said she's just trying to be realistic about the second. My point is that I know the percentages - Nicola researched them and we discussed them before we made our decision about transplant - and not one medical professional has mentioned it since the initial assessment. It was discussed with an anaesthetist prior to my signing consent forms, and then we've all let it lie. Except the Transplant Coordinator who seems to feel the need to labour the point. We spoke for perhaps forty-five minutes with the door closed covering a wide range of issues, and all in all, I'm happy with the outcome.

The newsagent in the hospital sells plain paper A4 pads so I bought one of those with the intention of mapping two processes. The first is what I'm calling the heart transplant preparation process, and the second the heart retrieval process. I made a start on them today, and Neil (former Transplant Coordinator) helped me a little in terms of the order of the steps for the heart to find its way from the donor to the recipient (see below). I'm not sure if Neil thinks I'm a crackpot – I believe it's rare for the staff to have a patient who does this type of thing. My goal is firstly to help other heart patients understand the processes, and secondly to track both processes next time an organ comes available for me.

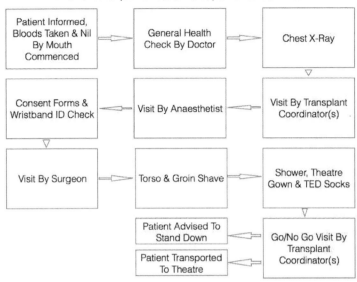

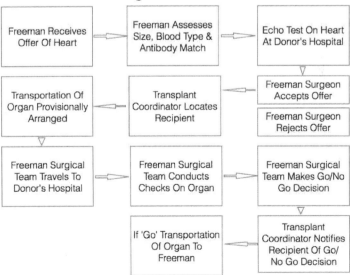

The Heart of the Woman (William Butler Yeats 1865-1939)

AMY: Phone just died, sorry. Xx

NICOLA: That's ok. I was struggling for ideas for Luke's birthday. Xx

AMY: You don't need to get him anything though. We're not that serious. Xx

NICOLA: Hmm. How not very serious? Xx

AMY: I didn't know there was a scale lol x

NICOLA: Yep. 1 – dating several people simultaneously to 10 – he might want to move in when his lease is up. Xx

AMY: We had a wobble yesterday – probably my fault – so we've gone from 10 to 8.5. How're things with you and T?

NICOLA: We're ok, thanks. Relationships are never easy at the best of times. I guess we're bound to have times when we're getting on each other's nerves. Have you sorted whatever led to 8.5?

AMY: Yes, I think so. He stays at his on Thursdays so it's nice to have space but also seems like the argument is on hold somehow. Well, it's over but we don't feel fully made up.

AMY: Haha, he's just turned up now.

NICOLA: I think it's difficult to make up when you have children. Less freedom. But maybe good that you are forced to have space. I guess in any relationship, however good it is, there's that period of 'storming' after the forming and before any norming. In that book by M Scott Peck, he said that when you first get together, love is kind of blind and,

> *a bit like a child doesn't see itself as a separate person before the 'mirror stage,' and in new relationships we don't see ourselves as separate either. We want to see ourselves as so alike as though we're two halves of one whole. Then we get past that and realise that we are two separate people who don't see everything the same way or agree on everything. It's only then that we can develop the relationship and help each other to learn and grow.*
>
> *Go and sort it, then. Whatever that means. But never, ever be afraid of being on your own. You will know if it's right and if he's the right one. Xx*
>
> *AMY: That's helpful, thank you. We don't have shouting, rowing matches. It never gets heated. But I don't like feeling that insecurity. I know it's baggage from my last relationship. And Luke handles that well ... eventually. He's worth the arguments, though ☺x*
>
> *NICOLA: Difficult, but relationships aren't easy. I guess we all carry baggage from every relationship – parents, friends as well as partners. But maybe that's part of the problem – we label it 'baggage' rather than 'what I learnt and how I grew through that experience.'*
>
> *AMY: It doesn't seem to be how I grew so much as how I can be really cutting and unemotional. Or appear it. Xx*
>
> *NICOLA: I think being able to identify those things is the first step in altering them. But you are also very warm and loving, so it's not all negatives. Nobody is perfect. We can all grow. That's what relationships are about – we learn from each other. And learning to trust takes time. xx*

It's a new situation for me, this 'distance mother' arrangement. Over the last few years, our family has been through a lot. Death features in that, and illness too, but other stuff that's just too painful and raw to write about here as well. During that time, on occasions Amy and Sam have switched roles with me and become the ones providing support. Other times have been more traditional and I've been there for one or other of them; most notably, Amy.

When my children were growing up, I worked long hours and found the battle between work and motherhood a constant challenge. Women working in management roles in the 1980s seemed to need to work longer hours than their male counterparts if they were to be taken seriously. I'm not sure even now we're 'there' yet in the UK, in terms of an egalitarian society, but at least flexible working is more possible ... and we lost the need for shoulder pads!

Since I retired, it's been lovely to have time to spend with grandchildren, so I think this forced separation from them feels a little difficult. Elodie, the youngest, came along a few months after Kevin was diagnosed as terminally ill. It seems irrational now, but before she arrived I struggled with thoughts of somebody having to die to make space for a new life. It was as though I feared the arrival of a new baby in our family was intrinsically linked to Kevin's looming death. But, from the beginning, she was a bundle of joy; an incredibly cute and cuddly infant, who always seemed to love being a baby. Even now, if anybody suggests she might be a 'big girl' she quickly corrects them and insists that she is in fact 'a baby.' Perhaps we can expect a remarkable level of intelligence: someone this little has figured that life's much less complicated if you can't be expected to take any responsibility for anything since you are just a baby. That resonates with me – many, many times in my life I've felt like I'm definitely not old enough to deal with what I'm facing.

8th February 2016

I have a feeling that the second week after the 'no go' experience will be tougher to get through than the first. Last week I felt very reassured that the system was looking out for me, whereas this, the commencement of week thirteen, sees me wavering between, "It's definitely going to happen," and, "is it ever going to happen?" Everything is back to 'normal' for me now - I have weekend leave, I show up at The Freeman on a Monday morning, have my cannula put in, receive a quick check of my fluid level from Dr MacGowan and sink back into the routine (I almost typed 'abyss') until lunchtime leave on Wednesday and weekend leave on Friday. I do know it's going to happen, but the wait is a long one judging by the 'averages' for The Freeman. Joking with the nurses and healthcare assistants is a lot of fun, but of course, they have work to do, and they do their best to support me.

Emma, the Social Worker, found a piece of work for Nicola and me to do. She asked us if we could update and refresh the accommodation alternatives to be given to patients and their relatives hailing from outside the Newcastle area. I shake my head and smile when Nurse Andrea and the Transplant Coordinator advise me that 'we already do that' and 'we can't make recommendations.' When I arrived here in July 2015, we were given nothing: no help, no advice, no guidance, no pointers. Organisations have 'maintain the status quo' and 'resist change' so deeply ingrained in the most unusual ways.

15th February 2016

The paradox is that I'm in a temporary yet semi-permanent situation; I'm waiting for a donor organ to come available after which I'll be able to start a recovery process. Having said that, my temporary situation has lasted thirteen weeks and during that time it has been essential to establish routine, order and structure to my days, with a reasonable sprinkling of variety. What I'm trying to explain is that my temporary 'life' has become semi-permanent due to its longevity. My temporary life of waiting may be over this evening, or in six, maybe even nine months' time. There are two challenges associated with this - staying in the best physical shape to undergo a major operation, and staying in the optimum mental shape to cope with the impermanence of my life.

I experience days of positive, optimistic thought patterns, as well as those of a more pessimistic nature, asking myself, 'What if it never happens?' and, 'What does death from multiple organ failure look like and feel like?' Thankfully, the negative days come by relatively infrequently and I do work hard with Nicola at warding them off. The weekly leave of absence on Wednesday lunchtime is helping because I know that I'll see daylight, breathe cold winter air, and most often watch the waves crashing into Longsands Beach at Tynemouth. I know I had bad dives, frustrating diving days when my equipment was not functioning correctly, and was always told that you have to experience the bad in order to truly enjoy the good. I still find the ocean calming and reassuring and in the ten years or so I lived alone, I could only find perfect peace and relaxation pottering around the ocean bed looking for critters. I was so very lucky to dive Florida, Fiji, Papua New Guinea, Malaysia, Indonesia, Thailand, French Polynesia as well as numerous locations in Australia. And lucky too to meet Dr Dave Harasti, who taught me so much about marine biology, and who became such a great friend.

Looking ahead to this week, I've been given a second leave of absence so as to see Amy, Luke, Millie and Elodie who're coming up to Newcastle to visit us. The girls bring joy into my life - innocence, fun, happiness and sometimes a cuddle. So, we drift into week fourteen.

22nd February 2016

Another week of routine and drudgery, during which time I promised to write down for my psychologist Dr Lucy Attenborough, the nature of the events that bring me into gloom:

1. The loneliness of the long-distance runner, by which I mean the monotony of the routine which, paradoxically, is both mind-numbingly boring and comforting at the same time.
2. My physical condition - bloated stomach, the weight of carrying fluid around, and the itching caused by my poor kidney performance. The closer I come to transplant, the more desperate I am for these to disappear from my body. Regarding my swollen stomach, I am disgusted by what I see in the mirror. If I put my heart under the slightest strain, my stomach swells and bloats. I can both feel and see my physical deterioration.
3. It's not the best metaphor, but one I use is the way in which my physical limitations paint me into an ever-shrinking corner. I adjusted to my inability to cycle, and some weeks or months later, had to adjust to my inability to walk in the countryside. I found some time later, that I could no longer work in the garden, and about the same time realised I couldn't wash the cars anymore. Add to this all the food and drinks that had to go too, and knowing that each adjustment caused me sadness and regret as my physical condition defined my quality of life more and more.

4. The others are in a group of lesser but nonetheless important factors: anxiety associated with the fear of being removed from the transplant list; sleep deprivation; wearing the same clothes over and over; relationships with my sons; missing friends and relatives; and the rules of the ward, which are administered in a 'hit and miss' fashion, meaning some nurses apply them while others don't.

29th February 2016

The telephone rang expectantly at 00.15hrs as Nicola and I had drifted off to sleep. It was Sunday evening, the early hours of Monday morning, and a Transplant Coordinator, calmly explained that a potential heart had come available and that I should make my way into Ward 38 of The Freeman within the next couple of hours. The same process as before, more or less, unfolded over the next several hours: interminable waiting punctuated by visits from ever more senior medical professionals. At least I had the luxury of being able to lie on a bed and doze, poor Nicola had to sit on a chair for the duration. Dr MacGowan arrived at the beginning of his working day and from his conversation with staff, we understood that the heart was in Ireland. At around 10am, Professor Dark, one of the most experienced heart surgeons at the hospital informed us that he was sad to say it was another 'no go.' "I had the retrieval team send me photographs of the heart, and it was an easy decision to make as it was quite badly diseased. We will not take chances with you Trevor, because we want nothing but the best for you. When it comes to hearts, we'll continue to be patient. I'm sorry it's not better news."

The feeling is a mix of disappointment at not going ahead, with an elation that the quality control procedures are so rigorous. I've never experienced anything like it. We thanked him for his efforts and made our way up to my 'home base' of Ward 27, which by now was 'open for business,' on a bright and sunny Monday morning.

The Traveller Heart (Vachel Lindsay 1879-1931)

This time, we were called in to The Freeman just as we were settling down to sleep on Sunday night. After the summons, we got up fairly quickly, showered, dressed and made our way to Ward 38 where a cubicle had been made available for Trevor to wait in.

Trevor was 'booked in' by nurses who seemed unsure why they'd been burdened with this additional work, and junior doctors who couldn't understand how someone who claimed he was an in-patient had been away from the hospital. The notion of 'weekend leave' clearly escaped them. Eventually, Trevor went through the hitherto rehearsed procedure of preparing for theatre. Showered, shaved and gowned, he soon fell asleep on the bed. It struck me how exhausted he became quite quickly now. As he slept fitfully, I tried to find a comfortable position in a chair beside the bed; sleep would have been nice, but my brain was cantering ahead and my body was prepared to sleep neither sitting up nor leaning on Trevor's bed-table. It was a relief when a nurse offered to make me a cup of tea. She also offered to switch on the lights but I didn't want to risk waking Trevor – he'd have long enough to worry when he woke, there was no point in stirring him up now.

When Dr MacGowan came on duty early the next morning, he called in to see us and we learnt a little more about the potential donor heart. There's a reluctance to provide any information about where the donor heart is from and I accept this since confidentiality of the donor and family is important. But it would be helpful to be given some information about the likely timescale for a team arriving at the donor hospital. Dr MacGowan was entirely pragmatic and we learnt that the heart was from a patient in Ireland and this would mean a fairly lengthy delay in flying the retrieval team to the hospital.

At around 10am, we learnt that the heart wasn't suitable. The retrieval team had sent Professor Dark images of the heart which was seriously diseased, and he was one-hundred percent confident that this heart was not an option. It seems curious that someone with such significant heart disease has actually died of something else. Maybe they're lucky to avoid a prolonged period of chronic heart disease with all its limitations. I wonder if, given the option, they would have preferred that to the death they succumbed to. I notice that my perspective of death has altered massively over the last few years. It's such a taboo subject in this country but my experience of Kevin's prolonged death, following a slow decline during which each of his faculties was gradually taken from him, has certainly affected my outlook. My mother's death was inevitable and yet medical professionals continued treatment for what seemed an inordinate amount of time. I found it difficult to understand why she was having drugs, other than analgesia, as we all sat around the bed waiting. It's as though there's a need to squeeze every last breath out of a person, no matter what. Meanwhile, Charlie's death was peaceful, dignified and humane as the vet sensitively put an end to his suffering. And my Dad's, his was the best death we could get for him, but required a great deal of input and negotiation to ensure support from hospice nurses.

Perhaps, if we talked about death a little more authentically we could be more prepared and less passive. As a society, we've constructed a considerable lexicon to communicate this state: we shuffle off our mortal coil; turn up our toes; come to an untimely end; meet our maker; pass away; croak; check out; give up the ghost; kick the bucket; pop off; bite the dust; and succumb, to name just a few. But we shy away from words which accurately describe the process of dying, or the needs of those involved. Our unconscious incompetence with its inherent limitations doesn't become apparent to us until the final curtain draws around a loved one of our own. It's only through constructive communication that we can have any hope of securing dignified and pain-free death that meets the needs of the dying person and their loved ones, as well as healthcare professionals.

CHAPTER TEN

Losing Heart

4th March 2016

It's taken me almost a week to summon up the energy to write this entry. My emotions have ranged and raged - I've felt anger, frustration, crushing disappointment, disbelief, confusion, immense sadness, and resignation. Resigned to what? To my fate, I guess; to the possibility of not receiving a new heart after all. Nurse, Clive, - a QPR fan for his sins - and Healthcare Assistant, Victoria, woke me at 5am and told me that a potential heart had come available and I needed to be readied for the possibility of surgery. Excitement filled my veins, despite the fact that only blood came out when the junior doctor arrived to take samples. It felt more relaxed and more comfortable to be in Ward 27, my home base where the nursing staff knew me. Let me spare you the repetition of describing what are basically the same process steps of readying the patient for a heart transplant. Nicola came through about 7.30am and we smiled our smiles of greeting and hope, balancing carefully the possibilities of both 'go' and 'no go' options. At least we had a better idea of how long the process takes from beginning to end - between ten and twelve hours - so we bunkered down for the long wait. I manage the 'nil by mouth' reasonably well, I suspect because the adrenalin starts to flow. A few mouthwashes of cold water keep me going.

As before, and in somewhat random order, appeared a procession of medical professionals, junior doctor, transplant coordinators, anaesthetist, surgeon as well as their assistants, students and deputies. Sometimes they ask the same questions as their immediate predecessor, but the sense of hope and elation was such that I didn't care. Around noon, the Transplant Coordinator told us that things are looking extremely positive, and around 2pm, her boss accompanied her to give us the news that the transplant would definitely proceed. Their smiles were massive, as were ours. The theatre staff would come to collect me around 2.45pm, and yes, I'd be permitted to walk there if I wished. Total joy and elation. Just the best feeling in the world! Imagine for a moment, you are suffering from an illness that is slowly killing you, and which will result in multiple organ failure. Probably your kidneys will go first, and then it's dialysis two or three times a week in order to postpone the inevitable. Then a person walks into your room and explains that you're going to have an operation, very soon, that will not only cure you of these ills but allow you to return to an active life. What an explosion of hope and joy you'd experience! Over the next hour or so, my mind began to walk through the dozens of activities that I'll be free and able to do - jog, cycle, walk, hike, eat, drink, play, swim, shower (without rest), shop, garden, take on stairs and slopes, tie my shoelaces, and many, many more. The picture of a new life was clearly forming in my mind's eye. I called my brother Robert as well as my sons Christopher and Daniel. These were short calls as none of us wanted to get into 'possibly final goodbye' scenarios but they were of course filled with happiness and hope.

I nipped off to the toilet, during which time Nicola was asked by a nurse if they are permitted to come in and share their happiness at the good news. So on my return the room started to fill with nurses, healthcare assistants, and cleaners, about half of whom were shedding tears of joy as they hugged me. I was keen to avoid these scenes until we received the definite go-ahead, but it had come and we celebrated. The group left and Social Worker, Emma Sowerby, who's given us fantastic support throughout, arrived with her beaming smile. She closed the door and expressed her happiness for us both. About five minutes later, Hazel returned along with the surgeon Mr Shah. Even though we were an hour late for my collection, I still didn't entertain for a moment that anything was wrong. Until Hazel dropped the bombshell. The operation could not go ahead. An antibody had been discovered in my blood, one which had not appeared before, and this increased the chances of rejection of the new heart by my body. Mr Shah left, as did Emma, and Hazel remained to support us for a while, but it was clear she was almost as devastated as we were.

The next hour was spent putting into reverse all preparations, and because it was Friday, Nicola and I packed to leave for the weekend. At one point Nicola left to go to the nurses' station and returned to tell me that there were many tears of sadness there. She also mentioned that she had seen Hazel weeping in the empty daycare wing. As we left, I had this awful feeling of shame that I had let these people down. We struggled to make eye contact as none of us knew what to say or how to say it. One nurse said that in over twenty years of working with transplant patients, she had never experienced anything like this before. She had questions, we had questions, Hazel had questions, but it was clear to me that there were to be no answers. Everyone understood the technical aspect of antibodies and rejection, but nobody understood how the plug could be pulled fifteen minutes before I was due to enter theatre. It seemed to me that something had gone badly wrong - hospital staff seemed as confused as me and Nicola - but no-one was willing to discuss it.

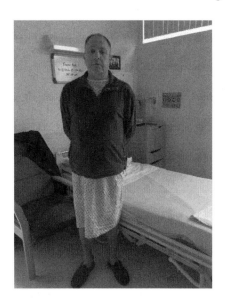

Never Give All the Heart (William Butler Yeats 1865-1939)

This time, Trevor was in hospital and was told early in the morning that a potential heart was available. Again, I went in and sat with him while we waited. The usual comings and goings of medical and nursing staff went on and there were lots of positive and hopeful noises. The time passes very slowly when you're waiting to see whether a heart is suitable. You look for hints in words, expressions, timings ... anything really. Is the fact that nobody has come by for two hours a good thing or a bad thing? Would we have heard something by now if it was going ahead? Or could it be a good sign that we haven't heard anything? Was the anaesthetist trying to tell us something when he said, "See you later"? Every word is dissected and scrutinised in your head.

The staff all seem to play their cards close to their chests. It's difficult because, as I said previously, I can see that it's important to maintain the confidentiality of the donor and their family. The last thing the transplant system needs is any lack of transparency that has the potential to further reduce the number of organs available. But it would really help the sanity of the patient requiring a transplant and their family if there was more consistent and better communication. Maybe I won't care about all of this when it's over and Trevor has his heart, but at the moment, one of the most difficult things we face is the torpor between being told a heart has become available and a decision being made.

Over the next few hours, we got occasional updates but in the main, Trevor and I sat in the cubicle on Ward 27 and waited for eight or nine hours before we were told the remarkable news that the heart was suitable. It was a healthy heart, in good condition and Trevor would be going to theatre in thirty minutes. It was definite. No going back. It was happening.

Half an hour passed. Then an hour. I wasn't sure whether Trevor had noticed that time was ticking by. I find it difficult in that type of situation to know whether to say anything or not. If I say something, he may not have been aware of it and I've drawn his attention to a problem that he will then worry about. But if he is aware of it, he may not be talking to me because he thinks I haven't noticed, and then he hasn't got anybody to talk to and is bottling it up for fear of worrying me. When we were first told that the transplant was going ahead, Trevor had popped out to the bathroom and some of the nurses who'd heard the news popped their heads round the door and asked if I thought Trevor would mind them coming and saying, "Good luck," before he went down to theatre. I said that I didn't think he'd mind – although he'd been worried about people being in any way positive before the heart was confirmed, this had been confirmed and was definitely happening, so how could that be a problem? They'd come in and we'd smiled and laughed and been so happy. But that was forty-five minutes ago.

Emma, the Social Worker, had also heard that the transplant was going ahead and she'd come in to wish Trevor well before he went down. It was while we were talking to Emma that the Transplant Coordinator and Surgeon came into Trevor's cubicle. I didn't really have time to notice how they looked, but it must have been pretty glum as they came to say that the transplant wasn't going ahead. At the last minute a problem had been identified - something to do with a mis-match in anti-bodies which meant there would be a greater chance of rejection than the surgeon felt was safe. Emma looked more like a rabbit in the headlights than anybody I've ever seen. We must have all looked shell-shocked. A thousand questions went through my head but I asked nothing; what was the point? The words that came out of my mouth were the much rehearsed stuff about it being better to find the right heart than just 'a' heart; it not being anybody's fault; it being a difficult job for the Transplant Coordinator to have to convey news like this.

When I popped out to the loo a few minutes later, I passed the Transplant Coordinator in the corridor. She was weeping and other nurses were trying to comfort her. The ward nurses looked bereft. They sobbed. We comforted. Odd.

I recall that I felt a strong sense that something very peculiar was happening. The stress we were being put through was so intense that it was difficult to understand how this could be part of any normal healthcare process. I genuinely wondered whether there were hidden cameras in Trevor's cubicle filming us in order that either a) a bunch of psychologists could analyse our response to extreme stress, or b) viewers could phone in to vote somebody off. When I talked to people afterwards and explained what happened, they asked how we got through it. I guess the answer is that you really have no choice since the only other option is to fall to pieces and I'm never quite sure how one does that.

Once again, we collected together Trevor's belongings and wended our way back to the apartment. I felt raw. I absolutely didn't have a clue what to do with or for myself, or for Trevor. I needed a grown up to hug me and tell me it will all be okay in the end. Trevor couldn't do that. He needed me to help him. But my tank was on empty: I had very little left to give.

I suppose it shouldn't have come as a great surprise that we fell out. Blamed each other, somehow; if not for the transplant being aborted, then for every minor hiccup that weekend. Our emotions were shot and I didn't have any idea how we were going to pick ourselves up and go again.

16th March 2016

The week after the third 'no go' was very tough, beginning with a weekend of bitter arguments between Nicola and me. I failed to link the cause of the discontent to the stress of the previous day, failed to summon enough emotional intelligence to see the obviousness of the predicament we were in, and failed to manage both my tone and my irritability. Returning to The Freeman on 7th March, I fell into a period of negativity, disillusionment and scepticism. Several visitors over the coming days came by, and the two most powerful conversations were held with Transplant Coordinators, Neil, and a few days later, Gill. Neil warned me that he wanted to speak to me as a friend rather than as a patient, and powerfully explained how disappointed in me he would be if I walked out on this process. "You've come too far, and while you've made a heavy investment in this, it's easily matched by the investment this hospital is making in you. You'd be letting down all these people who genuinely care for you, who stand in tears when you get a 'no go,' and who truly want you to have the better life that lies at the end of this. You have to dig deep," he said.

The conversation with Gill occurred on the Friday and was heavily cathartic in nature. Tears flowed again and we reached a point of calm honesty. Her eyes held her emotions: sadness, grief, disappointment, a steely determination that this transplant is going to go ahead, we are going to see it through. We spoke in practical terms of how we might go about rebuilding my trust in the system, and how information and communication were critical to this. Despite the lateness of the call on the antibody issue, all decisions had been taken in my best interests by deeply experienced professionals. Deep down I knew this, but I needed to hear it. Indeed, I've noticed that this is a pattern with me – I need to hear over and over from medical professionals that it *is* going to happen. Then I can dig deep. Then I can dig in.

Seventeen weeks now completed, and today's the commencement of eighteen. I have a quilt on my bed now, more decoration on the walls from Millie and Elodie, and, courtesy of Nicola who stayed at the Hilton for her Uncle's funeral, a reversible Do Not Disturb/Please Make Up My Room sign that hangs on the outside of my door. If I must go through this, I want to do it with a smile on my face.

Naomi, my dear friend from Australia, despatched to me a koala teddy bear she'd been given as a child over fifty years ago. It's her healing talisman, her lucky charm, and is very precious to her. Unspoken, is the fact that he'll make his way back home when I have a new heart and am in recovery. Na as she's known, is the manager of the Maitland Neighbourhood Centre in New South Wales, and has enough love in her heart to satisfy a small African nation.

23rd March 2016

Despite the fact that I'm losing muscle definition because of a sedentary lifestyle of sitting and waiting, the mental challenge is becoming far greater than the physical. My certainty that a heart will definitely come along now sometimes wavers. My brain starts to play with scenarios involving either being removed from the transplant list or a heart simply not becoming available at all. The chapel here at The Freeman is a place of sanctuary and calm where I spend time meditating each day, keen to find that same place of sanctuary within myself. I must achieve this; it's essential to staying focused, healthy, optimistic and positive.

30th March 2016

I watched a documentary called West of Memphis, about three young men wrongly accused and convicted of the murder of three eight year old boys. They served eighteen years' imprisonment before they were released, and even then a condition of their release was that they plead guilty to the crimes. During this period of incarceration, one of them spoke eloquently on his reflection of 'time.' He wrote:

"We spend much time dwelling on the past, but in truth the past exists only in our memory and it can never be repeated. Likewise, we spend much time dwelling on the future, but the future exists only in our imaginations, and it never comes. Time may be useful for arriving at meetings and appointments but I still prefer a world in which every time we look at our watches, the watch face simply shows the word 'Now.'"

I found a number of topics coming together; Buddhism, Gestalt Psychology and ACT (Acceptance & Commitment Therapy) to name but a few. How must I apply these notions to my own circumstances? If I accept that I've entered a period in which the mental challenges are greater than the physical, what are my commitments? My goal is to minimise the amount of time I spend dwelling on my former life, both before cardiomyopathy and before the onset of greater limitations to my physical state. I cannot change the past and nothing beneficial comes from spending time, thought and energy there. I strive to look upon my history with great fondness and eliminate the tendency to desire those days to return. They cannot. My goal is also to minimise the amount of time I spend dwelling on the future, and especially, 'when is the transplant going to happen?' and, 'what will my life be like in recovery and post-recovery?' The future lies only in my imagination and each transplant is different, each recovery is different, each 'new life' is different. I seek that special place in my mind where I lose the anxiety of wondering what the future holds and accept there is nothing I can do to influence it. Let it go.

This leaves what Gestalt practitioners call 'the living present' and is where I wish to spend my time, thoughts and energy. I aim to focus on what I can change and influence in my life. If I succeed in this, I'll be able to appreciate the present moment, and my watch shall always display the word 'Now.'

CHAPTER ELEVEN

Take Heart

18th April 2016

The phone rang at fifteen minutes past midnight as Nicola and I were dozing off. My Transplant Coordinator called us in with the news that a heart had become available and at this stage it looks a good match, fitting all the criteria. We knew the drill and arrived to join the preparation process a couple of hours later. After the previous last minute refusal, I had a very, very open mind as to whether or not we'd proceed, and constantly reminded myself of the 50:50 at best chance of going ahead. I received the news that Mr Shah and Professor Schüle agreed it was an excellent match so it was all systems go. After the obligatory twelve hour 'prep' time, I was wheeled away. The wonderful staff of Ward 27 stood in line giving tearful hugs, kisses and well wishes, to such an extent that the porter had to wrench me away - we were in danger of being late for an important appointment!

    Nicola came with me and I felt relaxed, joyful and positive as I lay there and signed the consent forms. The transplant coordinators reassured me there is no chance of a refusal at this stage, so it really is going to happen. In front of me was a guy on a bed saying goodbye to his wife, and in a conspiratorial whisper, it was explained that I would be receiving the donor's heart, and he would be receiving the same donor's lungs. Everyone seemed in such good spirits as Nicola and I kissed goodbye and I was whisked away into the next room for anaesthetic. I drifted off.

My Heart Goes Out (Stevie Smith 1902-1971)

When 'the call' came shortly after midnight on Monday 18th April, we were in bed and had just switched the light out. Having experienced the whole 'early hours of Monday morning call' previously, I think we both settled into the now familiar routine. I must admit, we lay in bed a touch longer than we should have; aware that we wouldn't arrive at Ward 29 by 2 am as instructed, but wanting to savour this time on our own before the NHS machine, and its uniquely unfathomable timeframe, once again consumed us.

Albeit reluctantly, we did eventually get up. Curiously, Trevor insisted on showering in the main bathroom, rather than the en-suite. I was surprised by this choice because he'd previously expressed a preference for the pleasure of standing under the powerful rainfall shower, as opposed to the less impressive shower over the bath. Although it didn't occur to us at the time, this may have been a decision he later came to regret.

Carrying out my morning ablutions so soon after my bedtime ones felt a little Groundhog Day-ish - one of the previous calls had come on a Sunday evening, just after we'd turned in. On auto-pilot, I boiled the kettle for tea; took my morning medication; showered; washed and dried my hair; reinstated make-up; dressed with comfort in mind; put my e-reader in my handbag. And prepared for another futile session.

Outside, the air was milder than I'd expected. The apartment complex was peaceful: the silent lights-out routine in anticipation of another working week. An overwhelming sense that nobody, except Trevor and I, was aware of our drama.

Radio 2 was on the car stereo during the short journey. I recognised the voice of the presenter: Janice Long. Whenever I hear her voice, a stream of consciousness leads me to thoughts of her brother and how irritating I find him, so, I guess similar thoughts were processed that night. On reflection, I think my conscious was split into two discrete sections: one sharply focused on filtering every thought before voicing it to avoid the potential ensuing atmosphere worthy of a cheese grater. The other, set to personal cruise-control, programmed to deliver us safely to The Freeman. Trevor and I didn't exactly have a conversation. I attempted to fill some of the silence: noticing there were very few cars on the road; turning onto the High Street was easier than usual; somebody had placed an unlit skip at the side of the road; parking at the hospital shouldn't be a problem. For a moment, I let down my guard and pointed out that the song playing on the radio seemed ironic: D-Ream's 'Things Can Only Get Better.' Usually, Trevor and I would have shared a smile. Today, we didn't. We were both completely lost in our own thoughts. I was contemplating how many more times we can do this; not just because of the massive stress it brings, but also since Trevor's deterioration is progressing unabated. I know the time will soon come when it's now or never.

When we arrived on Ward 29, the nurses were expecting us and showed us to Trevor's bed on a six-bedded bay. Curtains closed around each of the other beds shielded the inhabitants from prying eyes. It was only later we learnt that Ward 29 is 'lungs.' In hindsight, the cacophony of rasping coughs and violent expectoration stuttering from each partitioned area would have given us a clue. Trevor had always feared being on a bay in these circumstances: he worried that the noise of preparing him for theatre would disturb other patients. But the additional disruption associated with Trevor's admission blended into the hubbub.

Trevor's observations were quickly monitored and recorded, the usual swabs taken for MRSA screening, and Trevor managed to squeeze out sufficient urine to allow the necessary checks.

The on-call Transplant Coordinator visited at around 2.30 am and updated us on progress so far. As she'd explained during the call to invite us in, the donor was known to have an infection which may or may not be active. This was not considered a contraindication to transplant and she explained the procedure for management of any risk. The Cardiothoracic Surgeon, Mr Shah, had checked with Professor Schűle, as the infection was not something he had come across before, and both were happy to proceed if the heart was considered suitable. Antibodies, we were assured, had been checked and rechecked to ensure that this time the donor heart was a good match. Those words, 'this time,' lodged briefly in my conscious, but it didn't seem advisable to ask about 'last time.' Tests undertaken so far suggested that the heart was good, but the retrieval team had not yet been sent. We were told that there had been a recent change in procedure for the dispatch of teams, and this had created some confusion. However, the Transplant Coordinator assured us, this was now resolved and the retrieval team would be leaving shortly. Whilst she had initially expected to know by 3.30am whether the heart was transplantable, this had now shifted to around 6.30am. She left, assuring us she'd return between 6.30 and 7.00am to update us.

Finding the right words to say once Trevor and I were left alone again was less of a problem than I'd anticipated. Trevor was uncomfortable with the bloating and fluid retention on his abdomen. He was really struggling. He obviously just wanted quiet. Sleep didn't come easily to him but, I turned the light out and sat soundlessly amongst the relentless rally of sputum fire, willing Trevor to be able to find some relief.

Before he'd managed to settle, a nurse came and told us that Trevor needed an x-ray. I'd already suggested to him that if this was needed, he should concede to being transferred in a wheelchair. He really was finding any exertion too much. If I'm honest, I had one eye on the consequences for the next day when inevitably the transplant didn't go ahead. Trevor would be left, once again, in greater physical and emotional distress through late medication and the demands the night's activities had placed on his failing body.

A wheelchair was brought. The nurse asked if we needed her to accompany us, but I insisted we would be fine. There was a hiccup when we arrived at the main X-Ray Department and couldn't get in, but some domestic staff kindly helped us out and the radiographer was found. The chest x-ray was done very quickly and we returned to the ward. It struck me that this interlude had been a welcome time-robber. It was now 4.00am.

Returning to his bed, Trevor tried once again to sleep. We looked at each other as the neighbour executed his entire repertoire of snoring. Whistling, wheezing, grunting, gasping. Guttural. Each mode lasting five to ten minutes before switching to the next. From the other beds, the sound of coughing, thick with mucous reverberated around the bay. Remembering I had headphones in my handbag, I connected to my iPhone and listened to a meditation app. Under the circumstances, it was surprisingly relaxing. I encouraged Trevor to try it, but for him it was just another irritation among the many.

He tried to find a comfortable position and some sleep. I listened to Elbow.

At around 6.00am, the ward began to groan into consciousness. Nurses circled the ward, weighing patients and recording routine observations. Men began to make the noises men make in a morning. It's fascinating to observe male behaviour in this setting: dense salutations, bids of a hearty, 'Good morning.' All suggestive of a night of peaceful slumber, as opposed to one of universal insomnia.

Trevor was shaved and instructed to shower and put on a theatre gown. Having used Ward 29's facilities, he commented once again that the hygiene standards of men appalled him.

A welcome distraction appeared in the shape of a Consultant Anaesthetist who seemed very knowledgeable. He was accompanied by a glum junior doctor who received what I trust was an exceptionally important text message during the consultation. The Anaesthetist asked whether anybody had explained to Trevor what would happen during the operation. Trevor's, "No," appeared to justify a detailed explanation of every risk associated with a heart transplant, the most serious, apparently, being death. Trevor focused on an increasing urgency to empty his bowels, and I attempted to zone out whilst maintaining the appearance of somebody who was paying attention. Like Trevor said later, it was all academic: he was so poorly, what choice did he have? It's an interesting quirk of the British healthcare system that extremely difficult and intensely private information of this nature is delivered in a six-bedded bay, with all the privacy afforded by a flimsy cotton curtain.

Shortly after the Anaesthetist departed, a Healthcare Assistant swept back all of the curtains around the beds on the bay, insisting that she needed to, 'Do the bays.' With continued disregard for the patients, she then opened the main blinds disgruntling one chap who was stuck in his bed and blinded by the sunlight. Trevor and I gave it a minute, and then, realising that whatever 'doing the bays' involved it was not something that would affect us, I firmly pulled the curtains back around, preferring the shred of privacy this secured.

We listened to the inane chattering of men between each other, and between themselves and the nurses. I decided that there was very little chance of Trevor getting any sleep, and a very serious risk of me eventually demanding quiet.

My request that we be allowed to return to Trevor's cubicle on Ward 27, where we could both have some peace to prepare ourselves for the inevitable disappointment, was met with approval by the Ward Sister. I quickly purloined a wheelchair, installed Trevor in it, and navigated the lifts and corridors to the sanctuary of his cubicle, where Trevor lay on his bed and I sat in the chair beside him. The peace was palpable. We were mainly left on our own. A couple of nurses did the usual checks; Mr Shah, the Surgeon, visited; the Transplant Coordinator came and told us the transplant would be going ahead ...!!

Neither of us could really believe it. We skirted around the topic and avoided saying any version of, "Well, hey, that was a long wait, but it's actually happening." Mainly, I guess, because we didn't believe it was. In some ways, it was like playing a game of 'Chicken': which one of us would cave in first and hint that we were pleased, excited, or hopeful?

Time passed and nurses introduced words or sentences such as, "I think you're going down soon." But we kept schtum.

The Transplant Coordinator appeared again to tell us there would be two transplants done at the same time. Along with the heart being transplanted into Trevor, a man would be receiving the lungs. This meant a slight delay, but Trevor would be going to theatre in about an hour. It seems strange, reading this back, that the dehumanisation of body parts in this way seemed entirely normal at that time. We had become so accustomed to the vocabulary of transplants that there was no discernible reaction in either of us to the harshness of discussing the organs of a recently deceased person in this way.

After this, Trevor wondered whether he might like to speak to Elodie. We chatted about it and agreed that children have the wonderful ability of minimising anything, so this might be a good idea. At least it would break the tension and distract us from our overwhelming, yet unspoken dread of another cancellation. Amy answered her mobile quickly and Trevor asked if he could speak to Ella. Although Ella was tired, and not in a chatting mood, the prospect of talking to her 'Treasure' was too much to pass up. Trevor asked if Ella could keep a secret and explained to her that nobody else knew, but he might be getting a heart. Squealing, Elodie dropped the phone and rushed off to tell her mum's friend. So, not much distraction for us there, then.

A few moments on the phone with Amy and then just the two of us again. Not daring to voice our fears; not daring to indicate anything that may be construed as joy; not daring to speak for fear of saying the wrong thing. Trying so hard to remain cautious, while wishing with all my heart that this would be 'the one.' And acutely conscious that wishing doesn't work. The last six months had shown me that. Neither did praying. Nor visualising. Not even, remaining positive.

And then things began to speed up. A trolley arrived with a porter who told us he was taking Trevor to theatre. Alison, another Transplant Coordinator, would accompany him. At first, Trevor was reluctant to get on the trolley; he'd always strongly expressed a preference for walking to theatre when it eventually happened. But, I think by this time he didn't actually care how he got there and he was quickly settled on the trolley. Nurses from Ward 27 lined the corridor and the porter had to stop again and again for each nurse to hug Trevor as he was wheeled past. Trevor 'joked' that he'd doubtless be back in fifteen minutes.

Three of us walked, and one rode, the short distance from Ward 27 to Theatre Reception. We joined a line of theatre trolleys waiting in turn to be checked by a theatre nurse. When Trevor's wristband was checked, it made us smile that the nurse was the first person in many months to remark on his birth date: "Oh, a Christmas baby." What seemed like a lifetime away, this comment had begun to really grate as every single healthcare professional we came across had used those exact same words. Today, it was fine. A small price to pay.

And that was it. Trevor and I said goodbye. No mushy stuff. We've done all of that. We were just impatient to get this party started before somebody snatched the opportunity away, again.

It probably sounds odd to hear that saying goodbye was really quite easy. I think that after such a long wait, we were both desperate for the transplant to happen. Trevor has been so uncomfortable and so poorly that there was no way I could have any doubts at all about this. I felt entirely comfortable that the professionals whose hands I'd left him in would look after him. He was safe. Soon, he would receive an anaesthetic and I felt such calmness in the thought that he would be able to sleep without restless legs, or itching, or pain, for the first time in months.

Alison showed me how to get to ICU, and explained how I would be contacted and when this was likely to happen. When a Transplant Coordinator joined us for a moment, we talked about how poorly Trevor has become and how relieved we all are that a heart has, at last, become available.

As I walked to my car, to pick up my wheeled crate to transfer Trevor's belongings from the ward, I phoned Christopher, Robert and Sam to give them the news we'd all been waiting for. Chris suggested he speak with Daniel. I reassured each one that I would contact them as soon as I knew anything.

During that walk, there was a very surreal moment. Many times over the last few months, I had passed a particular theatre porter, dressed in green theatre scrubs, carrying a small red cool bag marked 'Blood Products.' The cool bags reminded me of the small picnic version that people use to carry their sandwiches to work. I'd often mused on this, wondering whether these were donated organs on their way to theatre, and taunting myself with thoughts of other people receiving their gift. When I'd left Trevor, this now familiar porter was sitting in theatre reception. As I now walked towards the hospital entrance, I passed him in the corridor. I was walking away from theatre; he was walking towards it. We glanced at each other, and my gaze fixed on the two red cool bags he carried, one over each shoulder. One lungs, one heart? I'll never know, but it seems very likely that Trevor's new heart and I passed in the corridor.

Returning to Ward 27 without Trevor felt strange. But not unpleasant. Rachel made me a cup of tea; I took down the pictures and photograph; packed his clothes and toiletries; stripped the bed; threw away the rubbish. Then I said my thanks and goodbyes to the nurses, reassured them I would be back with cake, packed the car, and returned to the apartment, phoning Amy en-route to confirm that Trevor had in fact gone to theatre.

At first, I thought about sitting in front of the television for a while, but then realised it would be more sensible to keep myself busy. Get on with some chores. A couple of hours soon passed sorting washing, doing some ironing, and catching up on housework. After that, I relaxed on the sofa for a while with the telly on in the background and managed to sleep for half an hour or so. When I woke, I phoned my Aunty Marion to let her know. And then I had a bath.

As I was drying my hair at about 6.30pm, I'm not sure what made me think about it but I checked Trevor's phone and discovered it was switched to silent but there were three missed calls from an undisclosed number. The first had been at 5.11pm. This did worry me a little since Trevor hadn't gone to theatre until 1.15pm and the operation was due to take 7-8 hours. A moment after I put Trevor's phone down, mine rang: it was the nurse from ICU letting me know that Trevor had been back from theatre a little while, the operation had gone well, and I could go in and see him when I was ready. They had thought that Trevor's number was the one to phone, but after several attempts had realised that this probably wasn't the right number since the phone went to answerphone and it was Trevor speaking. It seems ironic that despite being asked my mobile number several times over the course of the last five months, and seeing it written in Trevor's medical casenotes, at the critical point when it may be necessary to contact me urgently two phone numbers were erroneously transferred to his ICU notes: Trevor's first and mine second. It transpired that after three failed attempts to contact me on the first number, the nurse tried the second number. Frustrating, especially when Mr Shah and the nurse said they'd been trying to contact me for a while and I felt like I was being accused of going AWOL. So, note to self: if ever you're supporting someone through a heart transplant again, remember to personally check that the correct phone number is handed to the ICU nurses.

Entering ICU for the first time was a little confusing, but the staff were reassuring and explained where I needed to go. Trevor was in Cubicle 14 which had an air-lock to minimise the chance of infection. This meant that entry into the cubicle was through a door into an ante-room where I needed to hang my coat, and wash my hands with Hibiscrub. When I went into the cubicle, Trevor was on a ventilator and was sedated. He had a large number of infusions, both bags and syringe drivers. There were also many screens displaying graphs and numbers in different colours. Lots of beeping. The hum of a ripple mattress vibrating beneath him.

I talked to Trevor a little. It's always difficult to know whether somebody who's unconscious can hear you, but I stroked his head, reassured him that it was over and that I had let his sons know he was okay. I stayed for about an hour. The nurse, Johnny, had arms covered in tattoos and a head and chin covered in stubble. So very different from nurses in 'my day.' But still very capable and professional. He reassuringly explained what was happening and what to expect next. And that Trevor had a urinary catheter and was passing urine. Again, I noticed how confident I felt that Trevor was in safe hands. He looked so peaceful and I felt happy that he was sleeping, and the signs of tension that I feared had become permanently etched onto his face, had relaxed.

Later, when I texted Christine and said that I thought Trevor was receiving very good care, she pointed out that in the light of my exacting standards, if I thought the care was good, then it must be very good. That reassured me too. She's right. I have very high standards and am quick to notice when something isn't right. But everything I saw on ICU felt right and gave me confidence.

By the time I left, Johnny had been replaced by the night nurse, Mia, who gave me the direct line telephone number for the cubicle. I asked if it would be okay to phone in the morning, and Mia promised to phone if there was any significant adverse change overnight.

Pulling into the car park at the apartment complex, I became aware of thoughts that had begun flickering in my conscious. Once I'd parked, I sat for a moment to mull over precisely what I was thinking. I noticed that these thoughts were about Trevor and me, and the things we could look forward to. Our future. It struck me that I had begun to think of a 'future'; a thought which would have seemed anachronistic just twenty-four hours earlier.

The apartment seemed quiet. Quieter than usual. Odd, since Monday nights are usually spent on my own in our normal Freeman week. But, we'd entered a new version of normal. Trevor's absence felt almost palpable. I glanced at the bottle of Hunter Valley wine he'd opened the night before. We'd had a glass each as we ate olives and watched Sunday evening television. Together. I dismissed the idea of pouring a glass; it's something we'd shared. I need to hang on to that. It needs to be left unfinished.

Surprisingly, when I called Cubicle 14 at 6.20am, Trevor was awake and able to talk to me briefly. Mia told me that he'd been extubated and woken at around midnight. Trevor and I only spoke briefly, but it was heartening to hear his voice and hear him say that he was okay. I said that I wouldn't be able to see him until 2.00pm as visiting was from then until 8.00pm, but Trevor was anxious that this was a long time to wait. He asked the nurse if this was correct, and she explained that as it was his first day post-transplant, I would be allowed to visit briefly in the morning.

At around 8.00am, I walked into Trevor's cubicle to find him awake, propped up in bed, and drinking sips of water. He didn't complain of any pain, but, to be fair it looked like he had a fairly heady cocktail of drugs entering him via various tubes. When breakfast was delivered, Trevor asked for orange juice and a cup of tea, but nothing to eat. Swallowing orange juice caused him to wince and complain that his throat hurt. We talked about the possibility that this was because he had been intubated for several hours and the tube may have caused a sore throat. The nurse reassured Trevor this was quite normal and they wouldn't usually be concerned unless it persisted for several days. I stayed about three quarters of an hour, until I was conscious that the nurses wanted access to Trevor and I didn't want to get in their way.

19th April 2016

I had no idea of the time or even the day. I heard a voice calling my name in an insistent way, repeating it again and again. An ethereal voice was asking me to grasp the railing of the bed as a signal that I could understand. My brain told my body to do as requested but that's where it ended. My hand just flapped around. I couldn't speak and I didn't know why. Panic rose as I figured I was trapped inside my body, unable to communicate. Is this it, am I locked-in? I found a person's hand and squeezed it, holding on for dear life, gripping tightly to let them know I was conscious. The same process was repeated a few minutes later and I grasped the railing - the whole episode (I was later told) is a normal part of reversing the anaesthetic to bring me round. The unfortunate ICU nurse later explained to Nicola that an almost-broken hand is an occupational hazard.

20th April 2016

Returning to consciousness, I was aware of Nicola's presence, and that of a nurse, and being in a cool, dark room. Some hours later, the nurse gave me instruction on how he would help me move to a chair so that I could have something to eat and drink. I felt a little groggy but not enough to limit my feelings of euphoria probably caused by the morphine being administered. Eating and drinking was very painful, each swallow of lukewarm water gave a stabbing sensation in my throat, soreness from the tubes used in the operation. I persevered though and was relieved when the nurse told me that in the event of coughing, hiccups, burping, sneezing, to just let it happen; no damage could be done. Nicola said goodbye as I needed sleep and rest and I asked where the call button was placed. She smiled, gently telling me that this was ICU and I wouldn't need a call-bell as a nurse would be present in my room throughout. "But where are they going to sleep?" I asked in puzzlement, at which she laughed and said that they don't sleep, they watch over me. I drifted off into another remarkably peaceful sleep.

I've been asked by a nurse if I felt anything at all that was different about my chest, my body, my brain, and the answer is a clear 'No.' Such a sweet question to ask, and I feel so privileged in being able to reply from a position of experience!

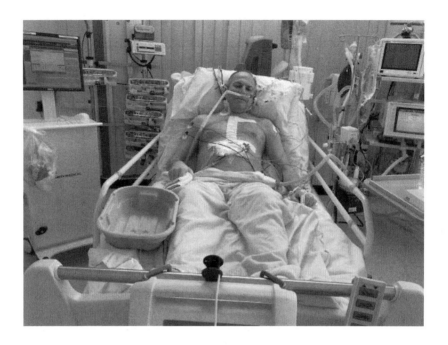

23rd April 2016

I've decided to keep the medical information to a minimum as I always wanted this to be a journal of the sharing of experience and of reflection. This is as much as I'll write – on this day, the nasal cannula was decreased from 40% to 20%, pleural drains removed, oxygen mask replaced with HP nasal tube, a lower dosage of morphine administered, soreness of throat decreasing, exercise and a full meal taken, heart beating unaided with an external pacemaker backing it up. Here in front of me is the mountain I've craved for so long – just climb it through rehabilitation and exercise and I'll be fit and free for living life to the full. Little did I know of what lay ahead.

CHAPTER TWELVE

My Aching Heart

How is Your Heart? (Charles Bukowski 1920-1994)

On Tuesday when I visited, the nurses were just finishing inserting a cannula into Trevor's neck to connect him to a dialysis machine. This felt disappointing, but we were reassured that after a heart transplant patients frequently need dialysis for a short time. It was still hoped that Trevor's kidneys would regain their strength with the increased perfusion from his new heart. We'd previously been told that when the heart is failing, blood isn't pumped through the kidneys at high enough pressure to enable them to filter blood effectively. Also, during the heart transplant, the kidneys (along with all other organs) are shocked by the trauma of the procedure. We would have to wait and see whether Trevor's kidneys would recover.

Trevor was moved down to Ward 38 which feels like enormous progress. He's in a light, airy dual-aspect room near the nurses' station. The room is en-suite and much more comfortable than ICU. We have a new group of nurses to get to know, which isn't easy. I wonder whether this is something the transplant service should consider? The transition between wards and ICU could be a great deal smoother if patients and carers had a familiar face or two. Would it be impossible to give patients an opportunity to meet some of the nurses, physios and other professionals who will be looking after them post-operatively? It might be argued there's a chance patients may not get an organ so it would be a waste of time introducing them to people who may or may not look after them. But patients awaiting a transplant are generally a captive audience and it would be possible for them to in some way be familiarised with the environment they hopefully will be going into.

My days have taken on a new shape. Visiting on Ward 38 is fairly open, but generally restricted to afternoons. I've been trying to encourage Trevor to drink plenty of clear fluids as I do want him to do everything he can to kick-start his kidneys. After six years of restricting fluid intake, he now needs to drink more.

I have had some welcome respite; it's half term so Christine was able to come and stay overnight again. We went out for something to eat which was a bit of a wake-up call for my seriously neglected stomach. As Trevor's on Ward 38 and allowed visitors, Christine came to see him with me. His first visitor. It's strange, but it was remarkably reassuring to visit him with someone else; as though it reduced the pressure on me because another person could verify that he looks ok. I've spent the last week or so counting the hours, and then the days and relating these to 'transplant survival statistics.' I know it doesn't make any sense, but everything I've read tells me that the first 24 hours are critical. I was mightily relieved to get through those. Now I'm virtually crossing off days on the countdown to '30-day survival' – almost as though if he makes it to thirty days, he'll be fine.

The level of anxiety I feel hasn't really changed yet: when Trevor was waiting for a heart, my anxiety was all about whether one would be found. Now, I'm on a constant state of alert in respect of progress. The medical and nursing staff are continuously monitoring him, and he has a remote heart monitor which links to a screen at the nurses' station, so if anything happens I know they will respond immediately. But I want to know whether the progress with his heart is as it should be; whether his kidney failure is normal; whether the amount of fluid accumulating in his arms and legs is expected; whether he's exercising enough ... or too much.

24th April 2016

Continuous dialysis began as a result of increasing creatinine levels and a poor volume of urine being passed. I had the remaining chest drains removed - slightly painful procedure that lasts only a minute or two - and felt terribly low in spirits the whole day. After almost six years of being supplied with insufficient quantities of blood, as well as the hammering they took during the transplant, my kidneys have not sprung back into life. I exercised in the morning but felt just too tired and lethargic in the afternoon.

28th April 2016

Dr MacGowan conducted the first of my heart biopsies to check for signs of rejection, reassuring me that I'm making a good recovery. After fairly painful bone marrow and kidney biopsies, I feared the worst, as it turned out totally unnecessarily. A local anaesthetic, and certainly no worse than a visit to the dentist. I was returned to a cubicle I'd been given the previous day, as I was now a post-transplant patient of Ward 38. Luxurious was how I'd perceived having my own space on Ward 27 but boy, was this a step up a notch or two?! Private bathroom, lots of space, my own exercise bike, and beautiful, wonderful, stillness and silence at night. I enjoyed a pleasant breakfast (always tasty after a nil by mouth period) and agreed with the staff that I'd be responsible for recording fluids in and out.

30th April 2016

Five minutes on the exercise bike, thirty repetitions of dumbbells to build up muscle again, and walking four laps of the corridor. Dialysis continues because there's a need to reduce the potassium levels in my blood but the connection into my body at the neck wasn't working properly, so after three hours it was abandoned. Dr MacGowan swung by to tell me that the results of my first biopsy are good, with no signs of rejection. Whilst taking my evening medication, I began to vomit probably caused by trying to take too many pills at the same time. Another day with a mixed bag of results, ups and downs when it comes to my mood and spirit.

1st May 2016

Awoke feeling dreadful and this continued throughout the day - lethargic, insipid, listless, uninterested in everyone and everything. My body weight continues to increase by at least one kilo per day as fluid goes in but next to nothing comes out. I worry about one side effect I experience - when nodding off in Nicola's presence, I create in my mind an alternative picture of the 'living present.' For example, I doze and quite suddenly I'm in a conversation in my head with Nicola. We're speaking to each other but in my head, not in reality, then out of nowhere I say something out loud to Nicola that's a part of the conversation. It's what I imagine hallucinating to be like. Of course, I hear and speak one continuous thread, but Nicola only hears the final words as I return to reality. For me, there is no difference between the two states. Let's hope it's the medication.

2nd May 2016

Nicola comes in every day and does a shift of between eight and ten hours. Despite her back problems, she takes on the rock hard chairs - at least I have a bed to move to when I need a change. Every single day she looks lovely, and the nurses on this ward have also begun to benefit from her cake baking. An Easter one was delivered with rose petals handmade in chocolate.

Nurse Andrea Kane, who works on both Wards 27 and 38 is precious to me because she provides continuity between my pre- and post-transplant phases. This helps quite significantly with my mental health; a familiar face over the last six months, a genial approach that allows us to slip into being cheeky effortlessly. I'm convinced this post-transplant phase is harder for Nicola than for me. These days, my recovery regime is closely monitored by experienced post-transplant staff, while her role has changed completely in terms of the support she provides. Having said that, interesting, stimulating conversation is what we love the most, and for that we're never lacking.

Derek Airey, who's the chairman of the Freeman Heart & Lung Transplant Association came by and shared his passion for the Transplant Games. We had a few laughs as he tried to sign me up for cycling, swimming and squash, Nicola being unable to choose between me in Lycra shorts and Speedos. It was flattering to be approached but I'm conscious of being careful about a) running before I can walk, and b) becoming obsessed with exercise and competition.

Increasingly, I'm managing to put permanent kidney dialysis on the 'back burner' and focus on the benefits of the gift of life. Nicola confessed that in the last weekend before the organ became available, she was starting to be seriously worried about how soon I'd need seven-day hospitalisation. Now, I have life itself and that I shall never take for granted.

3rd May 2016

Today I was visited by my heart surgeon Mr Shah, in the presence of Mr Butt. Delighted at the excellent results of my first heart biopsy, the other message was 'we now see how it goes' with the dialysis, the fluid increase in my body being not at all unusual for heart transplant patients.

The brief meeting with them caused me to reflect on what exactly is a 'good day at the office' for surgeons like Mr Shah. Is he one of the few who can go home at night and say to himself, "I had a good day, I saved a guy's life today"? Or does the teamwork of Dr MacGowan, Mr Shah, Professor Schüle, and Dr Parry, effectively mean none of them go home thinking that? Or have they done it all and seen it all before so that the professional enjoyment comes not from the operation, but say, having a research paper published? I'd love to sit with them and explore this subject.

Rob, my Physiotherapist, came by and gave me some guidance on a safe exercise regime. He's a smashing bloke, always keen to walk with me, and supervise the exercises I'm doing. He's honest enough to say that he needs to prioritise patients who're reluctant to exercise over me, as he feels he can leave me to get on with it. Nicola showed me the patients' day room, where there's a better wi-fi signal and a place to watch tv.

The nursing staff are fine but there are so many of them, a different name every single day. Typically, they fall into two categories; those who're happy to spend a few minutes chatting, and those who clearly think they could get their jobs done quicker and better if it were not for those pesky things called patients. Asking for a piece of toast this morning, well, you'd think I'd asked for the Crown Jewels. The Healthcare Assistant sighed and tutted her way to providing it, but oh, what a chore it was for her; I was truly spoiled on Ward 27.

A Renal Registrar called in - I was alone – and she told me that within a day or two, they propose to put a permanent line into me and that the bad news is I'm going to need kidney dialysis three times per week for the rest of my life - that's three times four hours per week. She left me shell-shocked, confused, hurt, reeling from the news...and alone. Just where did that come from? Nicola arrived about half an hour later, took one look at me and asked what had happened. We talked about how we can cope with anything that's thrown at us, together, and as she often reminds me, "We're going to get through this, together." After a couple of hours, Nicola found Sister Ali, a young, talented nurse, who in turn contacted Dr Parry, the Cardiologist responsible for post-transplant care.

Wow, how he reassured me! First, he apologised for not having visited me earlier - he'd been at a conference in Washington DC. He listened to my story and visibly bristled. "I've been working here since 1991," he asserted, "and in that time I can recall only one patient that we've sent home after a heart transplant needing dialysis permanently. You are my patient and only mine - I have full responsibility for you and not a single thing is done to you without my permission." I'm not stupid, I know there can be no guarantees, but the relief at hearing these words was enormous. The roller-coaster I stepped on today took me up, threw me over the edge and brought me back up again. Nicola has the tenacity, determination and skill to know exactly when to intervene, how to do it, and with whom. The incredible value in knowing how a hospital – and its associated hierarchies – works.

So, We'll Go No More a-Roving (Lord Byron – 1788-1824)

Today was incredibly difficult. As arranged, I went in to see Trevor at lunchtime – since it was the weekend, there was no problem parking, and I breezed through to Ward 38 - I felt quite upbeat. That was until I walked into Trevor's room, saw his face and realised something was very wrong. I found him sitting in the chair beside his bed looking totally bereft. Apparently, a Renal Registrar had been in to see him about his kidney function and had asserted that Trevor's kidneys have stopped working because of chronic kidney failure, and not an acute kidney injury caused by the surgery. Up until this 'Harbinger of Doom's' revelations, we had understood that Trevor's kidney failure could be temporary. The Registrar's parting shot was that Trevor's kidneys will not work again and it's extremely likely he will be on dialysis for the rest of his life.

To set this in context, it's a Sunday; Trevor was on his own in his room; no information whatsoever was provided about the implications of permanent dialysis; and no nurse, psychologist, or loving wife was present during the conversation to ask questions, or pick up the pieces afterwards.

To begin with, I tried to talk with Trevor in the hope that I could make him feel a bit more positive. He strongly felt that he didn't deserve the transplanted heart; that it should have gone to someone who was fit and strong and could lead a full life. There was nothing I could find to say to help him understand or come to terms with what was happening. It felt so unfair: Trevor has just been through a massive operation; he's coming to terms with the psychological impact of having someone else's heart beating inside him; he's on a cocktail of drugs that his body has to adjust to; the levels of different enzymes and hormones in his blood are completely irregular; he's carrying a vast amount of fluid, mostly on his legs and abdomen; he's in pain; he's frightened. And I don't have the answers!

It dawned on me that this categorically shouldn't have happened. As far as I know, nothing in his blood results or condition has changed since yesterday when we saw the Cardiologist who didn't mention anything about permanent dialysis. Trevor's condition didn't appear to have deteriorated and I couldn't understand on what basis the doctor was making this clinical judgement. It occurred to me that this was the key term: clinical judgement. It's that 'professional opinion' trump card that doctors have. In the doctor's 'professional opinion,' Trevor's kidneys are completely wrecked; this doctor doesn't have to provide evidence to justify this, and another doctor's professional opinion might be completely different. But this is fine – the Renal Registrar can't be accused of unsatisfactory practice in any way because it's simply their 'opinion.' That's frustrating. And even more frustrating is the fact that this doctor dropped this bombshell when there was nobody present to support

Trevor, on a Sunday morning, when absolutely nothing is going to be done about it, even if it is the correct 'opinion.'

I asked Trevor if he was happy for me to speak with the nurse in charge to get an understanding of what has changed and why the news has been delivered now. And also to find out where we can obtain information to give us an understanding of what permanent dialysis looks like. Trevor agreed and I explained to Alison, the Sister, what had happened and how this had left Trevor feeling. Alison hadn't known anything about the conversation with the Renal Registrar and was surprised the nurses hadn't been informed. She assured me she would ensure this was brought to Dr Parry's attention and that we receive some explanation.

And that's more or less how we met Dr Parry. A slim, dark-haired, well-groomed, smartly dressed man burst into Trevor's room, accompanied by Staff Nurse, Claire. Dr Parry seemed very unhappy that permanent dialysis had been introduced. He'd been away on a course since Trevor was transplanted and this is why we hadn't met him yet. He explained in no uncertain terms that he is the Post-Transplant Cardiologist, Trevor is his patient, and he will decide what happens. Dr Parry didn't come across as the type of person you'd want to make unhappy about anything you'd done. I really didn't fancy being in the Renal Reg's shoes.

4th May 2016

Psychologist, Lucy, was meeting with Nicola and me when a knock on the door interrupted us. A porter requested that I go for an echo on my heart; we were almost finished anyway so I stood and went over to the wheelchair. I felt a bit woozy so was relieved to get into the chair. Then, at least six faces peering over me as I lay on my bed, complete with oxygen mask. I asked what was going on, whether or not these were students brought in to examine me. Who were these people?

Once in the wheelchair, I'd apparently lost consciousness and slumped over to one side – I'd fainted and been out for about thirty seconds, during which time a bunch of people had quickly arrived to lift me onto my bed. Mmm...familiar territory for me, standing too quickly and fainting. I felt so disappointed with myself, and embarrassed at having caused so much fuss and bother to so many people.

Dr Parry arrived on the scene quite quickly and with the help of Nurse Claire carried out some checks on the leads of my external pacemaker, his brow furrowed in concentration. He left and soon returned to say that he had consulted Dr Lord, The Freeman's resident pacemaker expert, and they'd taken the decision to install one internally. I have such incredible faith in these men's ability to make me well again, as well as having experienced an ICD for almost six years, consent came quickly; it would be a pleasure to go under the knife of Dr Lord, who'd been so kind to me over many months. He had two still to fit and would stay behind, getting to me around 8pm. I thanked him and he spoke as if it was nothing, as if it was no more trouble than giving a bowl of sugar to a good neighbour. He squeezed my shoulder before he left.

Later, Nicola told me she'd bumped into Dr Lord on Ward 27 as he searched for a consent form for me. She was delivering a cake to the nurses, so he had a slice before he came down and conducted the procedure on me. I wonder if this is a first? The surgeon stays behind and he's a little bit peckish. He enjoys a slice of cake baked by the patient's wife, and then gets stuck into the job at hand. Brilliant.

During the procedure, which was under local anaesthetic, Dr Lord spoke to me in just the right tone, providing me with just as much information as I needed to know. It was a little surreal, yet reassuring, to listen to the roll call of tools and equipment conducted by Dr Lord and his team, ensuring no nuts, bolts or wristwatches had been inadvertently placed alongside the pacemaker. When he was done, he looked at the wounds from my transplant and said he was delighted with their cleanliness and state of heal. He decided that even though he was trespassing on the nurses' territory, he may as well whip out the stitches while he has me and the kit easily to hand. I tend to accumulate quantities of anxiety about procedures for which I am given a few days' notice, so this was perfect for me. He bade me goodnight and left with instructions to his surgical assistants to apply a pressure bandage to the pacemaker wounds as I'd apparently bled quite a bit. Too much information!

5th May 2016

Dr Lord called in to see how I am and reminded me to take it easy for a few days as both a transplant and a pacemaker within two weeks of each other had left my body somewhat battered and bruised. "Sorry it had to be done this way but it's for the best," he said, his countenance filled with concern for me.

There was a scary interlude one afternoon: Trevor and I were speaking with Lucy, the Psychologist when a porter came to take Trevor to X-Ray. He got up quickly to move to the wheelchair and in doing this, became dizzy and collapsed. A great many nurses and doctors appeared in the room immediately. Assessing the situation quickly, I decided the best place for me was out of the way. I stood in the corridor for a few minutes and then was shown to the Day Room. After a while, a nurse came to say that Trevor was fine and they were monitoring him. When I went back to his cubicle, he was in sitting up in bed, chatting normally, but wasn't clear what had happened.

    Subsequently, it was decided that the external pacemaker monitoring Trevor's heart post-transplant, wasn't working properly. One lead had come loose. A pacemaker is put in during the transplant to regulate the heart until it establishes its own rhythm. His new heart was quite slow in achieving this. Interestingly, in my extensive reading on heart transplants, I've read somewhere some American research which suggests a correlation between patients who have been prescribed Amiodarone pre-transplant and transplanted hearts taking longer to establish their own rhythm. I sometimes wonder about asking Dr Parry about this, but he doesn't seem the type of doctor who appreciates questions from mere mortals like me. Anyway, it was decided that Trevor needs a permanent pacemaker and Dr Lord kindly agreed to stay late and do this after his routine list has finished.

    I think Dr Lord is one of those really 'human' consultants who shows tremendous compassion and cares about people. While Trevor was waiting for his heart, Dr Lord would frequently pop into his cubicle just for a chat. So often, doctors, and especially consultant grades, can be portrayed quite negatively in the media - that old adage that they spend most of their time on the golf course! Whereas, in reality, hospital consultants will often put themselves out. I remember as an NHS manager, sitting with an ENT surgeon one Friday evening, phoning patients to ask if they could come in for surgery the next day. This was because the admin staff had 'forgotten' to send for any patients and we didn't want to waste the theatre list. We left work that evening at 8pm, happy that ten patients would have their operation the following day. Admittedly, there are a few difficult consultants – usually linked to over-sized egos – but this is by far the minority and failings in the NHS, ironically, tend to be associated with staff intended to support the clinical process.

    Before I left the hospital, I called in at Ward 27 to collect my cake box. Having promised to continue making cakes for the nurses there after Trevor left the ward, I'd made them a carrot cake to celebrate his transplant. During his five-and-a-half months there, we reached a point at which I began to receive specific cake requests – a red velvet cake being but one. As I was updating the nurses on Trevor's progress, Dr Lord happened to come onto the ward before he went back to theatre to fit Trevor's pacemaker, so had a piece of cake to 'sustain' him. It sometimes feels like Trevor and I are part of the team and not simply users of a system. Like we belong, somehow.

10th May 2016

An update email to friends in Australia:

> Hello Newcastle NSW, Newcastle Tyne & Wear calling
>
> Thanks for your patience; I've not been in touch for a while. If ever you're worried, Nicola says you can mail her any time. Here's a crack at an update, and I've tried to be honest rather than my tendency to paint too rosy a picture.
>
> I am dealing with three issues at the moment. First, recovery from the transplant, which is going really well. My second biopsy came through clear of any signs of rejection. I had a good talking to by a nurse and Nicola on the wisdom of proactive pain management, so that's helping a lot. My wounds are healing very cleanly and quickly. Second, two weeks after the transplant, I fainted and so the doctors agreed on a pacemaker going in. I'd had an ICD for six years so had no qualms about this, but Dr Lord who placed it explained that my body has taken a bit of a beating when transplant and pacemaker are put together. Still, I'm doing well and now using dumbbells above my head on both sides. Third, and believe it or not by far the worst, is the accumulation of fluid in my legs and left arm. Professor Fisher told me this is common in 40% of heart transplant cases, but he reassured me no end by saying they will get rid of it, I will get my own legs back, and my kidneys will kick in at some stage. Since 2010 my kidneys have not received a proper supply of blood so it's unreasonable to expect them to leap into action. In the meantime, it's dialysis.
>
> In terms of the psychology, I have massive up and down days but I get regular therapy on this too. Of course, I'm on steroids which makes me more emotional than usual. Since the transplant, I've had two faints and two near-faints but this is all part of the tweaking process. I have to admit that the whole fluid thing took me by surprise - 11 litres in just over a week - as if someone has given me new legs and I have to learn

to drive them again. They are bloated and unrecognisable as my own and I'm completely embarrassed by them (see below). Equally embarrassing is when I become emotional, but again, Professor Fisher said they call it the 'three-week blues,' and it's normal.

Nicola has been putting in 8 - 10 hour shifts every single day, post-transplant. I couldn't have come through this without her - she has much knowledge about how hospitals work, when to question, challenge or intervene, and when not to. I tend to be a conformist patient and haven't the skill to challenge either the staff or the system, or to know when to do it.

The hospital is incredible, having a wealth of top talent, so professional and experienced. Every one of the consultants is published, has a firm handshake, immaculately dressed, talks in layman terms, and has great eye contact. You would never believe the wounds and scarring, it is much smaller than you'd expect and so very neat. The two surgeons who transplanted me came by and told me I was one of the shortest ops they've done - 4.5 hours - and that physiologically the heart was a perfect fit. Seconds after Nicola and I parted prior to the op, she passed a guy in the corridor carrying a cool box - so she had the unusual experience of walking by my new heart on her way out. One of these surgeons, Professor Schüle, told me my heart was completely knackered, so big and floppy that he has never taken one that size out of a person who's still alive.

Recovery is a remarkable process, too. Sitting in a chair within 12 hours of coming round, exercising after 48 hours, fantastic physio support, equipment that stays in my room. Tell you one thing about hospitals, there are too many sick people in them. What I mean is, people who've convinced themselves they are sicker than they really are, who say they can't do this, can't do that and refuse even to try. Exercise is key to physical and mental health recovery, no doubt.

Finally, I had an echo done last week. It's hard to describe seeing my new heart for the first time on the screen, and even better, hearing it. My third heart biopsy is this Thursday. They've warned me that all organs are always rejected at some stage, it's just a case of to what extent. I feel philosophical about my life ahead; I feel I've been given the gift of life, from being close to death a few weeks ago, to this. Only transplant patients can ever have this new perspective on life and I feel I'm such a lucky guy to be one of them. When I think of the bullshit we spend time worrying over, needlessly!

Best wishes,

Trevor

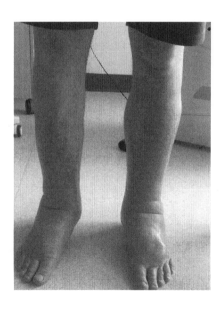

I Carry Your Heart With Me (E.E. Cummings – 1894-1962)

I've tried to keep Amy, Sam, Christopher and Daniel updated as much as possible with Trevor's progress. It's difficult that they're all so far away: Christopher and Daniel in Norway, and Amy and Sam a three-hour car journey. I try to explain to them what's happening and why, and what they can expect. They're all worried about his kidneys not working and knew how anxious he was before his transplant about the prospect of dialysis. Perhaps my emails are too long, but I try to make sure I explain everything so they understand what's happening and why. Maybe that's cathartic for me too.

Today, I wrote to them all to explain the situation as I understand it with Trevor's kidneys:

> *Hi there,*
>
> *We talked with a doctor for a while today and learnt a bit more – I thought you might be interested. A few days ago, the cardiology consultant and nurse advised that Trevor should have a high protein diet although the renal people might not support this wholeheartedly. It was suggested that I take in some high protein foods, but these also need to be low in sodium, potassium and phosphate to avoid increasing the level of these in his blood. That was a bit of a challenge! Everything I found that was high in protein was either high in potassium, phosphate, or sodium. Home-cooked chicken might have been ok, but because of his immunosuppression, we need to be extra careful to avoid any risk of infection. And, of course, heating, cooling and transporting chicken could be risky. But, he's not allowed oats, dried fruit, chocolate, nuts, hard cheese, oily fish, cream, shellfish ...*
>
> *I did some research and hit on these bars which are intended to boost you when doing sport. They contain the same amount of protein as a chicken breast or steak. And most importantly, Trevor likes them – I've been encouraging him to eat three each day.*

I asked the doctor exactly why high protein is good, and he explained: when you've had any surgery, your body requires protein to heal. This would be the same even if you'd just had your tonsils out, but a heart transplant is probably the biggest operation you can have, so the need for protein is even greater. But add to that the difficulty with Trevor having been unwell for a long time, and particularly over the last six months while he's been in hospital. His muscles have wasted on his thighs and arms, and he virtually has no bum. Other organs in his body have also suffered. So, he needs enough protein to rebuild muscles and strengthen organs, as well as to heal the bones and vessels damaged in the transplant. His muscles need enough protein because it's only when they recover that his blood can pump around his entire body more efficiently, his blood pressure can raise, and, hopefully, his kidneys will get sufficient flow and pressure to kick back in.

He had dialysis today and was quite tired; they managed to take a litre of fluid off. He had some low moments but managed 2 x 15 minutes on the bike as well as a short walk. Xx

11th May 2016

Cycling away with headphones on, I caught a movement out of the corner of my eye and turned to find three persons from the renal team, including a Consultant, waiting to speak with me. It's reasonable to feel trepidation when three physicians walk in, asking for my attention. I finished the twenty minute bike ride, and listened to what they had to say. The Consultant explained that it was their opinion, the reason my weight is not falling is that too much fluid is going in daily, and I should consider a limit of 1000ml. I replied to the effect that Dr Parry has told me no limit, to aim for 1000ml as an absolute minimum, and hitting 1500ml is fine. "Well, if you were solely a renal patient, I would limit you - that's my recommendation but you are Dr Parry's patient so please discuss it with him." I begin to feel like a political football being kicked between two sides, cardiology and renal.

The dietician then went through my food intake with me, as the last bloods I gave showed a spike in phosphate content. I stick to the renal menu that's provided, even then always choosing the 'low potassium, low phosphate' foods. I showed her the protein bars that Nicola has begun to buy for me, the reason being that the cardio team explained my recovery will be improved with a high protein input. The dietician looked at the bars and sucked in air over her teeth, as if she was a mechanic pricing up a job while looking at my car engine. With all the trademarks of a person who was dealing with a complete imbecile, she pointed out that the bars are not good for me as the protein source is milk-based products. This was quite a discourse and I waited patiently for her to conclude. When she had, I asked politely if she could explain why the dietician from her team who visited me and Nicola a week ago, fully endorsed the intake of these same protein bars. Ah. Silence. Then the backtracking started which concluded in her approving the bars, but no more than two per day, which is exactly what I take.

Talk about eats, shoots and leaves! I find it incredibly frustrating when a delegation descends on me alone, gives me conflicting advice, and disappears. My mind races and without wanting to sound like a wimp, it's easier all round if Nicola is present to soak up the dietary information. The meeting was finally interrupted by a porter arriving to take me down for more dialysis so these issues were left hanging and unresolved.

The Trevor Hall who arrived for dialysis was completely different from the Trevor Hall who left three-and-a-half hours later, 2.7kg lighter. On return to the ward, I recounted to Nicola the visits from renal and dietetics. Nicola spoke with the nurse in charge and requested a meeting between us, members of the renal team, members of the cardio team and nursing staff. Let's see what that brings. On our side it will be a request for consistent instructions that I can then follow.

After that, Nicola suggested I have a shower and arranged with the nurse that my heart monitor could be removed for long enough for us to do this. I think I feel refreshed from being clean, but it was in equal parts exhausting and terrifying. As much as the wires hanging from my chest are annoying, I also know they're my direct line to the nurses. My umbilical cord. Taking them away, even for a short time, made me feel vulnerable. I had to sit on a chair while Nicola hosed me down with the shower-head, lathered me with soap, and hosed me down again. There's certainly no dignity in illness! I hate having to put Nicola through so much strain on her back. She says it's not a problem, but I know it is. When I was clean, dry and feeling a bit more human, Nicola said my scars are healing well and it was time for another photo – the tubes sticking out of my neck are for dialysis, and the dressing on the left of my chest is where the pacemaker was put in.

Back on the bed, with my wires once again in place, Nicola put cream on my lower back which she starchily refers to as my 'pressure area' and then massaged cream into my feet and lower legs. It's a strange sensation for the fluid that's sloshing around in my feet to be pushed back up my legs. I know that as soon as my feet are back down when I'm sitting out, the fluid will gather again. But even temporary respite is welcome.

My exercise regime today was 2x20 minutes cycling, 2x15 minutes cycling and 40 repetitions with the dumbbells. Nicola's insistence, persistence and dogged determination to push and challenge me are key to this.

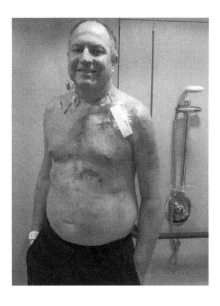

12th May 2016

I felt very positive today, after my weight dropped by almost two litres from yesterday. It was another busy day, with line removal, third biopsy and a meeting with Psychologist, Dr Attenborough. The line removal was done on the ward and I was distinctly unimpressed with Nurse Jody being interrupted by a colleague toward the end of the job. Aside from another patient's medical details being discussed in front of me, the line removal was delayed by a good five minutes, mid-procedure.

The third heart biopsy came and went, and my anxiety was immediately allayed when I realised Dr MacGowan was doing the procedure himself. If it's another 'all clear of signs of rejection' I'll be very happy. I was tired at the end and the position of the new line in my neck makes it sore when I turn my head, but otherwise, I felt good. My focus during local anaesthetic procedures is to concentrate on two things: first, my spine melting like an ice cube into the gurney and second, the picture of a new and independent life at home. If I've turned the corner on the fluid reduction, then I'll start to recognise progress again.

The psychology support is superb, Dr Attenborough and I having another good session. She asked the very pertinent question, "Today is an 'upper' because of the weight reduction, but what will happen if tomorrow you increase in weight?" We had a long conversation about how to focus on the things I'm in control of, such as fluid intake, exercise and the like, while leaving the medical issues to the team caring for me. The 'downer' days tend to be associated with (possibly) a poor quality night's sleep and the challenge of exercising with 12 litres of excess fluid in my body. (If you'd like to try this at home, place 12 litre-bottles of lemonade into two carrier bags and carry them around the house for an hour or two). Lying on the bed with my feet elevated helps to spread the fluid more evenly, particularly around my midriff. Standing for half an hour to alleviate the pain of the pressure points on my bottom causes the fluid to come crashing back down to my feet and ankles. It's a 'damned if I do, damned if I don't' scenario' – I need to exercise daily to recover from the operation, but exercise is very difficult when I'm carrying the excess fluid and have sore pressure points.

Having decided not to renew the tv subscription, it's interesting to see that I'm enjoying my evenings of a movie and a book. Why on earth do we channel surf and settle on watching mindless drivel?

It was good to see Amy, Luke and the girls at the weekend. With everything that's happened over the last few weeks, it seems like a lifetime since I saw them. Before we went to visit Trevor, I warned Amy that his sense of humour has entirely failed. Usually there is some banter between them, but Trevor's finding life very difficult at the moment: he's permanently in pain or discomfort from the excess fluid he's carrying. That's made considerably worse by the lack of consistency from medical professionals. It appears that 50% believe his kidneys will kick back in and the other 50% seem almost determined they won't. Meanwhile, we're bounced around in this pinball machine and it's impossible to know which direction we're heading in. I appreciate that nobody has the answer, but I really wish they'd all stop sharing their opinions and just have some kind of unified approach to the problem.

On the way to The Freeman, we picked up some food from M&S and had a picnic in the dayroom with Trevor. It felt like the first 'normal' thing we've done since the transplant. When the girls first saw Trevor, they were a bit unsure, but in that unique way that children do, they soon accepted the situation and got back to being themselves. Millie was her usual serious self and enjoyed talking to us about what she'd been doing. Elodie initially kept her distance from Trevor, but got closer and closer until she was sitting on his bed beside him, sharing food. Normality restored!

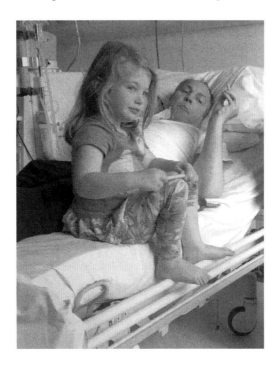

Trevor seemed to really enjoy spending time with Amy and the girls; I could see a little bit of the 'old Trevor' emerging from the chrysalis in which he has been cocooned. Maybe he can see that there are still reasons to live even if life doesn't take the shape he'd hoped for.

After we'd spent a few hours with Trevor, we took the girls to let off steam in Jesmond Dene Park. There were animals to look at and a park with play equipment. The sun shone, the girls showed off their acrobatic skills, and it was great to breathe in some fresh air and relax. We had dinner in the apartment and I bathed the girls which is always fun. Once they were in bed, the grown-ups shared a bottle of wine and caught up until I couldn't keep my eyes open any longer. It wasn't the best night's sleep, I have to admit. Sharing a bed with Elodie, albeit a double, is complicated: she seems to prefer lying horizontally across the bed with her feet sticking into my ribs. And thumb-sucking is a noisy affair. But it was lovely to wake up with her beside me and Millie soon joined us. Just Trevor missing.

Trevor was made up when Amy *et al* returned to see him on Sunday morning before driving home. He wasn't expecting to see them again so was delighted that they called in. Dialysis was underway in his room and after a few squeamish moments the girls were fascinated to learn how Trevor's blood was circulating through a machine to clean out the toxins. The nurses were lovely, answering questions and letting the girls help out a little.

I stayed with Trevor for a while and massaged his feet and legs before I left. It's becoming part of our routine: leg massages, pressure area care, and circuits of the ward.

14th May 2016

As soon as I saw our granddaughters, my spirits rose. Understandably, they looked a little frightened at first, especially by the lines emanating from my neck, and perhaps the dialysis machine to which I was later connected. That's unimportant though, because at one stage Elodie climbed onto Nicola's lap for a soothing rock and cuddle, and it was joyful to see Nicola's batteries being recharged before my very eyes. If ever I were asked to give advice to a person waiting for a transplant, I'd say the most important point is to always bear in mind that because you are the patient, this experience is not 'all about you.' If you have some challenges ahead, then so does your partner; they are of a different kind but they are no less mighty than yours.

Eating a picnic lunch in the day room as a family was wonderful - taste bud explosion from Marks & Spencer, platter sharing and great company. It's another example of how often we take such simplicities in our lives for granted. I learned in Asia that there is such a feeling of togetherness and bonding when food is shared and passed around. As always, the girls were beautifully behaved, a real credit to Amy.

I had three litres of fluid removed, felt physically lighter and better, and later in the evening walked a record five laps of the ward, earlier having done a total of 85 minutes on the exercise bike over four sessions (see below). A nurse asked me where I'm cycling to. "Home," I replied.

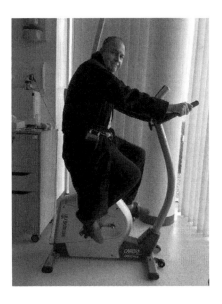

17th May 2016

When we're both 'up,' it's easy. When one of us is 'down' and the other 'up,' it's not a problem because one energises the other. But when we are both 'down,' it's very, very hard. This has been the case over the last few days so there have been plenty of tears on my part as my emotions are let loose. I can see Nicola's exhaustion as soon as she walks into the room, plus she tends to notice her pain much more. She tells me she misses home dreadfully and my thinking channels to 'if only it weren't for me and my condition, she'd be there.' When she's down, there're no smiles, laughter or gentle reassurance of, "This is only temporary, we're in it together, and we're going to get through it." I don't know why those few words give me strength and succour but they do. Nicola speaks them often so when they are absent, I feel as though I can't manage.

We've also struggled to converse lately about non-medical subjects and boy, how I need and rely on those! Friends, family, current affairs, sport, politics, future plans - conversations on these keep me focused on the big picture and out of the quagmire of day-to-day medical issues.

This morning an almost 2kg loss in weight cheered me up; I'm now down to 90.9kg. Still, I know that every day I put fluids in and my kidneys fail to pass fluids out, it's a step in the wrong direction. The positive is I can see progress while the negative is that gravity pushes some of the remaining fluid into my knees, calves, ankles and feet. Worse of all is the fact that I can't find any position in which I'm comfortable. Sitting, it goes to my feet and they start to burn. Feet up and it drains to my calf areas. Inverted in bed, the fluid spreads more evenly but the pressure points on my bottom become painful. The exercise bike relieves my calves, but pushes the fluid to my feet, and doing walking exercise with enormous swollen feet is painful. The only way to control this is for my kidneys to 'kick in' and start to expel waste products of their own accord, or to have dialysis thrice weekly so the machine works for them. The big danger is that each dialysis session sends a signal to my kidneys that they can stay asleep as someone else is going to do the work. A difficult and challenging balance is sought but ne'er a day goes by without my mentally willing, nay imploring them to 'kick back in' and begin expelling urine. Patience.

21st May 2016

Nicola and I drew up a list of the various ways in which we seek to enrich our lives when eventually I'm discharged and become an out-patient at The Freeman. We concentrated on the changes we'd like to make when we are home together in Moortown, to recreate the very special relationship we had:

- Sharing each other's preferred music through the house, taking turns between radio and albums;
- As soon as permitted, I'll do 80% of the driving for the first year, so Nicola can have a break;
- Less TV and Facebook, more conversation, choosing programmes to watch, no channel surfing;
- 'Growing' together through gardening together;
- Joining a local gym, exercising and swimming together;
- Me taking more responsibility for choice of restaurant/pub/activity;
- Teaching me some culinary tasks so we can prepare meals together;
- Mastering the making of homemade pasta together;
- Sitting together to find and design trips away, as opposed to dividing up the work;
- Less time apart in separate rooms with me on the desktop and Nicola on the i-Pad;
- Planning further home improvements together.

What we're aiming for is to try to obtain the maximum benefit, spiritually and emotionally, from this transplant experience. We've made such an enormous investment we feel we owe it to ourselves and my donor to gain a return from it. We want to grow, and to help each other grow. We've been averted from a disaster at the last possible moment and have been given potentially another twenty years together. What did we learn? How do we introduce change into our lives? How do we lead good lives? How do we become better people, richer for an experience few others have? How do we ensure that we appreciate time? And recognize that time together is finite?

A visit from Chris made my day. It was so good to see my son, and I found it particularly joyful to witness Nicola and him in conversation. Sadly, Daniel continues to leave me at the margins of his life, and I can't establish from him the reason. It seems to be something to do with my relationship with Nicola, her children and grandchildren, but I can't be sure. Regardless, he has chosen not to visit me in hospital after a heart transplant, and the reason for that I doubt I'll ever understand.

I'll close today with the words of Steve Jobs, founder of Apple, who died of cancer a couple of years ago. I find that it resonates with me. I find it 'speaks' to me:

I have come to the pinnacle of success in business. In the eyes of others, my life has been the symbol of success. However, apart from work, I have little joy. Finally, my wealth is simply a fact to which I am accustomed. At this time, lying on the hospital bed and remembering all my life, I realise that all the accolades and riches of which I was once so proud, have become insignificant with my imminent death.

In the dark, when I look at green lights, of the equipment for artificial respiration and feel the buzz of their mechanical sounds, I can feel the breath of my approaching death looming over me. Only now do I understand that once you accumulate enough money for the rest of your life, you have to pursue objectives that are not related to wealth. It should be something more important: stories of love, art, dreams of my childhood. No, stop pursuing wealth, it can only make a person into a twisted being, just like me.

God has made us one way, we can feel the love in the heart of each of us, and not illusions built by fame or money, like I made in my life, I cannot take them with me. I can only take with me the memories that were strengthened by love. This is the true wealth that will follow you; will accompany you. He will give strength and light to go ahead. Love can travel thousands of miles and so life has no limits. Move to wherever you want to go. Strive to reach the goals you want to achieve. Everything is in your heart and in your hands. What is the world's most expensive bed? The hospital bed. You, if you have money, you can hire someone to drive your car, but you cannot hire someone to take your illness that is killing you. Material things lost can be found. But one thing you can never find when you lose it, is life. Whatever stage of life where we are right now, at the end we will have to face the day when the curtain falls. Please treasure your family love, love for your spouse, love for your friends...Treat everyone well and stay friendly with your neighbours.

23rd May 2016

"You'll almost certainly be needing kidney dialysis three times per week for the rest of your life," said the on-call Renal Consultant with a weak handshake and a colleague in tow. He asked me for data on my historic creatinine levels (shouldn't he know these better than I?) and sucked air in over his teeth, shaking his head, when he learned that after almost five weeks of dialysis, my kidneys have still not kicked in. Hence, the proposal to insert a tunnelled neckline, which Dr Parry - my doctor - has already discussed with me. I asked the Consultant why he walks into my cubicle as the harbinger of doom, and yet Dr Parry is hopeful they'll kick in. "Members of the renal team fill me with doom and gloom, while the cardio team inspire me and give me hope," I protested. The Consultant snorted and laughed at this and interrupted me with further words. He became uncomfortable when I asked him to please not interrupt me, and then I politely gave him feedback on his bedside manner, which basically sucked. Pulling faces, shaking his head, laughing, interrupting - he seemed somewhat surprised when I pointed out the impression he gave me as a patient.

Trying to have the renal team and the cardio team speak with each other in this hospital seems to be asking too much. Consequently, any degree of consensus in respect of my treatment and communication is clearly out of the question. The renal team looks at me as purely a renal patient, while the cardio team, arguably quite rightly, look upon me as a cardio patient with renal problems. But the effect on my spirits of this apparent power-struggle is quite profound: once again, I was left totally deflated.

Arriving soon after they left, and having spoken to Nurse Holly who'd been present, Nicola pulled up a chair and over five minutes gave me a good talking to, which made me see sense. She spoke of my responsibility not to allow these renal people to 'get to me.' "After all, what has changed regarding your case, your condition, your blood results?" That's true – like she always says, "The fat lady hasn't sung yet!" Having said that, continually having to reassure me and help me get back on track with a positive attitude is energy draining for Nicola. I know it is. I have an obligation to her to be more resilient.

However, it frustrates me somewhat that my case seems to be growing from a heart transplant, to a heart transplant and a pacemaker - a pacemaker whose top lead by the way doesn't work; dealing with fluid build-up on a long-term basis; a tunnelled neckline with its associated ban on swimming, bathing and showering; and kidney failure which necessitates dialysis thrice weekly and severely limits my lifestyle. The picture I have held in my mind for so long - a strong and healthy recovery and leading a normal life as many transplant patients do, increasingly feels shot to pieces. There is but one fact I must hold on to - whatever this condition throws at me, I get to build a much longer life with Nicola. "Let's focus on what we can do, rather than what the condition takes away from you," she counsels, and she's right. After seven months in hospital, I'm at the stage where I'll let them do anything to me so long as it gets me out of here and living with Nicola again. But, in the face of this unexpected adversity, it's impossible to stay 100% positive, 100% of the time.

Exercise-wise, the day was very positive. Nicola suggested that when walking laps of the ward, I quicken my pace a little - she reminded me that I now have a new heart and can begin to move back to my pre-cardiomyopathy state. This is what she's perfect at, providing gentle encouragement without getting in my face about it. I completed no less than fifteen laps of the ward (previously, the most I'd done was five), I climbed the stairs twice, did sixty repetitions with the dumbbells and a total of eighty-five minutes on the exercise bike.

I vaguely remember feeling quite upbeat as I drove into the car park at The Freeman. Trevor had seemed more positive since Amy's and Christopher's visits. However, as I stepped out of the car, my phone pinged with a message from Trevor: 'Renal Consultant says I need permanent dialysis for the rest of my life ...'

Arriving on the ward, I stopped at the Nurses' Station to ask what had happened and fortunately Holly was there. She'd witnessed the conversation between the on-call Renal Consultant and Trevor, and strongly felt that Trevor hadn't helped the situation. "If he asks the question, the doctor will give his opinion. Trevor needs to stop asking the question."

To be fair, I think it must be very difficult in Trevor's situation: of course you want to know that progress is being made, or what the outcome of something is going to be. The difficulty is that nobody has the answer he's searching for. Of course, nobody can tell him that his kidneys will start to work again at a certain time on a certain day. And that's the response he's desperately searching for. The one he'd like most. But neither can they tell him that his kidneys definitely won't work again, and that he will require dialysis and what the arrangements are for this. At least even with that, he'd have some certainty about what life will look like. The most authentic response a doctor can give is that they just don't know and every patient is unique. But doctors can be very bad at saying they just don't know. That's funny since the Read Codes through which every hospital episode is entered onto a computer system, has a code for the abbreviation occasionally entered by doctors into patients' case notes: GOK (God Only Knows). Despite this, some doctors just can't find it within themselves to admit this to patients. Maybe that has something to do with ego, or maybe it's fear of not meeting the expectations of patients, or perhaps a symptom of a litigious society in which there has become a tendency to practice defensive medicine. I'm not sure any of us visits a doctor in the hope they'll tell us that medicine is an art and not a science and therefore they think 'x' is the problem, but equally, it might be 'y,' so who knows?! We've all grown up with the expectation that we see a doctor who will tell us precisely what is wrong and how it will be treated. There's fault on both sides with that, but doctors surely have a responsibility to communicate sensitively.

I was quite stern with Trevor. I positioned a chair so I could sit facing him and explained that whatever the outcome, he needs to get through this time. We both need to get through this. I sympathise enormously with his need to know what the outcome will be, and I understand that sitting in a hospital ward hoping to get better leaves very little else to think about, but he needs to stop asking every doctor 'the question.' There isn't an answer. Nobody can give an answer. Doctors will try. And given that fifty per cent of his care is through renal doctors, he can assume that at least fifty per cent of the time, he won't get the answer he wants. I urged Trevor to look at the facts: nothing has changed in his condition. He isn't producing more urine, but he isn't producing less. His blood results haven't improved, but they haven't worsened. He needs to focus on what he can do to help himself: eat protein to help rebuild muscles, drink enough fluid to keep his kidneys hydrated, take frequent exercise to strengthen his muscles including his heart and get the fluid moving round his body to reduce the swelling. And take some responsibility for maintaining his sanity. That's his part in this. I need us to be on the same page and I can't be at the hospital all of the time to act as his minder.

Trevor took it remarkably well and I felt mean for being so direct, but I think he needed a wake-up call. He said that he will take on board what I said. I hope he does because I know that depression is a risk after any major surgery, and especially something like a transplant. When you're ill with something that takes a long time to recover from, it's easy to become consumed by negatives and feel like you never will feel better. I tried hard before his transplant to talk to him about the rehabilitation process – the two steps forward, one back kind of experience. But he was frightened and it was difficult to contribute to that. The 'Transplant Handbook' we were given was next to useless; to be fair, it was well out-of-date, but also written by healthcare professionals who generally speaking have not experienced a heart transplant. All they can write about is the process from a clinical perspective, not a patient one. I know each case is different and recovery isn't the same in every person, but just some insight into what to expect as 'the patient' would have been helpful.

Since I was taking no hostages today, when Trevor and I walked around the ward, I also mentioned something I've noticed recently. He's walking like a person with a heart condition and not someone who has a strong healthy beating heart. I asked why he's walking so slowly and suggested he could try going a bit faster now. Treading on eggshells here, but I think it all had the desired effect. When I got back to the apartment, Trevor texted to say he'd completed twelve circuits of the ward and is going to do some more when he's had a rest. That's progress!

24th May 2016

It's the picture of that simple, meaningful and independent life post-heart transplant that slowly seems to evaporate with each passing day. I'll eventually return home to Moortown with a tunnelled line coming out of my chest, unable to swim, shower or take a bath. I'll likely be unable to wear the clothes in my wardrobe as I'll need to hide the lines, which are about four inches long. I have to become obsessive about infection control around the lines. I'll have to find a specialist supplier of shoes that can fit my fluid-filled feet comfortably. That means walking down the high street in a pair of Velcro slippers. I'm currently passing between 60ml and 90ml of urine daily, and Dr Parry says that needs to be at least 200ml before we can say my kidneys are starting to wake up. I'll be on dialysis at Grimsby Hospital three times per week, for four hours at a time. The more I am dialysed, the lower the chance that my kidneys will awaken, as the machine is doing their job for them. I face alternate days of dialysis and battling with fluid build-up. I face limitations on the amount of exercise I can do because on non-dialysis days, I'll be carrying extra fluid. My biggest concern is the danger I'll potentially bring to my relationship with Nicola. With this negativity, I drain her of energy, sapping her resolve, straining relations between the two of us.

    The irony is that my heart grows stronger everyday - there are consistent signs of zero rejection - and my exercise tolerance increases and increases. I thought I was coming in for a heart transplant that would save my life, and with a little determination and dedication allow me to return to an independent lifestyle for possibly twenty years. No ties. Free to work in the garden unhindered, as well as a thousand other activities. I imagined I'd be able to go out for lunch or dinner with my wife, and choose sensibly from a menu with minimal dietary limitations. It's easy to describe the challenge I face to appreciate that I'm alive and capable of having a meaningful, loving relationship with Nicola, family and friends. And yes it's true, what was the alternative? My own death. So I chose the 'live life' option; it's just that I feel I've been hit by a bus. My only hope is to put my faith in the view of The Freeman's cardiology team, each one of whom is confident my kidneys will return. The renal people disagree to a man, the harbingers of doom. Those who enter here, abandon ye all hope.

25th May 2016

An email written to Naomi Rees, who has been so helpful in providing support to Nicola and me from Newcastle, NSW to Newcastle, England:

Dearest Na,

I mean this - you have been through more pain with dental treatment than I ever went through with a heart transplant. I have been managing my pain for several weeks now on daily Paracetamol, and about one Codeine tablet a week. I told my brother that I have so much respect for his son, a relatively healthy Cystic Fibrosis sufferer who regularly has to pee kidney stones. They say it's excruciating.

Hey, try not to let the work stuff get to you, eh? Hold it lightly, not tightly. It's hard when you're a caring person, but in the grand scheme of things, it's small stuff, and they say 'don't sweat the small stuff.'

I had two really good sessions with the Psychologist today, one with Nicola present, one alone. I've been looking at this all wrong, Na. And as with all good practitioners, she didn't have to say a word, I reached the conclusion myself.

I went into this wanting a new heart, to lengthen my life so we could be together. I wanted a future relationship with Nicola, a spiritually rich and rewarding one. That's more or less in the bag, well, things are looking good. Now, I have a choice. I'll have the tunnelled neckline inserted next week, probably on Tuesday, if not Thursday. This will give better, cleaner and more long-term access for the dialysis nurses. I will not be allowed to swim, shower or bathe, effectively I can't get it wet. Choice one is that I'm devastated at possibly never again being able to swim, go swimming with the girls, experience that incredible feeling of refreshment from a great shower, go to the spa etc. Choice two is not to look at the limitations, but instead look for the opportunities. If I can't swim with them, what can I do with them? I can take them out for afternoon tea, I can picnic with them, go to the park, watch them grow. If I can't shower, there are some alternatives such as hand held shower heads. Not the same, but that's the limitation, the opportunity is that I emerge from the shower into a relationship with Nicola – all I ever wanted, and which fills me with contentment every day.

We gave away our tickets to see Caro Emerald when I came into hospital. I saw that in April 2017, she's appearing at the Royal Albert Hall. I said to Nicola that we'll have to wait and see what dialysis looks like and she said no way, we don't revolve our lives around dialysis, we live our lives, and we make arrangements at a London hospital if necessary, so we fit in dialysis, if I'm still needing it then. So tomorrow we'll buy two tickets, and then Nicola will book us into a plush London hotel.

I call it Opportunity not Limitations. We are so lucky. We're both retired, neither one of has to get back to work. More and more, we realise that our savings are just that, they are not our children's inheritance. I'll have several dietary restrictions but hey, I eat anything and everything, so when I have to do without this, that and the other, I'm going to turn to what I can have. I had a choice, either have a heart transplant and give up shellfish, or until my impending death (as was the case) eat as much lobster as I want!

All I can do is follow medical instructions, and my kidneys will either come back or they won't. I must not spend my life worrying and becoming depressed about their malfunction. I have life, a strong heart, Nicola, and the ability to feel pleasure, to breathe, to appreciate, to love and to discover new experiences. Compared to some of the people who have struggled in their lives, such as those you know from work, I'm a very lucky man.

Nicola and I started playing Scrabble last night through an app on our i-Pads. It felt lovely to be in touch! Me in hospital, her at the apartment. Anyway, she has pissed me off royally, beating me by about 100 points. She put down the word 'Li' so I challenged it and the computer says it's ok. I wrote her and said since when is a Chinaman's name in the English Language? She said it's a unit of measurement in

China and is a legitimate English word, just like foot, inch or yard. Grrrr...

Oh yes, the tunnelled neckline will go in next week. As it's Bank Holiday weekend, Dr Parry said I can keep the lines at my throat and go home to Gosforth Saturday, Sunday and Monday, leaving the hospital in the morning each day, and returning in the evening. Oh boy, to be alone with Nicola. I mean the intimacy from holding hands, from talking, cuddling in our own place, sharing food, going for a drive. Heaven.

Love and best wishes, Trevor

I'm not sure how much longer I can cope with NHS culture. It's totally bizarre and people working within it seem unable to look outside of their bubble. When I trained as a nurse, something called the 'nursing process' had recently been introduced. Primarily, this was intended to move away from systems where one nurse took all of the patients' temperatures, another washed them, another handed out medication, and so on. The new process meant that each nurse on a shift was allocated a small cohort of patients for whom she had total responsibility; undertaking all the needs of those patients and liaising with medical staff as appropriate. After I left nursing, this appears to have evolved into the 'named nurse' system where each patient is not only looked after by a particular nurse, but also has the name of that nurse written on a whiteboard above their bed.

Unfortunately, it seems that nurses have become so engrossed in their processes they've forgotten to look up and ask patients whether it works for them. Today, as usual, I went in to see Trevor around lunchtime. My heart sunk palpably when I looked at his face: he was slumped in his chair, unshaven with the air of somebody who, getting to the end of a marathon had been told they'd taken the wrong route. It transpired he'd had another night without any sleep. His legs were painful because of the fluid build-up and he felt totally miserable. His sacrum was sore and he couldn't find a comfortable position to rest in.

It was frustrating as a few days ago a nurse informed Trevor that whilst he 'preferred' his wife to look after his pressure areas, they would now need to take this over. Unremarkably, since this announcement, his pressure areas have been ignored.

Metaphorically rolling up my sleeves, I decided there was only one thing to do. Although I'd planned to only stay for a couple of hours today, I figured that the only way to get anything done in the way I felt was required, was to do it myself. I suggested to Trevor that we manage his daytime activities, and I would stay that evening until he was asleep. We made sure the day nurses were okay with this and began mission 'Get Trevor a Night's Sleep.'

Firstly, I helped him to get a wash and change of clothes. Once he felt a bit brighter, we spent the day alternating between exercise and rest, but each time Trevor rested, I insisted that he lay on his bed with his feet elevated.

After his evening meal, we walked a little more and sat for a while in the Dayroom. I transferred a footstool and pillows from his room in an attempt to make him a little comfortable. As usual, I made his bed up freshly - I'd learnt fairly quickly where the linen cupboard is on Ward 38. It seems that bed-making has been completely removed from the Nurse Training Curriculum and each day, I've re-made his bed; the only nurse who seems to do it properly is Andrea. How difficult is it to understand that you need to tuck the head end of the bottom sheet in first if there is any hope that the patient won't untuck it as they get in, and slide down, the bed? At about 9pm, I suggested we go back to Trevor's room so that he could lie with his legs elevated for an hour, giving him the chance of starting the night without pain.

Before he got on the bed, I made sure he'd absolutely done anything and everything that required his legs to be on the ground. Medication, drink, small amount of urine, blood pressure. I massaged Trevor's legs for thirty minutes or so while he lay with his head as low as he could tolerate. When the swelling in his legs had reduced, we returned the bed to a horizontal position, sited extra blankets in case he woke up in the night cold, and put everything within reach. The nurse came in and did his observations.

The day nurses had been kind enough to give me his sleeping tablets early so that he could take these twenty minutes or so before I left. As he drifted off, I felt a tremendous sense of relief. He would get some rest and it had all been worth it. As I left the ward, I stopped at the nurses' station and explained that he had settled and was asleep so please could they avoid disturbing him as he really needed some quality sleep.

Imagine my surprise as I arrived at the apartment, my phone pinged and it was Trevor: 'The nurse woke me up to take my temperature; I really shouted at her. I can't get back to sleep!'

Aaaaarrrrrggggh!!

29th May 2016

Waking up in a rented apartment, alone, on your birthday, for the first time in your life, is a tough experience. That's what Nicola had to experience today, and I felt for her. I had been given leave for the day, but on condition that I depart around 10am and return to the ward around 10pm. So Nicola collected me and we dashed off to the apartment to open her cards, and have breakfast together. I'd reserved a table for afternoon tea at the swanky Vermont Hotel in the city centre, and for her sake, overcame my anxiety about wearing hospital sandals to cater for my feet, badly swollen with fluid. The food was delicious and Nicola looked beautiful.

Plans were almost dashed however, by Nicola's son Sam, springing a surprise visit an hour or so before we were to shower and get ready to go out. Still, all worked out fine in the end because as they all went off to Tynemouth, with an arrangement of meeting back at our apartment later in the day. I have to say, Sam is hilarious. He must be the most naïve guy on the planet in the sweetest way. I asked if he'd arrived using a GPS - he said not, and that he thought he'd just follow the signs to Newcastle. So they'd driven around the suburbs for quite a while. Sam's nature is just to 'wing it' often with comical consequences. He's a great guy though, and would do anything for anybody, a really generous person.

2nd June 2016

"Well you're a first for us, Trevor!" said one of the nurses as the job of implanting the tunnelled neckline in me was being completed. "You're the first patient who has fallen asleep whilst we carry out the procedure!" I asked how they knew I'd fallen asleep because often I try to meditate myself to a faraway land, to which she replied, "Well, the snoring kind of gave it away."

Earlier in the day I'd had my fifth heart biopsy and the line removed from my neck. I'd been returned to the ward, given a very quick breakfast, and then wheeled off for insertion of the tunnelled neckline. By the time lunch was served, I felt pushed and pulled around. The only way in which this line may be permanently removed, is if my kidneys 'kick in' and start working again. The renal doctors say there is no chance of that happening now, whilst the cardio doctors say there is still a possible chance, they just don't know when. I hate the renal 'doom and gloom' merchants who appear at my bedside like the Grim Reaper, and I so dearly want to prove them wrong. As the line now emanates from my chest, rather than at my neck, there's no real need for me to be taking up a hospital bed. Discharge to outpatients is on the horizon, as is sleeping in the same room as my wife.

I confess that I'm rapidly approaching the end of my tether when it comes to my staying power. Perhaps it's the light at the end of the tunnel that's exacerbating my feelings of depression. Frankly, I don't care what they do to me now, I just want home. Whatever the constraints on my life, Nicola and I will work around them. I've made a note of the comments she makes that I find inspirational, that bring me back to being centered and grounded:

- We're in this together, side by side.
- Everything about your condition is temporary, nothing is permanent.
- Was that your chimp (emotional) talking just then, or your computer (logical/rational)?
- No matter what is thrown at us, we'll find a way to overcome it.
- Never forget to look behind you and see how far you've come in such a short time.

PART III

A Heart in the Right Place

CHAPTER THIRTEEN

Heart and Soul

6th June 2016

At last, the day I have longed for has arrived - discharge day. Today, I become an outpatient, remaining under the care of Dr Parry, but being treated with kidney dialysis by the renal team. Dr Parry believes I have suffered an acute renal injury, while Renal maintain I have unrelenting chronic kidney disease. Frustrating that ne'er the twain shall communicate, much less meet! Dr Parry fortunately has the final say and he's keen to find the right balance of dialysis - too little and toxins build up in my blood, and my body retains fluid, while too much sends a signal to my kidneys that something else (a dialysis machine) will do their work for them...permanently.

Nicola and I bade farewell to the staff of Ward 38 and went up to Ward 27 to do the same; after all, the staff there took care of me over the twenty-two week pre-transplant phase. We then walked out of The Freeman together, with a sense of a chapter closing and a new phase beginning. I reflected on my mixed feelings towards my condition - so many issues seem to have arisen that have taken me by surprise - a pacemaker inserted (with a faulty top lead at that); the whole dialysis issue with cardio and renal kicking me around like a medical football; two lines emerging permanently from my chest; so many foods to avoid on a renal diet; a ban on showering and swimming; intensely bloated feet; and more besides. Still, as I remind myself, I have a brand new heart that has so far shown no signs of rejection, and seems to be going from strength to strength.

We drove to the Eldon Centre where we bought some Hugo Boss clothes for me. In the changing room, it was so hard for me to look at myself in the mirror, and when I did I simply felt an immense sadness. This was not how it was supposed to be – bruised, battered, swollen, haggard, tubes emerging, and more besides.

> AMY: Hope you're having a more restful day. Lovely weather here
>
> NICOLA: Thank you. I made Trevor take two sleeping tablets last night. Threatened to put them in pieces of cheese if he didn't – like I did for Charlie – and shove them down his throat!!! Labradors are far easier to manage! We both slept well! Nice here too ☺
>
> AMY: Glad you slept well. Must be knackering.
>
> NICOLA: Weeks seem to be going by quickly with the new normal of getting up at 6.30am at least three days-a-week for hospital stuff. We popped into Newcastle to take some jeans to be shortened. Had a cuppa and a scone in the café in Fenwicks. Daren't tell him, but he's not supposed to have scones – baking powder ☹

After a trial over the Bank Holiday weekend, Trevor was finally allowed home. To be honest, the difference between him being home and being in Ward 38 appears relatively minimal. He sleeps here. When I say 'sleeps' this isn't entirely accurate, since sleep is quite a struggle: the bed is too small, he's too hot, the room's too light, his legs are too swollen. Most of the days seem to be taken up with appointments – Cardiology, or Renal, or Psychology, or Dialysis, or a combination. But at least we have some time in the apartment together.

Trevor went through a massive crisis of confidence when he was discharged. Deeply unhappy in any of his clothes and still can't get shoes on. Before he left hospital, I bought him some sandals from Clarks; ones with adjustable Velcro fasteners so he can fit his feet in however swollen they are. They're an improvement on the footwear provided by the hospital, but he has always taken a pride in his appearance – that's one of the things that first attracted me to him – so it's difficult for him to not look his best.

With this in mind, I persuaded him that we should go into Newcastle and look in the Hugo Boss shop for something that a) fits, and b) he feels comfortable in. He found it difficult in the changing rooms. Looking in a full-size mirror at reflections of scars and tubes, and trying to find clothes that masked any lumps where the tubes protrude, was a challenge. It doesn't matter how many times I tell him that I don't see the scars or tubes, I just see the person I love who's alive. I think time is the only thing that will help. We did find some clothes and I think even just the process of going into a shop and buying something made him feel a little more human.

Food is still quite a challenge. The list of forbidden fruits provided after the transplant includes shellfish, paté, soft cheeses, rare steak; anything luxury, really. And the list from Renal includes virtually everything else you might want to eat. Vegetables have to be boiled within an inch of their lives and I'm spending an inordinate amount of time studying food labels in Sainsbury's looking for low salt, low phosphate, low potassium. Most labels don't go into much detail but I've installed an 'App' on my phone which helps me to figure what I can serve up. Shopping is fast becoming a nightmare for me and torture for Trevor who, with doleful eyes, holds up packages to which I respond, "Sorry, you can't have that." On occasions, you can feed the air between us into the bread slicer. Difficult. But I'm not giving in on this one: if his kidneys are to have a chance of working, it's important that we don't damage them further.

Eventually, I hope to convince the renal doctors to give us access to Trevor's blood results so we can see what effect his diet has. It's really difficult to get Trevor to stick rigidly to a diet regime without being able to tell him whether any difference is being made. Unless we have access to blood results, we could be limiting certain foods without it being necessary. And of course, we could be not limiting some foods enough. The dialysis nurses just seem to connect Trevor to a machine with no interest whatsoever in diet, or bloods. They just weigh him and programme the machine to take off a certain amount of fluid. I'm also struggling to get him to drink enough to give his kidneys a chance. The dialysis nurses have convinced him that his priority is not to gain weight – or fluid – between sessions. But the Cardiology theory is that he needs to drink at least a litre each day to perfuse his kidneys. Living in the apartment with me must sometimes feel like he's in a hostage situation! Waterboarding as fluid is forced down him, and no sooner has he sat down than I've got him up and exercising again.

9th June 2016

Dialysis was done on Monday of this week and my body passed 70ml of urine. Tuesday, which is dialysis day +1, brought the passing of 175ml, and Wednesday, dialysis day +2, saw me pass 400ml! See? The longer I go without dialysis, the better my kidneys are at waking up and functioning. Now, we are still a long way short of 1000ml passed, but 400ml is a massive step in the right direction. I can't wait to tell Dr Parry at my clinic appointment tomorrow, when presumably, he will decide if my next dialysis will be Friday 10th or Monday 13th June.

Meanwhile, Nicola and I walk about two miles each day; me on terribly swollen feet bound in sandals held tied with Velcro fastenings.

14th June 2016

A very frustrating week after my discharge, with my being called in to the hospital for numerous clinics, appointments and dialysis. We still struggle to come to terms with the waste, inefficiency and delay that appears to be institutionalised in the NHS; how the system treats us like compliant automatons; the archaic paper-based systems; and so on. On one occasion, sitting in front of Dr Parry, Nicola and I waited patiently while he took from his desk drawer a reel of paper 'ring binder' reinforcers, and stuck them onto each hole punched in the papers in my file. All the while, a nurse was perched behind him on a stool, doing absolutely nothing. How can it be acceptable for a senior consultant's time to be taken by such trivial administration tasks? So this week, I will have been called in for dialysis on Monday, Wednesday and Friday, and Dr Parry's clinic on each of these days, too. Each clinic day, I am despatched to different departments for an ECG and X-Ray, followed by an appointment with Dr Parry, at which little is said. Each Cardiology appointment lasts a minimum of two and a half hours; whereas, my clinical contact time is around fifteen minutes. Under her breath Nicola mutters phrases like, 'one-stop clinic,' and 'patient-focused service.'

As the days roll by, I prepare myself for the worst and hope for the best when it comes to my kidneys. If it has to be dialysis, so be it. If this does prove to be the case, I will always think that my heart transplant has not been, well, fully capitalised on. Why not transplant a heart and a kidney at the same time, knowing that my kidneys have been sleeping for five-and-a-half years? Perhaps this is not the right time for me to be asking such questions, but I just feel that both The Freeman and I have an obligation to the donor to get the most out of his gift.

Meanwhile, I've drafted a letter to the family of my donor, and this is what I've decided to write:

Dear Donor Family

First of all, may I express my sadness at the loss of your loved one, and the enormous gratitude I feel at his (and your) donation to me - a stranger - of the gift of life itself. I can't begin to imagine your loss and how much you must miss this man in your lives every day.

Mere words can never express how I feel towards you and him. In 2010 it seems that I caught a virus that led very quickly to chronic heart failure. I was a fit and healthy 50 year old who'd never abused his body and regularly visited the gym. I made a strong-but-partial recovery and continued with a reasonably good quality of life. However, my health started to deteriorate in 2014 and my Cardiologist made it clear that I needed a heart transplant if I were to survive.

In 2015, after further deterioration, I was placed on the UK 'urgent' heart transplant list and I waited in hospital for five-and-half months. I experienced the pain of three 'no go's,' in which I was prepared for surgery that was subsequently cancelled because the match was not good enough.

Your gift to me means that I can continue with my family life, with luck for many years to come. I can watch my granddaughters grow, I can play with them, and I can make a meaningful contribution to family, friends and my community. Inside of me beats a strong and healthy heart. I think of my donor and his family every single day; of the miracle of your generosity to me, as well as that of medical science. Please rest assured that I'll continue to take great care of my new heart; it's the least I can do to honour my donor and you, his family. Thank you once again, from the bottom of my new heart.

Yours sincerely, Trevor Hall

> P.S. Please forgive my not writing this letter by hand, but one of the side effects of my drugs is that my handwriting is very shaky. The doctors tell me this will pass.

It's part of my sense of closure as I've been discharged - we surrender our apartment on 10th August - and I'll be attending The Freeman only for heart clinic appointments, and most probably Grimsby for renal consultation and dialysis. I've started rehabilitation, revolving at present around a daily walk of between 2 and 4 miles, as well as some seated cycling with pedals.

Sometimes, a donor family chooses not to respond, and that would be perfectly ok with me. Dealing with loss must be very difficult and different from family to family.

28th July 2016

Dr Parry explained we might well have to concede defeat. In the history of The Freeman, the longest a pair of kidneys has taken to kick back in after a heart transplant is twelve weeks, and here I sit, still waiting, after fourteen. But the data clearly encouraged us to hold out hope. I've been passing increasing amounts of urine as the weeks pass, though I do accept it isn't just an issue of quantity – it's also a question of the quality of the waste products being sieved and expelled. During the dark days of passing 25ml daily, I fancifully promised Nicola that one day I'd emerge from the bathroom punching the air and shouting (in the voice of a darts match scorer) 'One Hundred And Eighty!' Dancing around the bathroom, a wiggle here, a shimmy there, at the passing of a mere 180ml of urine in a single go, is an act I never thought I'd be doing.

A few days ago, the Sister of the Renal Ward asked me to conduct a 48 hour urine sample and to bring it in at my next dialysis session. In that period I passed well over 2 litres of urine. I could pee for England. But though I am clearly kicking out the fluid, am I kicking out the toxins, too?

Nicola was in the bathroom getting ready to go to bed and I was sitting in the lounge. Nothing much to do so checked my phone as I normally do before turning in. I found an email had arrived from Renal Consultant, Dr Charles Tomson, which read:

> *Dear Mr Hall*
>
> *I have the results of the inter-dialytic urine collection that you gave in yesterday. The urea clearance was 17 ml/min, creatinine clearance 27 ml/min, giving an estimate of overall glomerular filtration of 27 ml/min. This is extremely good news, because it indicates that you have indeed recovered sufficient kidney function to make further dialysis unnecessary. You do not need to attend for dialysis tomorrow night, and I will ensure that the dialysis unit know not to expect you.*
>
> *We will need to make arrangements to remove your tunnelled neck line, depending on exactly when you plan to move back to Grimsby. Before we do that, we will need to know that your blood platelets and blood clotting are OK, and I hope it will be possible to get these tests done in the heart transplant clinic. You will definitely need continued careful follow-up, but I suspect that at least while you remain in the North East, that would be best provided by Dr Parry. You may well continue to need blood-pressure-lowering drug treatment and/or diuretic treatment to help the kidneys regulate blood pressure and fluid balance.*
>
> *Best wishes, Charlie Tomson*

Stunned, I read it again. And again. It seemed unequivocal, no ifs, buts or maybes, he is saying it's over. All the disappointment, guilt and sadness associated with still being on dialysis left me like a hot air balloon rising into the stratosphere. I charged into the bathroom and showed the mail to Nicola. We danced, we laughed, we cried, we hugged (mind the line, girl!), we screamed it from the rooftops; this news came out of nowhere and knocked us for six in the best possible way. At long, long last I felt an emotion for the first time - sheer elation about my heart transplant - and simultaneously, an overwhelming sense of wonder at what the human body is capable of. How do I thank my kidneys? Thank them for finally deciding to get off their miserable backsides and come to the party? I read that mail over and over, and out loud the words, "We will need to make arrangements to remove your tunnelled neckline." Twenty-two weeks waiting for a heart transplant, followed by fourteen weeks of post-transplant dialysis, ten of which were spent staring into the abyss, trying desperately hard to make the best of it. At last, I can feel I've done justice to my donor and his family. The recovery mountain stands before me, and free of shackles I begin the long haul up to Fitness Summit.

I'd just taken my make-up off when Trevor came to the door of the bathroom, handed me his phone and asked me to read an email. Looking at his face, I thought something serious must have happened, but was in no way prepared for what I read. His kidneys have come back. After all the measuring, monitoring, arguing, persuading, hoping, and - despite not being religious - praying, it had happened. Dialysis is no longer required and his permanent lines have become temporary.
A bit like the time I learnt Elvis died, the twin towers had collapsed, and the tsunami hit Japan, this moment is etched on my mind forever. The moment we finally felt we'd made it.

Since gaining access to Trevor's blood results a few weeks ago, I've been keeping a spreadsheet to record blood results and urine output. Although initially, Dr Parry said Trevor needed to be producing 1000ml of urine each day before discontinuation of dialysis could be considered, it transpired that this isn't the full picture. The 'quality' of urine is more important than the 'quantity.' For the last few weeks, Trevor has been producing increasing quantities of urine each day – the much awaited cry from the bathroom of 'one-hundred-and-eighty' has been achieved and surpassed for a while now. The challenge has been getting anybody to listen to us. As I mentioned previously, dialysis nurses are focused on the process of hooking the patient up to a machine and getting them through the system. There is no interest in the patient, just the task. It has sometimes felt as though some renal doctors, and particularly those close to the renal registrar with whom we'd originally had an issue, have a perverse incentive to prove Trevor's kidney failure is chronic and not acute. We did find one renal registrar who spoke to us like we were human and reasonably intelligent – although, even he explained in words of one syllable the meaning of the word 'osmosis' and how a teabag works! Presumably, the assumption is that if you're not a doctor you didn't manage to complete secondary education. To be fair, he was reasonable and listened to us, but he was then transferred suddenly to another hospital so that route closed as quickly as it opened.

I was becoming increasingly frustrated because each time Trevor went to dialysis he returned home looking more and more like a prune. The amount of fluid removed each time is linked to some anecdotal perception of 'dry weight.' Usually, a person's dry weight is measured first thing in the morning after passing urine and before having a drink. But because dialysis inevitably takes place at varying times of day, the dry weight on which fluid removal is based can be taken first thing, or after you've eaten three meals and drunk three pints, or anywhere in-between – and Trevor's was taking no account at all of the litre or so of urine he was passing naturally. Consequently, he was struggling to get the nurses to listen to how much fluid he thought should be removed. I was receiving text messages each session in which Trevor expressed his frustration. It was difficult; I'm conscious that dehydration can adversely affect the kidneys and we really didn't want to risk upsetting them if or when they finally decide to give it another go.

After a week or so of this, I suggested Trevor should ask if he and I could meet with the nurse in charge of the unit. If this meant going in for yet another appointment, so be it. The senior nurse we eventually met with was helpful. She looked at the data I've been collating and agreed with us that Trevor's dry weight needs to be managed differently to avoid him being dehydrated after each dialysis session. Hallelujah!! She also agreed to discuss Trevor's case with a Consultant who is a specialist in dialysis. I have to admit, it came as a bit of a surprise that nobody had thought of that sooner: a patient with a complex history who has suffered an acute kidney injury and requires dialysis wasn't referred to a dialysis specialist? Really?! In the meantime, the Sister assured us she would set Trevor's dry weight at 82kg and make sure a note was put on his file instructing the nurses to discuss his dialysis regime with him prior to each session. That does seem a tad ironic. In order for nurses to do their job properly, there needs to be a Post-it Note attached to the patient's case notes. But, Trevor and I smiled and nodded, just grateful that at last someone was taking us seriously.

Subsequently, the dialysis specialist asked Trevor to undertake a 48-hour urine collection. The dialysis nurses seemed quite perturbed when Trevor asked for two one-gallon containers. We were both delighted when he managed to fill one and needed to use the second. The urine was duly delivered to the renal unit and the rest, as they say, is history.

We now have confirmation that as well as meeting the quantity target, Trevor has also surpassed any quality control requirements. We're there. We're alive. We're free!

CHAPTER FOURTEEN

Home is Where the Heart Is!

Enlightenment

I have many reflections, but the strongest is that the psychological challenges were greater than the physical. My body felt very little pain throughout the ten months; sure, some procedures were painful for a short period, and I had a massive feeling of discomfort when carrying litre upon litre of excess fluid, but they were incomparable to the psychological issues I dealt with.

Pre-transplant, I had fortnightly sessions with a Psychologist, and post-transplant we agreed to increase these to weekly. They resembled a cross between therapy and coaching, with Dr Lucy Attenborough expertly balancing listening with challenging, occasionally providing suggestions for coping strategies. For the most part though, she facilitated my reflection so that I could manoeuvre around the road blocks and out of the cul-de-sacs of my own thoughts. There are three types of reflection: first, thought alone - disjointed, haphazard, freewheeling; second, journaling - the transference of thought into structured, documented sentences; and third, the formation of thought into sounds which are then spoken out loud. We rarely speak in structured, orderly sentences. The important point with the third is that I can hear myself think: I hear my own reasoning, which is an essential part of my 'sense making.' Imagine thoughts being created in my mind, run as a tape to hear what they will sound like, emerging from my mouth in the shape of sounds, flying into the ears of both the listener *and* me, and then being run through my mind a second time as a tape. During that final run, the sounds on the tape are quality checked for sense-making. If they make sense, they're noted and stored.

Naturally, our conversations were always confidential, and I appreciated Lucy's summarising (and seeking my consent to) what would be said in her team meetings. Sometimes, she would offer to intervene and speak with a senior person about an issue, and always I was given the choice on such matters. "No thanks," from me was fully respected.

It's easy for a transplant patient to believe they have all the support they need from family and friends, but the benefit of speaking with an independent person, who has no history, no prior knowledge and can listen without judgement, is invaluable. He or she looks through a totally different lens. Pre-transplant, the emphasis was on dealing with the wait, the uncertainty, the risks and the effect of my deteriorating condition on those close to me. I realised that the transplant created as much mental strain on my wife as it did on me - they were strains of a different nature but no less important is the need to confront them. Post-transplant, the emphasis was on dealing with the frustration of my physical condition and especially the worry of the prospect of permanent dialysis.

Some of the thoughts I needed help with were probably predictable, whilst others took me quite by surprise:

1. The heart of another human being beats inside me and the implications around his soul, his being, his anonymity, and especially the guilt of my family's joy occurring simultaneously with his family's sorrow. The nobility of my donor and his family's gesture, along with my feelings of humility and gratitude.
2. The philosophical discussion around the heart itself, why we use that organ so often to describe emotions; the division we make between the emotional state (heart) and the rational state (brain), and our reluctance to look at the human form holistically.
3. My hopes and ambitions for the future; the fact that I had a limited time left to live and suddenly, I face a rosy future; the unique perspective on a new life that only a transplanted person can experience.
4. The fear associated with the prospect of permanent dialysis, the frustration that this came at me unexpectedly and that I was mentally unprepared for dealing with it. The guilt I felt in not being able to do justice to my donor and his family by making a 'full' recovery.
5. The issues surrounding loss and limitations (a deficit based view) and the danger of depression caused by my physical condition.
6. Feelings of envy towards others who're making a recovery quicker and more fully than me, and the guilt towards those who have not received an organ, and for whom time is running out. Add religion, God, fate and personal beliefs into the mix.

Over time, our psychology sessions took on a different form; they experienced a change of direction though this was very much an organic process. Change emerged of its own volition and we allowed it to lead us. We used cognitive behavioural techniques, meditation and various tools such as the creation of a positive image of the future. At one point, I felt I was becoming depressed and I'm convinced it was having someone to talk to that helped me stave off this danger.

Positive Image of the Future

During meditation, Lucy asked me to create a positive image of the future in my mind, this image being what I wanted to see, experience and be a part of at some stage in the future. With eyes closed, I transported myself away from fluid-filled legs, pressure point sores on my bottom, dialysis lines emerging uncomfortably from my neck, and into a scene in which I enjoyed the company of family and friends, free of pain, limitations and hindrances. Over several weeks I created two or three scenes that I'd regularly revisit during meditation and despite sometimes feeling this was a futile exercise, I persevered. I studied appreciative psychology during my career when working on the creation of positive work environments but doing it myself was more challenging than teaching others to do it.

Only four months later ... Elodie joined me on the kitchen floor of our home, sitting between my legs as we pretended to row a boat towards Millie who was lying down colouring. Millie took a whiff of the imagination-fueled boat-on-the-water scene and leapt up, spreading her books across the floor, announcing that they were stepping stones across the river. Elodie climbed out of the rowboat and stepped onto a stone, just as I too abandoned the boat and turned magically into a hungry crocodile, snapping at the ankles of the girls as they screamed and jumped from stone to stone. If they missed their step, they fell into the water and the crocodile took them; they screeched and squealed in delight as the ravenous reptile wreaked havoc. What fun! They left soon after and as I collected the debris from the floor, it dawned on me that we'd unwittingly acted out a scene I'd created in my mind in hospital - a fully recovered Trevor playing with the girls in our home, making them scream and laugh; Amy, Luke and Nicola present and smiling. I'd created a scene of normality that at the time, seemed so far away, so distant, an unreachable land. I sat on the floor, leaning back against a cupboard, and my emotions caught up with me. Struggling in a state of poor health seemed so recent, yet I was through it: I'd emerged on the other side, fit, healthy, happy and without limitations. I felt back to my old self, with bells on.

From A Whisper To A Scream

The greatest challenge to Nicola and me as a couple, was the change in our relationship, from patient and carer back to husband and wife. This topic needed several conversations over a number of weeks after my dialysis lines were removed and were critical to our spiritual and relational recovery. I honestly believe that few couples explore this territory, and instead continue with the roles they've become accustomed to. At the Transplant Outpatient Clinic, wives and daughters fuss over husbands and fathers, seemingly stuck in a pattern of behaviour they've become familiar with, perhaps even comfortable in. These, along with hospital staff, appear to believe that post-transplant the patient continues to be ill and in need of care. At no stage did I receive signals that I am now fit and well and the expectation is for me to continue to progress and shed the cloak of illness. More often than not, I'm the fittest person in the waiting room at the Transplant Clinic, surrounded by people who're just not being encouraged, pushed or challenged, either by their partner or hospital staff, to shrug off their habitual behaviour of huffing, puffing, sighing, stooping, limping, and conducting life at the pre-transplant snail's pace. The moment Nicola reminded me I have a new heart and should walk like a healthy person again was both cathartic and an epiphany. At a clinic check-up, I asked a doctor for advice on how to continue the improvement in my body's performance. He looked at me with a puzzled expression and said, "Why bother? You're alive, aren't you? Be grateful for that."

At another appointment, the registrar noted my high blood pressure that had been taken as soon as I took my seat. I asked if it could be related to the fact that I'd just been running up the clinic stairs, twenty repetitions, prior to being called in. "Now why would you want to do that?" he asked. "Because I can!" I replied with a beaming smile, but he didn't seem to 'get it.' We failed to understand each other - he couldn't look at the world through my eyes, for he hadn't known the awful anxiety of looking at a flight of stairs with a failing heart inside his chest, the despair of sinking to his knees to recover his breath at the top of one flight, the desperate longing for the fit and healthy glow his body used to exude...but doesn't any more. He can't look at those stairs through the eyes of a transplant patient and see the joy of the challenge, or feel the elation from having run up them. He doesn't have 'sparkly bits' like this in every one of his days.

Nicola had to cease her tendency to do things for me, things that I couldn't manage before. But it wasn't just those. I needed to recover my manhood in our relationship. I needed to share the driving again, to carry the shopping from the car to the house, to open doors for her (for a change), to fetch and carry, to nip up the stairs to bring something we'd forgotten, to do the DIY jobs around the house. It's a long list. We noticed that when on a 'power walk,' she'd flag a little over the last 2km of a 12km walk, but she'd urge me to push on, smiling, proud of me. I wouldn't, because all the way through this she's told me, "We're in this together."

The NHS - the Good, the Bad and the Ugly

Having spent the best part of 10 months in The Freeman, it was of course impossible for me to fail to make observations about the organisation that took care of me. Consulting on organisation was both my MSc. and my career for the last fifteen years of my working life. I tried to remain objective throughout, but it's hard to do this when, as a patient, you're so incredibly vulnerable for so much of the time. I smile at hospitals conducting satisfaction surveys amongst patients who've had pain taken away, are being questioned in their pyjamas, and basically have nothing to compare their treatment with. Of course they're grateful. Yes, a hospital is filled with people doing their best (well, most of them are), but that often disguises the fact they're working with broken, fragmented work processes; poor leadership; an absence of quality and cost awareness; inexperienced, unqualified, unskilled management; and absolutely no clue about continuous improvement systems. I lost count of the number of times nurses presented me with incorrect doses of medication before I lost patience and took back the responsibility myself. On another occasion, I explained to a nurse why she should inject me slowly with a drug over a period of several minutes, compared to her completing it within ten to fifteen seconds. Another nurse had previously explained to me the importance of that slow delivery, but not everyone knew about it. I have a thousand stories like this. I learned that nurses have a reputation for being 'angels,' such having come typically from elderly, vulnerable patients and their relatives. But it's not true. Not all nurses, by any means, are angels. Some are for sure, there's no doubt about that, but there's a significant portion for whom it's just a job, a means of income. And I met more than one who was simply downright lazy and avoided work at all costs. My biggest challenge - and for this I needed Nicola's help on so many occasions - was to have my wish to be involved in my treatment respected. Questions, especially challenging ones, were not always welcome and the dominant belief seemed to be that things would work so much better if I simply shut up and did as requested, even if that request turned out to be wrong or dangerous. Senior doctors at The Freeman are remarkably talented - I felt honoured to be treated by them - and I admire the fact that the hospital is able to attract and retain some of the most talented surgeons, physicians and doctors in Europe.

The NHS is *not* in crisis - it's way beyond that. It is broken, disfigured, dysfunctional and completely unable to meet the demands of today's society. It was designed for something totally different to that for which it is being used today. Pouring in more billions is not the answer - that's akin to pouring in more ingredients to a cake for which the recipe is wrong, it just won't help the outcome.

Changing it radically, redesigning it, and privatising more of it are the way to go. The country has an ageing population and it has an obesity epidemic; these two factors alone put an incredible strain on the organisation. The demand placed on it by illegal immigrants, health tourists, and poorly thought-out EU expansion is shameful; only the refusal by the General Medical Council to co-operate with identity checks is more shameful. A significant proportion of nurses working on heart wards of one type or another, are morbidly obese. They seem unable to 'join the dots' by themselves, to see that within just a few years *they* will be the ones in wheelchairs and mobility scooters, unable to move, suffering from heart disease and diabetes, in danger of losing limbs and possibly their lives. Not to mention placing more demand on an already over-subscribed system. It's so sad, and so clearly an issue of education and class, because you rarely see an obese consultant, surgeon or doctor.

That phrase about experience being something we get just when we stop needing it seems to have defined my life over the last few months. As a couple, we've learnt an enormous amount and hopefully grown a little. Even the words 'heart transplant' have shifted from an unfamiliar term that creates a sense of both wonder and alienation, to part of our everyday language. Trevor and I have undoubtedly changed both as individuals and as a couple. I've seen him at his most vulnerable and he's seen me at my most tenacious. Boudicca he used to call me when we began living together and he sometimes found me too intense or intimidating. I wonder what he will call me now.

We've also learnt a great deal about the NHS. I guess that not many people with our backgrounds have the opportunity to analyse this complex organisation from such close proximity. The hierarchy and bureaucracy is much written about, and there have been many attempts to modernise, improve, and reshape this national treasure to create something that meets the needs of a twenty-first century society with its many and varied demands. There are some great people working at The Freeman; some are brilliant at their job, others not so good. Some are excellent at a particular task: one nurse springs to mind who gets things done; the Rottweiler-type who gets her teeth stuck in and doesn't give up. She's good at that. Not so good at other aspects of the role. Some of the standards of nursing have slipped; the ward sister who makes absolutely sure that not a minute of any day is wasted is no longer in evidence. Linen cupboards are upside down, sluices are untidy, patients are unkempt, beds are neglected, communication is ad hoc, mistakes are common.

It seems that the NHS relies on its 'heroes.' That small number of individuals who do considerably more than their share of the work to make sure problems are resolved and progress is possible. In terms of management, it's not obvious there is much. The NHS seems to have descended into a jumble of diverse agendas that rarely match. Duplication, waste, and low standards have become the accepted norm.

From many nurses, I'm sure the rallying call, 'We're understaffed ... underpaid ... under-trained,' will be heard. Sadly, this can't be used as an all-encompassing panacea for what's gone wrong. During my second career, as a teacher, it occurred to me that modern secondary students begrudgingly attend classes but see any intervention by teachers as an interruption to their social lives. While Trevor was in The Freeman, it struck me that nursing is very similar. Our close proximity to the nurses' station gave us an insight into the working day of a lot of nurses. There is very little communication about patients; lots about social lives. Many nurses spend a much larger proportion of their working day around the nurses' station than with the patients. When I hear the war-cry, 'We're on our knees,' I smile. For the majority, it's certainly not because of the demands of their work. I accept that the shifts are twelve hours - sometimes thirteen – but these hours are far from all 'worked.' To be fair, because of working three long days, nurses are actually at work for fewer days each year than teachers.

If we are to have an NHS in the future, there are certainly changes that need to happen. Modernisation, including efficient use of technology as well as changes to working practices, is urgently needed. Those sacred cows which have been herded around the NHS since its inception in 1948 need to be slaughtered and replaced with systems which ensure effective use of finite resources. So often, we hear medical and nursing professions calling for more funds if the NHS is to survive; rarely, if ever, do we hear them suggesting that major change needs to happen.

Don't get me wrong, we're grateful that the clinicians caring for Trevor helped him towards his recovery, and some of the clinicians we came across during this journey were truly outstanding. But, I think it's also important to say that when we fly overseas, we're grateful that the pilot who is flying the aircraft did his job properly. And grateful that the gas engineer looking after our boiler did his job properly too. The people who work in the NHS are not providing a service out of the goodness of their hearts any more than other employees in other industries. And, like most people, the primary reason NHS staff go to work is to earn a living. It is important to recognise that the salary of each person employed by the NHS is paid by the taxpayer - the user of the service – and each person has the right to expect value for money, and to be treated with respect. I can recall as a fresh-faced student nurse being told by a clinical tutor, who seemed somewhat strait-laced at that time: "Nurses have come to be seen as 'angels' by many of the public, and some nurses evidently believe this. You need to get that out of your heads now. You are not angels!" Those words resonated with me many times over the last few months; I think what she said is still relevant today.

Our greatest thanks go to the donor's family who, whilst negotiating their way through the saddest day of their lives, were asked about donation of their loved-one's organs. Imagine for a moment their heads reeling from the awful news, their dreams of a future with husband and father shattered, not knowing which way to turn, what to do or say, desperately trying to make sense of events that have turned their worlds and lives upside down. In the midst of this, they managed to take a deep breath and say, "Yes," to the gift of life.

The Final Word

I don't know if it's the best thing that ever happened to me. It wouldn't surprise me if one day I say it is. I'm wary of coming across as a reformed smoker, stopping complete strangers in the street and telling them to seize the day, to put a smile on their face as things could be a heck of a lot worse, and asking if they'd like to see my scar. (My beautiful scar: a neat, vertical, barely visible hand-stitched work of art that adorns my chest.)

At the end of the day, it was an incredible learning experience, one that I never dreamed I'd go through. I discovered so much about myself, about life and how I should strive to conduct mine, what to focus my energy on, and what to let pass me by. I discovered the true value of that most precious of commodities, time. With six weeks left to live (in the opinion of the experts), a healthy heart came along. My size, my blood type, and my antibody 'fit.' Today, physically, I can achieve almost everything I could achieve in 2010 pre-cardiomyopathy, and there were times when I'd given up dreaming I'd be able to write those words. In addition though, my life is so much richer for the experience of having undergone this life-saving and life-affirming organ transplantation. I can't complain about the weather any more. No matter how miserable it is to everyone else when cold, dreary and raining, I can see only wonder and beauty. When I look at that weather, I feel the fireworks going off in my stomach, I feel the blood pulsing through my veins … and sometimes I see the rainbow. It's the same rainbow everyone else sees. Only mine has the sparkly bits.

EPILOGUE

A gentle push off from the side, arms outstretched in front, hands together, outward facing, a torpedo gliding silently through the water. Bubbles trickle from my mouth as kick and pull signals the first actions of breaststroke. My head breaches the surface, air momentarily sucked in, followed by a downward, forward push leading to the next kick and pull. "Stroke execution!" is bellowed by the grammar school swimming instructor, a plump matriarch who takes no nonsense from anyone; a woman obsessed with developing swimming talent; a woman who regards the pursuit of excellence as a combination of art and technique, who demands perpetual perseverance from every pupil. I have no idea why her voice still ricochets around my head with every stroke I swim some forty years later. But the Trunchbull of Barton Grammar certainly focuses my concentration.

Counting the laps silently, automatically, revelling in the joy of once again being completely surrounded, engulfed, consumed by water.

It's April 2018 and two years have passed since my transplant. My 'dry weight' is now 80kg wet-through. Three times each week I rise at 6am, spend an hour in the gym on cardio machines, delight in the sweat that safely pours from my brow: free of anxiety, free of excess fluid, free of lines and tubes. A quick shower and it's time for my 700m swim – always the highlight of my day – a combination of breaststroke and front crawl. I power through the cool depths, a determined impassive countenance on the exterior, a grin from ear-to-ear inside. Pushing on for those last few laps of front crawl, I emerge from the pool breathing hard.

Most days, I feel I could swim forever – energy seeps from every pore. None of the regulars at the gym know of my transplant, and I like it that way. Anonymous. My scar is almost invisible, still beautiful but very faint.

This is the gift of a life.

Printed in Great Britain
by Amazon